The Japanization of Modernity

Murakami Haruki between Japan and the United States

Harvard East Asian Monographs 298

The Japanization of Modernity

Murakami Haruki between Japan and the United States

Rebecca Suter

Published by the Harvard University Asia Center
and distributed by Harvard University Press
Cambridge (Massachusetts) and London, 2008

Published by the Harvard University Asia Center, Cambridge, MA 02138

The Harvard University Asia Center publishes a monograph series and, in coordination with the Fairbank Center for Chinese Studies, the Korea Institute, the Reischauer Institute of Japanese Studies, and other faculties and institutes, administers research projects designed to further scholarly understanding of China, Japan, Vietnam, Korea, and other Asian countries. The Center also sponsors projects addressing multidisciplinary and regional issues in Asia.

Library of Congress Cataloging-in-Publication Data

Suter, Rebecca, 1975–
The Japanization of modernity : Murakami Haruki between Japan and the United States / Rebecca Suter.
p. cm. -- Harvard East Asian monographs ; 298)
Includes bibliographical references and index.
ISBN-13: 978-0-674-02833-3 (cloth : alk. paper)
ISBN-13: 978-0-674-06076-0 (paperback : alk. paper)
ISBN-13: 978-0-674-30637-0 (epub)
1. Murakami, Haruki, 1949---Criticism and interpretation. 2. Murakami, Haruki, 1949---Appreciation--United States. I. Title.
pl856.u673z87 2008
895.6'35--dc22

2008008830

Printed on acid-free paper in the United States of America by Maple Press, 480 Willow Springs Lane, York, PA 17406 (www.maplepress.com).

The manufacturer's authorized representative in the EU for product safety is LOGOS EUROPE, 9 rue Nicolas Poussin, 17000, La Rochelle, France (e-mail: Contact@logoseurope.eu).

To Hans, Roberta, and Matteo

Acknowledgments

This work began as a research project for a Monbukagakushō fellowship, which subsequently became my doctoral dissertation at Università degli Studi di Napoli "L'Orientale." In my progression from Monbushō research project to dissertation to book, I benefited from the help of a number of institutions and individuals.

I should first of all thank my advisor at Tokyo University of Foreign Studies, Kutsukake Yoshihiko, for making the research project possible in the first place, and Toshiko Ellis and Shibata Motoyuki of the University of Tokyo, who helped to set my study on Murakami Haruki in motion during the early stages of my research in Japan.

I am also grateful to my teachers in Naples, particularly to Giorgio Amitrano and Paolo Calvetti, for their helpful insight on the dissertation, and to Donatella Izzo, not only the best possible advisor but also a constant source of inspiration.

In the academic year 2005–2006, I was the beneficiary of a postdoctoral fellowship at Harvard University's Reischauer Institute of Japanese Studies, which allowed me to turn my thesis into a book manuscript. I would like to thank Susan Pharr and Ted Gilman for their precious encouragement. I would also like thank my fellow post-docs Matthew Fraleigh, Haeng-ja Chung, and Yuma Totani, for thought-provoking discussions and for a great time together that made the whole experience not only more productive but also much more pleasant.

My greatest obligation is, of course, to Jay Rubin, whose insightful feedback on the initial draft was crucial in the rewriting process. And I am very much indebted to the two anonymous readers of my manuscript for their careful and stimulating criticisms.

I would like to express my gratitude to a number of people for inspiring discussions that greatly helped in reframing my work; there is no way to do justice to all of them, and I apologize to the ones I am most likely forgetting to mention. I would like to thank Eve Zimmerman, Hosea Hirata, Anna Elliott, Edwin Cranston, Adam Kern, Dani Botsman, Shigehisa Kuriyama, Christopher Bolton, Susan Napier, Ian Condry, David McCann, Theodore Bestor, Merry White, Victoria Bestor, Katrina Moore, Christopher Hanscom, Anna Andreeva, Ed Drott, Seth Jacobowitz, Aaron Moore, Christopher Bondy, Emer O'Dwyer, Marjan Boogert, Izumi Nakayama, and Jun Uchida.

I also want to thank my students in Japanese Literature 246 at Harvard, particularly Aaron Hames, Kevin Singleton, and Jessica Crewe, who were made to read a great deal of Murakami, and whose brilliant remarks in class often gave me cause for reflection in the revision process.

Many thanks to David Brophy, for his patient and careful proofreading, and for a thousand other things.

Finally, I would like to express my gratitude to Tada Hiroshi sensei, Maestro Silvio Giannelli, and Sioux Hall sensei, for helping me to keep *mens sana in corpore sano.*

Contents

Reference Matter

The Japanization of Modernity

Murakami Haruki between Japan and the United States

Introduction

The subject of my work is the role of the contemporary Japanese writer Murakami Haruki as a cultural mediator between Japan and the United States. Murakami is probably the most translated among contemporary Japanese writers; at the same time, he has been very active in introducing American literature to Japan, having translated writers such as F. Scott Fitzgerald, John Irving, Grace Paley, Tim O'Brien, J. D. Salinger, and Raymond Carver. Although many critics both in the West and in Japan have discussed Murakami's works, very few have analyzed his role as a literary and cultural mediator between Japan and the United States. My work proposes to fill this gap, in the conviction that studying the works of Murakami Haruki from a comparative perspective can provide a better understanding not only of the author and his works, but also of the status of contemporary Japanese literature within the context of world literature.

Furthermore, I am convinced that looking at Murakami's work as Japanese-American cultural cross-representation can provide original insights on two major interrelated contemporary debates, both full of varied and complex positions: on the one hand, discussion of issues of modernity and postmodernity, and on the other, theorizations of the concepts of postcoloniality and globalization.

Both the unique position of Japan vis-à-vis the West and the peculiar situation of Murakami Haruki's works within contemporary Japanese culture provide us with a unique vantage point from which to contribute to the discussion of these ideas. The concepts of modernity, modernism, and postmodernism, as we will see, have been subject to a number of varied and often contradictory definitions. However, while studying ongoing debates on these questions, I was struck by the fact that, despite the nuance and complexity that has been brought to these debates, these theoretical concepts still tend to be mainly West-centered, making it difficult to apply such concepts to non-Western cultures. This apparent disconnect would seem to call for a broader perspective.

To this end, I have tried to address (and question) in my analyses of Murakami's work a number of assumptions that feature in the discourse on modernism and postmodernism: above all, how these concepts stress the temporal nature of modernity, and how some of the basic themes of postcolonial theory and theories of globalization come into play, particularly the relationship between universalism/imperialism and particularism/nationalism.

The Japanese experience of modernization is full of anomalies and contradictions that can offer interesting perspectives on current definitions of modernity, modernism, and postmodernism, and can open up new critical windows on the discussion of Western cultural formations in the modern (and postmodern) era. Nevertheless, the Japanese case has been largely neglected by theoretical studies on Western modernity.

As evidenced by Karatani Kōjin, Japan offers an invaluable point of comparison for Western modernization, since in a very short span of time it underwent epistemological changes that in the West had occurred gradually over the course of three centuries, between 1600 and 1900. A particularly significant issue in the development of Japanese modernity is the formation of the notion of the modern individual subject, which has been one of the main concerns of Japanese literature since the Meiji era (1868–1912).

In this respect, the case of Murakami is illuminating: modern individuality is central to his work, but his stance on this issue is radically different from that of other Japanese writers of the post–World War II period. In this respect, Murakami may be closer to those writers of the Meiji era who first dealt with the problem of individuality and its relationship with Western culture, such as Natsume Sōseki and Mori Ōgai, than to such contemporaries as Ōe Kenzaburō, who insist on the necessity for the Japanese to acquire a strong subjectivity deeply rooted in history. I would argue that Murakami's work has given birth to an entirely new approach to modernity and subjectivity in Japanese literature. Therefore, the problem of the individual subject will be one of the main theoretical perspectives from which I will analyze his work.

The history of Japan's relations with the West also throws into question some of the basic notions of postcolonial theory. Japan was the only country in East Asia to successfully resist colonization and to aspire to a role of equality with the Western powers, becoming in its turn a dominant imperialist power in Asia. At the same time, it experienced a strong cultural colonization both at the end of the nineteenth century and during the U.S. Occupation following World War II. Yet, in both instances, rather than simply accepting a culture imposed upon it from the outside, Japan actively appropriated Western technologies and modes of thought. Some scholars speak of an "internalized colonization" of Japan, arguing that it escaped colonization precisely because it was quicker in "colonizing itself by itself." All of these features make this country a unique item of comparison for theories of colonialism and imperialism as well as issues of universalism and particularism, two other terms that have been subject to a number of divergent and often ambiguous definitions.

Furthermore, the case of Japan challenges some basic assumptions of the concept of Orientalism as formulated by Edward Said, which is mainly based on an "Orient" that coincides with the Middle East. Finally, in recent times, Japan has been one of the few non-Western countries, if not the only one, to pursue a form of "cultural imperialism" in Asia very similar to Euro-American neo-colonialism, a phenomenon that clearly problematizes the common Western-centered vision of globalization.

Although some of the issues raised in this study pertain more to the fields of intellectual history, sociology, or even international relations than to literary criticism, I will address them from the point of view of literature and use them as a framework for a textual analysis of Murakami's work. One reason for this is that I continue to find value in discussing narrative fiction against such a background, even though in recent times the approach to literature of so-called "Theory" has been contested by works such as Daphne Patai and Wilfrido Corral's *Theory's Empire: An Anthology of Dissent*, and by the birth of organizations such as the Association of Literary Scholars and Critics, which has revived an emphasis on the aesthetic appreciation of literature in Western literary studies. Most of all, I maintain this position because I am convinced that literature still plays a significant role in the formation of a national culture and in cultural cross-representations, and therefore I believe that an analysis of mutual literary representations can provide an invaluable insight in the study of the relations among cultures, especially in the case of Japan and the United States.

At the same time, I also believe that a comparative perspective is fundamental in order to understand modern Japanese literature, not only because it has been heavily influenced by Western culture, but also because the modern concept of literature (*bungaku*) was formed in Japan in connection with, and in reaction to, the impact of the West—a view emphasized by several literary scholars, including Karatani Kōjin in his landmark study *Kindai bungaku no kigen* (*Origins of Modern Japanese Literature*). In particular, Murakami's twofold role as writer and translator is especially salient in considering the prominent place of translations in the Japanese literary panorama, particularly in the early Meiji period and in the postwar years.

Murakami Haruki is particularly relevant to the discussion of all these issues, for a number of reasons. First of all, Murakami has deliberately set himself apart from both the literary elite (*bundan*) and from the class of postwar intellectuals aligned with the so-called ideology of *kindaishugi* (modernism), which I discuss at length in Chapter 1. For this reason, he has been accused of superficiality and has been criticized for his lack of political and social commitment by other writers such as Ōe Kenzaburō and by critics such as Masao Miyoshi. Because he is not a "modernist" in the *kindaishugi* sense, many critics have defined Murakami as a postmodernist, usually in a disparaging sense, stressing the commercial aspects of his novels and his compliance with the logic of late capitalist society.

In my opinion, though, Murakami's work cannot be categorized as "postmodernist" either; those critics who label him postmodern fail to consider his use of typically modernist literary strategies, such as his play with foreign language and with the Japanese writing system (particularly the *katakana* syllabary), his distrust of the ability of language to represent and communicate, his stress on the arbitrariness and deceptiveness of the linguistic sign, or his use of "fragments of Western culture" as a means to hold back chaos, reminiscent of the function of Joycean myth according to T. S. Eliot, a means to put order in the "immense panorama of anarchy and futility that is contemporary history."[1]

Other features in his work are indeed reminiscent of postmodernist literature: his use of metafiction, his attempts to undermine a univocal vision of reality, and the blurring of the boundary between "high" and "low" culture. We see this in his references to classics of the Western philosophical and literary tradition, treated as though they were cultural commodities for popular consumption, easily recognizable icons that give his texts an exotic appeal and a connotation of sophistication and cosmopolitanism.

I address Murakami's work in the light of Brian McHale's distinction between modernist epistemological doubt, which interrogates the possibility of knowing the world, and postmodernist ontological doubt, which questions the world's very realness. Murakami's works often oscillate between these two stances, once again undermining a clear-cut distinction between ideas of "modern" and "nonmodern" or, in this case, "postmodern."

I will scrutinize another frame of reference in this study: the contention that true art should be subversive and critical of the status quo. As argued by New Historicist scholars in regard to modern European literary theory, such a viewpoint is in itself a powerful instrument in containing dissent, since it relegates the subversive elements of society to more or less inoffensive artistic manifestations and brings such elements back under control. According to Tomi Suzuki, an analogous mechanism, precisely in relation to the potentially revolutionary impact of concepts imported from the West, was evident in Japan between 1880 and 1890, when the ideals of liberty and individualism lost their political connotation and simply converged in the newly born romantic literature and in the *watakushi shōsetsu*, or "I-novel."[2] Something similar happened again in the postwar years with the so-called *kaikon kyōdōtai* or "repentance community" advocated by Japanese writers and intellectuals, and with the related ideology of *kindaishugi*; by taking upon itself the function of addressing serious political issues, literature facilitated the disappearance of actual social action, and political activism gradually faded into a less threatening "committed literature."

Murakami Haruki, by refusing social commitment of a traditional kind and accepting the proposition that books are, among other things, commercial objects, that have to appeal to the public to be read, contests the myth of art as necessarily rebelling against the dominant economic and political system. He refutes a simple opposition between detachment and commitment that remains basically inside a binary system of thought, to tread a radically alternative path, a "complicitous critique," that is in some aspects similar to that of postmodernism and in other respects closer to the dynamics of postcolonial literature, but cannot be reduced to either.

Furthermore, this apparent absence of critical distance in Murakami's work is counterbalanced by the cultural and geographical distance that his texts maintain from the Western culture to which they refer. European and American postmodernist authors look at modernism from a temporal distance, but from within the same culture. Euro-American postmodernists consider themselves legitimate children of Western modernity and modernism, and while they relate to them in a critical way, they do it without the anxiety that the non-West has often felt toward modernity.

In my work I have tentatively defined Murakami as a "paramodernist" who relates to modernity and modernism not as "past" but as "foreign" things. As such, I treat his relation to modernist and postmodernist literature as something akin to the "mimicry of the colonized" as theorized by Homi Bhabha: not a passive imitation of Western models, but a parodic incorporation that transforms the original and ends up destabilizing it. By analyzing his work, I look at what happens when what Harold Bloom defined as "the anxiety of influence" intertwines with the relation between "the West" and "the Rest."

Murakami has introduced American culture to Japanese readers both by means of numerous translations and by incorporating elements of Western culture into his texts. I have chosen to focus mainly on his use of foreign elements in his stories, and I will not discuss specifically any of his translations; I will, however, treat his activity as a translator as a key frame of reference, especially insofar as his translations have influenced the Japanese public's reception of American culture, as well as the works of Japanese writers of the younger generation. As Miura Masashi notes in *Murakami Haruki to Shibata Motoyuki no mō hitotsu no Amerika* (Murakami Haruki and Shibata Motoyuki's Other America), young novelists such as Satō Yūya, Ono Masatsugu, and Yanagi Hiroshi are heavily influenced not so much by the style of American novelists directly, but by the Japanese translations of Murakami and Shibata.[3]

Murakami himself is aware of this role and has produced a number of metacritical reflections on the theoretical issues involved in translation, both in interviews and in the book-length essays *Hon'yaku yawa* (A Night Conversation on Translation) and *Hon'yaku yawa 2: Sarinjā senki* (A Second Night Conversation on Translation: War with Salinger), in collaboration with Shibata Motoyuki. Furthermore, with the conscious aim of introducing literature to a younger generation of readers, he has published *Wakai dokusha no tame no tanpen shōsetsu annai* (A Guide to the Short Story for Young Readers, 1997), a compendium of lectures from his visiting appointment at Tufts University in 1993.

In addition to his role as a prolific presenter of American culture to Japanese readers, Murakami is widely translated in the West and thus serves as an active conveyor of Japanese culture to Europe and the United States. Before analyzing his texts, I look at how Murakami markets his work to the West, particularly to the United States, and how he relates to issues crucial to Japan in the 1980s, the first years of his career as a writer, such as the idea of *kokusaika* (internationalization) and of *ippō tsūkō no bunka* ("one-way" or "trade imbalance" culture).

With the conviction that the image of Japan is shaped not only by its portrayal in American literature and in the media, but also by Japanese works that are translated into English and widely read by the American public, I want to look at Murakami's work as part of American literature, and I will therefore briefly examine the reception of his work in the United States and how it interacts with (and possibly helps to change) the American image of Japan. My contention is that Murakami belongs to a broader trend of Asian literature translated and published in the United States, an "Asian/American literature," incarnated by Asian intellectuals who live in the United States and simultaneously capitalize on their "Asianness"—often in self-conscious opposition to the notion of "Asian American culture" as internal to America and obeying its inclusive logic of inner diversification, thus challenging any unitary and essential definition of American literature. I therefore discuss the response of both American critics and the general American public to Murakami's works against the background of contemporary American views of Japan as they appear in, and are shaped by, literature and the media, particularly in the 1980s and 1990s. My main concern here will be with the concepts of aestheticization, domestication, and exoticization of foreign culture.

At the same time, Murakami clearly belongs to Japanese literature, and I want to highlight the way in which he addresses his role as a Japanese writer in a manner radically different from that of intellectuals such as Ōe. As I will demonstrate, Murakami's work is representative of a new Japanese mode of relating to the West: one free from the sense of anxiety, uneasiness, inferiority, or hostility that characterized much postwar Japanese literary production; one that actively uses the West's alienness as a hermeneutic instrument in a playful and ironic way.

Despite the contention of some critics that references to Western culture in Murakami, as in other writers of his generation such as Yoshimoto Banana and Murakami Ryū, are devoid of irony, that in these authors' works "quotation has been replaced by homage, that is the way in which contemporary Japanese novelists express their gratitude to their models,"[4] I would argue that Murakami's references to American and European culture do have an ironic function, which is not to create a distance *from* the West but a distance *through* the West, to move away from conventional reality using foreign literature and culture for their alienating effect.

Analyzing Murakami's oeuvre in these contexts, I have chosen to concentrate mainly on his short stories, not only because they are less widely known and less translated in the West than the novels, and would deserve greater attention, but also, and more importantly in my opinion, because they are free from the coherent and organic narrative structure of his longer works and are sites of bolder experiments, particularly in terms of metafictional techniques and the use of language.

It is worth noting, in this respect, that this experimental mode is the style in which Murakami first began to write. Although his first two novels *Kaze no uta o kike* (1979; *Hear the Wind Sing*, 1987) and *1973-nen no pinbōru* (1980; *Pinball, 1973*, 1985) would appear to fall into the category of semi-autobiographical fiction, they depart significantly from the conventions of both realist and confessional literature. They lack a strong plot (in fact, it may even be argued that they do not have any real plot), they are interspersed with metanarrative references to the act of writing, and even though, unlike later works, they do not contain any explicitly fantastic or supernatural elements, they are narrated in a rather anti-realistic style.

Another central element of these stories that has since become a defining feature of Murakami's fiction, in both short stories and novels, is the author's use of the nameless narrator *boku*. As Jay Rubin has noted, the choice to use almost exclusively the informal pronoun *boku*, instead of the more formal *watashi* or *watakushi*, sets this author apart from the tradition of the *watakushi shōsetsu*.[5] In contrast, Murakami creates what might be called a *boku-shōsetsu*, which, especially if we consider the way he explicitly distances himself from the *bundan*, we can read as a criticism of the dominance of confessional literature in the modern Japanese literary panorama. Unlike the protagonists of I-novels, Murakami's *boku* is invariably an "ordinary guy" who narrates events with a great degree of detachment and irony. As we will see, this element of seriousness through mockery is central to Murakami's idea of the role of literature in the contemporary world, as well as to his reflections on Japan's relation to Western modernity.

In fact, both novels and short stories often rely on Western culture for such ironic effect, and do so on many levels: *boku* constantly displays his knowledge of Western film, music, and literature, and this is what makes him a cosmopolitan and cool character; the narrator describes reality through metaphors taken from Western culture; and the texts make extensive use of loanwords from English and other European languages. As I mentioned before, I believe that the most interesting linguistic experiments are to be found in the short stories. On the other hand, the other main means in which Murakami distances realism, the portrayal of parallel realities and literal "other worlds," is central to the novels as well.

Starting with *Hitsuji o meguru bōken* (1982; *A Wild Sheep Chase,* 1989), Murakami increasingly introduced supernatural elements into his fiction. In this novel, we encounter once again the character Nezumi from *Kaze no uta o kike,* who is now possessed by the evil spirit of a Mongolian sheep; the story also portrays other surreal characters such as the Sheep professor and the Sheep man.

Hitsuji o meguru bōken revolves around the theme of spirit possession and uses fantasy mainly to explore questions of identity and consciousness; its sequel *Dansu dansu dansu* (1988; *Dance Dance Dance,* 1994) also introduces unreal spaces and other worlds, in the form of a hotel floor that only exists at certain moments in time, or, the novel at one point seems to imply, only exists for the narrator. The two novels thus embody the constant oscillation between epistemological and ontological doubt, between questioning of the possibility of *knowing* the world and casting doubt on its very realness, on the idea of a unitary and clearly defined "reality" that lies at the center of this author's fiction.

Murakami has also written in a more realistic mode. *Noruwei no mori* (1987; *Norwegian Wood,* 1989) in many respects reads as a fairly conventional *ren'ai shōsetsu,* a love story between college students. As such, it came as a surprise to Murakami's fans that were familiar with *Hitsuji o meguru bōken* and *Sekai no owari to hādo boirudo wandārando* (1985; *Hard-Boiled Wonderland and the End of the World,* 1991). Since then, and throughout his career thus far, Murakami has continued to alternate works in a more realistic mode and works that are more clearly fantastic.[6]

It is noteworthy that Murakami's more fantastic works are often also the most socially and politically engaged. Whereas *Noruwei no mori* is set in the years 1968–69, it purposefully avoids tackling the issue of the student movement and the New Left. On the other hand, *Hitsuji o meguru bōken* features a "Sheep spirit" (which turns out to be the obscure force behind most of Japan's history) through which the author investigates both the country's dark past in Manchuria and the underside of the economic boom of the 1980s. In a similar fashion, *Nejimaki-dori kuronikuru* (1993–95; *The Wind-Up Bird Chronicle*, 1997) revolves around a parallel reality that the narrator enters either in dreams or through a dry well in his neighbors' yard—a conceit that allows the author to deal extensively with Japan's colonization of Manchuria.

In *Supūtoniku no koibito* (1999; *Sputnik Sweetheart*, 2001), the uncanny experience of one of the protagonists, Miu, of seeing her doppelgänger making love with a man she hates results in permanent emotional trauma and possibly schizophrenia; however, this plot development also serves as an occasion to address the issue of her condition as a *zainichi*, a Korean national born and raised in Japan, and related issues of ethnic identity and social discrimination. *Umibe no Kafuka* (2002; *Kafka on the Shore*, 2005) shifts the focus to psychological and sociological ground, addressing the fifteen-year-old protagonist's difficult relationship with his father and hinting at the possibility that, by killing him in a dream, he might have caused him to die in the real world.

In this respect, one of the most interesting among the novels is *Sekai no owari to hādoboirudo wandārando*. This novel is structured on two narrative levels, with two different narrators (*watashi* and *boku*), who live in different "worlds." The first one is a sort of science-fictional future, a Tokyo that is home to strange creatures called *yamikuro* (INKlings, or Infra-Nocturnal Kappa, in Birnbaum's translation), as well as to *watashi*, a *keisanshi* (a "calcutec"), whose human mind contains a device that allows him to encrypt and decrypt data on a subconscious level, keeping them unknown to his rational mind. The other world is a fantastic walled city where *boku* is separated from his shadow and assigned the task of reading dreams, extracting them from the skulls of the unicorns that live on the outskirts of the town. We gradually discover that the two worlds are connected in the protagonist's mind: *boku* is a creation of *watashi*'s subconscious, a part of his system of data shuffling, and the story ends with the "death" of *watashi*, who will go on "living" in the imaginary world of *boku*. Although this story is often presented by critics on both sides of the Pacific as a paradigmatic example of Murakami's escapism, it seems to me to epitomize precisely his new notion of engagement. I will return to my interpretation of this novel in the last chapter of this study.

Some scholars in the West do interpret in political terms Murakami's use of the fantastic genre. Gareth Edwards connects his theme of the "other world" to the representation of a "hidden substratum of power" in Japanese society. This, Edwards argues, can be seen in the character of *sensei*, and in the sheep that "inhabits" him in *Hitsuji o meguru bōken*. Edwards interprets these "other worlds" as a means to explore the hidden side of Japan's "consensus society," arguing that "Murakami uses unreality to cast light into the shadows of a real world consensually idealized as safe, clean, and fair."[7]

Matthew Strecher also insists on the political aspect of what he defines as Murakami's "magical realism." According to Strecher, Murakami uses the fantastic genre to highlight the decline of the sense of individual identity in Japan in the generation born after the Second World War.[8] Strecher compares Murakami's novels to those of writers such as Gabriel García Márquez, in which supernatural events infiltrate their everyday settings. In his opinion, however, unlike Latin American writers, who associate this use of the supernatural with specific political statements, "Murakami's use of magical realism, while closely linked with the *quest* for identity, is not the least bit involved with the *assertion* of an identity."[9] He therefore sees Murakami's use of the fantastic as a critique of the way in which Japanese mass society suffocates individuality.[10] I share Strecher's view that Murakami's use of the fantastic is deeply related to his new form of social and political engagement; however, I see it neither as a critique of the loss of individuality nor as an assertion of identity, but as a reflection on the construction of subjectivity in contemporary Japan, which parallels Murakami's reflection on the relation between Japan and Western modernity. Although my main focus in this book is on the short stories, I will also include a brief discussion of the fantastic elements in his novels that are most relevant to my argument, particularly in Chapter 5, which deals with Murakami's use of fantasy.

The book is divided into five parts. In the first chapter, I provide a brief discussion of the theoretical framework in which I situate my study of this author's texts, addressing the current debate on the notions of modernity and postmodernity, universalism and particularism, imperialism and nationalism, Orientalism and globalization. In the second chapter, I give a short comparative analysis of the reception of his work in Japan and in the United States. In the remaining three chapters, through textual analysis of a number of Murakami's short stories, I look at the way in which cultural cross-representations and questions of modernity, modernism, and postmodernism emerge in his work. The third chapter is dedicated to linguistic strategies, based partly on the polygraphy of the Japanese language and partly on the introduction of foreign words in the *katakana* syllabary and sometimes in the Roman alphabet—approaches that highlight the artificial nature of language and the linguistically constructed nature of reality. The fourth chapter deals with Murakami's references to Western literature and popular culture, and with his use of a number of literary strategies that foreground cultural categories in order to subvert them, particularly the parody of Western genres and the use of metafictional techniques. The last chapter addresses the concept of literature as "other world" as well as the representation of other worlds in a more literal sense, different levels of diegetic reality. I examine the way in which Murakami's texts often border on the fantastic, staging parallel realities and distorted temporalities, and how these "other worlds" are related to the construction of individual identity, on the one hand, and to the problem of social responsibility, on the other.

ONE

The Japanization of Modernity

Modernism, *Modanizumu, Kindaishugi*

The term "modernity" is often abused and misused—defined so many ways that it seems to lose all meaning. In light of this overuse, one might be tempted to dispense with the term altogether; however, I believe we should still address it, looking at what the proliferation of discourses on modernity achieves and what it conceals, precisely because it is so frequently misused in contemporary debates on crucial issues. The term is employed with notable frequency today by Western journalism, be it to define Islamic terrorism as born of the incapacity to accept or deal with Western modernity; to connect issues of human rights in China to the country's reluctance or failure to modernize; or to urge Turkey to become more "modern" if it ever wants to be allowed into the European Union. Scholars and journalists writing on contemporary global politics often interpret international tensions in terms of a contrast between the West, bearer of modernity, and the rest of the world, premodern, nonmodern, or hostile to modernity, unwilling to modernize, resentful of modernity.

For their part, scholars of anthropology, sociology, history, and literature refer to the term as a problematic and problematizing theoretical category, and they, too, use it with increasing frequency to explain a variety of phenomena, attributing to it a wide range of nuances. The more the term is used, the less clear its meaning becomes. Especially in recent times, the term "modern" and its derivatives "modernity" and "modernism" have been subject to a great deal of contrasting definitions. In an essay titled "Definitional Excursions: The Meanings of Modern/Modernity/Modernism," Susan Stanford Friedman compares a series of excerpts from essays on modernity and modernism that are so dissimilar among themselves that they seem to refer to opposite phenomena. When one compares statements such as: "modernism . . . is the one art that responds to the scenario of our chaos" and "who says modernity says organization," the same term seems to take on completely opposite meanings.[1] Modernism can mean either the wavering of the certainties of Western tradition or the strengthening of the myth of rationalism and progress, either an embracing of the chaos of the world or the obsession of rational control over it—definitions not so much different as radically contradicting one another.

According to Friedman, "as terms in an evolving scholarly discourse, *modern, modernity,* and *modernism* constitute a critical Tower of Babel, a cacophony of categories that become increasingly useless the more inconsistently they are used" and "their use appears to threaten the project of scholarship/teaching altogether." However, she also maintains that these contradictory terms, by virtue of their resistance to consensual definition, form a fertile terrain for interrogation, "providing ever more sites for examination with each new meaning spawned," and therefore, "as parody of rational discourse, their contradictions highlight the production of meaning possible by calling attention to what will not be tamed, by what refuses consistency and homogenization."[2]

From the 1970s, the debate on what modernism and the modern are—or were—merged with the discussion on postmodernism, which is even more articulated and replete with varied and conflicting positions. Here the argument is further complicated by the fact that one of the crucial concerns of postmodernism is the refusal of definitions and the constant questioning of its own presuppositions.

A particularly significant but insufficiently studied issue in the debate on modernity is its connection to East-West relations. Modernity has often been portrayed as the exclusive domain of the West, to be exported to or imposed upon non-developed countries. However, Western modernity was also born of its relationship with such countries. Significantly, the modern era is usually considered to begin with "great geographical discoveries," that is to say, with the moment when Europe first came into contact with the "rest of the world," and set out to conquer, convert, assimilate, and modernize it.

Modernity was born in Europe in reaction to its encounter with the non-West and the consequent discovery of radically different cultures. On the one hand, this epochal event produced an opening to otherness that questioned traditional certainties; on the other hand, it generated various forms of parochiality and self-reassertion against the ethnic and cultural Other. These two reactions lie at the core of the contradictory phenomenon of modernity.

The acceptance of cultural diversity apparently prevailed in the shift from modernism to postmodernism, since the latter explicitly questioned the "grand narratives" and cultural assumptions of the West, instead valuing marginal identities and liminal positions. On the other hand, the very idea of *post*modernism, with its insistence on situating itself "after" modernism and/or modernity, reinforced the idea of historical progression implicit in the term "modern" as opposed to "premodern," concealing its cultural and geographical aspects. In this sense, the concept of postmodernism, with its stress on the temporal sequence premodern, modern, postmodern, further contributed to a progressive vision of modernity.

The concept of modernization as progress, as the path that every country should follow, lies at the heart of the concept of the "clash of civilizations," a paradigm often used to explain international relations in the era of globalization. Such an idea was first formulated in the 1990s by Bernard Lewis, the historian of Islam, and was brought to the world's attention by Samuel Huntington in his famous essay by the same title.[3]

Huntington reinterpreted relations between states in cultural terms, arguing that in the post–World War II era the fault lines of civilizations would be the battle lines of the future, and that in such times of emerging cultural conflict the West should forge alliances with similar cultures and spread its values wherever it could, acting in an accommodating manner if possible, but confrontationally if necessary. Other advocates of the "clash of civilizations" theory, such as William Lind, took a less aggressive stance, but retained the conviction that the great divisions among humankind, and the principal sources of conflict, are neither ideological nor political but cultural. The concept was subsequently adopted in the contemporary media and has become a current reference, especially in connection with Islamic countries, but also occasionally in regard to other non-Western cultures.

This "culturalist" stance closely resembles a post–World War II version of pre-war racism repackaged for the age of political correctness. In reinterpreting the racial menace to the white man represented by other races in terms of a clash of *civilizations*, this approach apparently allows for the existence of "civilizations" in the plural, thus taking a relativist stance that gives equal dignity to different cultures, but in fact results in a reaffirmation of the transcendental humanist paradigm of universalism that always takes the West as its standard. In this discourse, the concept of "modernity as progress" is a powerful instrument, one that implicitly assumes such Western values as democracy, freedom, and justice—concepts frequently recurring in Western (and particularly American) rhetoric on the new "white man's burden"—to be modern in themselves, and as such are the natural end of progress and should be the future goal of nonmodern countries.

The Japanese experience of modernization, however, throws into question these assumptions. The case of Japan foregrounds the intrinsically geographical and political nature of the concept of modernity, which in the West has traditionally been reconceptualized as temporal, i.e., as evolution *in time,* through the notion of progress. Japan's "concentrated modernization" from 1853 to the first years of the twentieth century significantly challenged the Western vision of modernity. The speed with which Japan acquired modern technology, a modern form of government, and a comprehensive social, legal, and military system, combined with its quickly realized aspiration to a position of equality with Western nations, caused in Europe and the United States reactions ranging from curiosity to uneasiness to alarm. The Euro-American powers repeatedly wondered how Japan could assimilate from the West so quickly all it needed to become a modern industrial society. Japan could not be easily integrated into its configuration of the world: it did not fit in the binary schema of a modern West and a nonmodern non-West. Japan's swift rise prompted the thought that modernity was not only a matter of progress, but was also predicated upon specific geopolitical conditions.

As Naoki Sakai notes, an answer to the "problem of Japan" came after the Second World War from the United States, in the form of a theory of "modernization" as the path that every state must inevitably tread, a universal value to which the particularistic instances of single nonmodern nations should conform. This theory of modernization thus assumed a specifically American tone. As Sakai puts it:

> A sizable amount of intellectual labor has been invested in order to render this peculiar object [i.e., Japan] innocuous in the discursive formation. In the United States, the consequences of this labor have usually been collected under the name "modernization theory.". . . What modernization theory has accomplished by introducing the opposition of universalism and particularism into the study of other cultures is . . . to reproduce the same kind of discursive formation within which the unity of the West is constituted—but, this time, with the centre explicitly in the United States.[4]

The questions of universalism and particularism are also relevant here and will be discussed in the following part of the chapter. However, the other important point that Sakai makes here is that the peculiarity of Japan's "second modernization" lies in the fact that it coincided not so much with its generic "Westernization" but with its Americanization. This process was clearly facilitated by the American-led occupation, during which Japan was obliged to reform its political, legal, economic, and civic institutions under the guidance of the United States. Japan was therefore the first instance of a phenomenon that became prevalent in the postwar world and is still in evidence today: the passage of the ideology of progress from Europe to North America, both in the sphere of ideals, where economic liberalism represents a new version of the civilizing mission, and in the sphere of economic and military power. After World War II, the Enlightenment project of universalist modernization, more or less abandoned by Europe in its strictly cultural or "civilizing" sense, was taken over in the field of economics by the American ideology of the free market. The United States thus became the new bearers of the universal (or "global") values that constituted the standards to which the rest of the world had to conform. As John Gray notes:

> The United States today is the last great power to base its policies on [the] Enlightenment thesis. According to the "Washington consensus," "democratic capitalism" will soon be accepted throughout the world. A global free market will become a reality. The manifold economic cultures and systems that the world has always contained will be redundant. They will be merged into a universal free market.[5]

In this sense, Japan can be considered a forerunner, because the United States has been its most important counterpart since the arrival of Commodore Perry's ships to Japan in 1853, and, most importantly, because Japan was the first and paradigmatic example of American-style postwar "successful modernization."

However, precisely by virtue of its ability to modernize, Japan has always constituted a destabilizing element within the Western representation of modernity, causing reactions that range from exoticizing fascination to open hostility, but also potentially offering a valuable contribution to the theoretical debate on the concept of modernity. Japan is non-Western but modernized, hybrid, and ambiguous, evincing in its relations with Europe and the United States some features typical of the (post)colonial phenomenon such as the "complicity of the colonized" exposed by Homi Bhabha; at the same time, Japan is impossible to label as an (ex-)colony, and as such challenges Western categories of thought much more than postmodernism, which questions them from within a fundamentally Euro-American standpoint. Japan's experience of modernity thus foregrounds the limits that Western-born universalistic notions—those that often continue to take the West as their standard—encounter when they cross their borders.

In this respect, perhaps, studying modernism in Japan as a literary and intellectual movement would be more illuminating than simply looking at its experience of modernity and modernization. Particularly challenging is the Japanese concept of *kindaishugi* ("modernism" or "the ideology of the modern"), an idea circulated after the Second World War among Japanese writers, philosophers, and intellectuals that gives a highly original contribution to the debate on the nature of "modernity" and "modernism."

In the early postwar years, a group of writers and philosophers led by Maruyama Masao articulated the need to restore the "incomplete project of modernity" that Japan had never fully realized. They advised Japanese intellectuals to come together as a *kaikon kyōdōtai,* or "repentance community," in order to face up to Japan's war responsibilities. To come to terms with the war's legacy, Maruyama advocated a new ideology of *kindaishugi* (modernism), making explicit reference to the famous debate on *kindai no chōkoku* ("overcoming the modern") held in 1942 by the literary magazine *Bungakukai* (Literary Society) in Tokyo and to the contemporaneous series of three symposia on the same issues organized by the publisher Chūō kōron in Kyoto.[6]

In December 1945, Maruyama published an article titled "Kindaiteki shii" (Modern Thought), in which he harshly criticized the project to "overcome modernity," arguing that

> Some of our most illustrious critics and scholars maintain that "modernity" has exhausted its historical function in the past, and that now even in Japan, or rather, most of all in Japan, it is time to

"overcome it." When we look at this attitude of the past years from the perspective of contemporary Japan, while we learn from MacArthur the foundations of civilization, it is hard not to feel a sense of misery and absurdity.[7]

According to Maruyama, Japan had never fully achieved modernity, much less overcome it. He therefore maintained that to rebuild the country in the aftermath of the war Japanese people had to become modern individual subjects, deeply rooted in history. Only a strong subjectivity, in his opinion, could mold citizens whose actions would be informed by rational knowledge and who would act responsibly. Maruyama pointed out that before and during the war there had been no clear line of demarcation between the public and the private domains in Japan, and this had allowed the state to dominate everyday life. The prewar category of *shimin* (imperial subject) led only to subjection; now, with the war behind them, the Japanese people needed to create a new kind of *shutai* (autonomous subject) that could negotiate between private and public realms and take political action. In order to do this, it was necessary for Japanese intellectuals to confront the past and acquire a historical consciousness. The ideology of *kindaishugi* and its image of a politically committed intellectual would be crucial for postwar intellectuals in Japan, and they are still a key concern of *junbungaku* ("pure" literature) writers today.

Interestingly, the "modernism" or *kindaishugi* of the postwar literati is in many respects the exact opposite of Western literary "modernism." In their famous study of modernism, for instance, James Bradbury and Malcom McFarlane mention as its essential elements "an emphasis on fragmentation, on the breaking up and the progressive disintegration of those meticulously constructed 'systems' and 'types' and 'absolutes' that lived on from the earlier years of the century, on the destruction of the belief in large general laws to which all life and conduct could be claimed to be subject."[8]

Whereas literary modernism in Europe represented a challenge to the master narratives of Western modernity and a constant questioning of the possibility to know the world and one's individual identity, Japan's *kindaishugi* coincided with an attempt, even though critical and fraught with ambiguities, to revive those same "grand narratives" in order to build a coherent, unitary subject, grounded in history and in national identity. Furthermore, a key element of so-called high modernism (represented mainly by the works of T. S. Eliot and Ezra Pound) was the insistence on the opposition between art and history: modernist writers and intellectuals saw art as a timeless aesthetic form that was capable of opposing the fragmentation and meaninglessness of the modern world and redeeming the "nightmare of history." This position, too, is the opposite of the insistence on social and political commitment on the part of Japanese intellectuals, and is actually closer to the ideals of the "overcoming the modern" debate, whose members rejected what they saw as a Western teleological vision of the world. According to Kobayashi Hideo, one of the participants in the discussion, beauty and art reveal to us the existence of timeless essence; beauty does not "evolve" in a progressive way and cannot be comprehended within the historically motivated perspective of the moderns.[9] To overcome modernity, in his opinion, did not mean advancing toward a new era, but being reunited outside history with the eternal forms of beauty and art—something very close to the ideals of Euro-American modernism.

The idea of Western modernity was central also to Japan's other "modernism": *modanizumu*, the literary movement that developed in parallel to the Euro-American stream in the 1910s and 1920s. This very contemporaneity was a central feature of the phenomenon. As Seiji Lippit remarks, the intellectual panorama of the Taishō period (1912–26) was defined by cosmopolitanism and the sense that Japan and the West were "inhabiting the same world," that Japan had finally caught up with Western civilization and become "modern." Significantly, for Taishō intellectuals, this cosmopolitanism and the related universalistic vision of the world were based mainly on the power of literature to spread universal ideas. After spending decades frantically translating literature and learning foreign languages, Japanese writers felt that the Western literary tradition belonged to them as much as to contemporary Europeans and Americans, and that acquiring this cultural capital had turned them into "citizens of the world."

In the 1930s, however, this cosmopolitanism eventually collapsed, and a sense of unease and a feeling of cultural homelessness became the new dominant features of Japanese literature and intellectual debate. The spread of modern technologies of communication and the consequent expansion of culture came to be seen as threats to national identity, and universalism turned into a sense of crisis. This was reflected in literature in a disruption of formal boundaries and a concern with the disintegration of the self, as exemplified by the experimental literature of Yokomitsu Riichi and Satō Haruo.

Central to this process is the Western concept of the individual subject, which had also been a major concern for Meiji writers. Since any sense of identity for Japanese writers of this period was deeply related to their literary conscience, the disintegration of the idea of literature resulted in dissolution of the self. Such a collapse of identity, in turn, was often represented in connection with foreign culture and, interestingly, with foreign language. This is evident, for example, in Akutagawa's short story "Haguruma" (Cogwheels), in which the protagonist's crisis of identity is objectified in the progressive disintegration of the narrator's speech into a number of foreign languages. In this respect, Japanese *modanizumu* seems to share many of the characteristics of contemporaneous Euro-American modernism: in its sense of crisis, its increasing criticism of the grand narratives of the modern West, and its suspicion toward the naturalness of language.

At the same time, however, there is one significant difference: no matter how much Japanese intellectuals of the early 1920s had felt that Japan and the West shared the same universal culture and coexisted in the same world, their critique of Western modernity was grounded in their sense of geographical and cultural distance from it, and their subsequent sense of crisis was inextricably linked to a conflict with Western culture. This became even more evident in the last phase of Japanese *modanizumu*, the "Return to Japan" phase that most writers who were part of the modernist movement in the early years of their careers, such as Kawabata Yasunari and Yokomitsu Riichi, underwent in their later works.

One element that complicates this picture, as discussed in greater detail in the next section, is Japanese imperialism in Asia. The colonial enterprise had elicited in Japanese writers a response similar to that of Euro-American modernists to Western imperialism, resulting in a literature that centered on the anxiety in the face of the hybrid, destabilized, and destabilizing colonial space, and on a criticism of capitalism as an imperialist mode of production and consumption. In the late 1930s, however, for a number of writers and intellectuals, the former sense of "modernist" exile and cultural displacement turned into nostalgia and an aspiration to reconstruct Japanese tradition and culture—an effort that, in many ways, was already evident in the 1920s, as documented by Marilyn Ivy in her study *Discourses of the Vanishing*. One of the most significant results of the spread of the "Return to Japan" ideology was the birth of *Bungakukai*, the "literary society" that organized the *kindai no chōkoku* debate.

Most importantly, the idea of a revival of Japanese values often appealed to Pan-Asianist sentiments, which in this sense became a substitute for the loss of the West as an ideal. In the second half of the 1930s, the rise of nationalism and the resulting government pressures on intellectuals resulted in a rejection of Western modernity predicated upon a "return to Japanese tradition" that was also identified with "Asian values." To quote Seiji Lippit:

> If the earlier modernist writings had reflected the collapse of a faith in literature and a fragmentation of a cosmopolitan subjectivity, we can see in the literary theory and practice of the late 1930s both an attempted reconfiguration of the institution of literature and, in a certain sense, a reconstructed conception of modernity organized around the idea of East Asian civilization.[10]

Japanese literary modernism, too, thus became a critique of modernity predicated upon the ideology of Pan-Asianism and a revolt against the West. This, in turn, led to the recuperation of Western modernity through the ideology of *kindaishugi* in the postwar years, as we have seen.

Thus Japanese *modanizumu* and *kindaishugi* add a new side to the discussion of what "modernism" is (or was), underlining the spatial dimension of modernity. Murakami's work is particularly relevant to the discussion of this concept, not only because he dissociates himself from the "modernism" of mainstream Japanese literature to the point that he has often been defined as a "postmodernist," but also because in his work he makes use of both Western modernist and postmodernist elements, looking at them from an ironic distance.

A crucial issue both in the *kindaishugi* ideology and in *modanizumu*, as we have seen, is the problem of modern subjectivity. This issue has been central to Japan's relationship with the West since the Meiji era, when, according to a number of scholars, the idea of the individual subject took shape. Karatani Kōjin traces back the birth of a Japanese subjectivity to the cognitive revolution he calls "discovery of landscape" (*fūkei no hakken*), that is to say, the birth of a separation between a knowing subject and a known object, and the consequent "discovery" of a landscape outside the self. This was paralleled by a "discovery of interiority": it is only through the birth of a subject possessing interiority that external reality is perceived as such, and vice versa. According to Karatani, this epistemological revolution happened in Japan as a consequence of the impact of Western modes of thought that were imported in the Meiji era together with Western technology. However, once constituted, the concepts of subject and landscape were naturalized and taken for granted, their recent origin was suppressed, and they were presented as natural and eternal characteristics of Japanese culture, or even of human nature.[11]

Literature was fundamental in this process of naturalization, as well as in the diffusion of the notion of individual subject. A particularly significant instrument was the *watakushi shōsetsu*, and its idea of literature as self-expression.[12] The confessional mode has remained a fixture in Japanese literature, from writers of the Naturalist school such as Tayama Katai and Shimazaki Tōson, to the "founding fathers" of *junbungaku* such as Shiga Naoya, all the way to contemporary novelists such as Ōe Kenzaburō, whose most famous novel is significantly titled *Kojinteki na taiken* (*A Personal Experience*). Murakami Haruki, on the other hand, takes a very different stance on this matter: he criticizes the idea of literature as self-expression (*jiko hyōgen*), and his work presents a new and unique approach to the problem of the subject.

Imperialism, Orientalism, Universalism

The case of Japan also calls into question certain assumptions of postcolonial theory, once again highlighting the geopolitical aspect of the concept of modernity. First of all, it offers a new perspective on the concept of Orientalism, famously formulated by Edward Said in his 1978 essay by the same title and developed in his later works, that has been crucial to reflections on East-West relations. Although Said's theory of Orientalism was ground-breaking at the time and remains an extremely valid and useful concept, confronting it with the case of Japan can provide a more nuanced vision of the phenomenon.

Koichi Iwabuchi criticizes Said for the "total absence of a consideration of Japanese imperialism/colonialism in his analysis of imperialism and culture."[13] Both in *Culture and Imperialism* and in *Orientalism*, Said deals only in passing with Japan because his work is mainly concerned with the Middle East,—not East Asia. Precisely for this reason, it is interesting to try to apply his notion of Orientalism to Western attitudes toward Japan. Richard Minear has analyzed early Western scholarship on Japan (in particular the works of Basil Hall Chamberlain, George B. Sansom, and Edwin O. Reischauer) in light of Said's theories, and has found many typically "Orientalist" features in these studies. The works of these three founding fathers of Japanese studies, in Minear's opinion, are based on an aestheticization of Japanese culture and an enthusiasm for Japan as "tradition" that reduces it to an exotic essence, an attitude very close to that of Said's "Orientalists."[14]

Japan's successful modernization threatened this aestheticized image, giving rise to expressions of concern about the impending loss of its pristine traditions that hinted at a concurrent preoccupation with the potential menace of its growing economic and military power. According to Neil Harris, who analyzes American images of Japan at the International Expositions of the late nineteenth and early twentieth century, "the dilemma of how to accept the prospect of Westernization crystallized American attitudes toward national difference generally: on the one hand, a tendency to see Americanization as a sign of progress; on the other, a desire to freeze national customs into a picturesque whole."[15] This ambiguous attitude is based on a fundamental desire to prove Japan's backwardness in order to reinstate America's role as an advanced world power. Although an appreciation of Japan's tradition and fear of its loss results in an affirmation of America's superiority as a modern country, praise for its modernization always underlines the derivative aspect of such progress and the essential backwardness of the country: it is only by "Americanizing" that Japan can "modernize." This discourse therefore allows America to constitute itself as the standard to which the world strives to conform. In this sense, too, American attitudes toward Japan reflect dynamics similar to those of Western, particularly European, Orientalism.

However, whereas the Orient described by Said coincides with the West's past, and is therefore easily represented as its traditional, backward, nonmodern Other, Japanese tradition cannot be considered the antecedent of Western modernity. Japan is essentialized as a country either of "beauty and tradition," or simply of backwardness, in the same way as the Arab world was, but it is distant in space, not in time. Japan's otherness is geographical rather than temporal, and this clearly foregrounds the geopolitical nature of modernity.

Furthermore, Japan's history challenges a fundamental assumption of postcolonial theory: the binary distinction between colonizers and colonized. Japan never became an actual colony: it is well known that after the first contact with the West in the sixteenth century, Japan was able to avoid almost any form of interaction with Europe for close to three centuries. Even after the Japanese were forced to open their ports to foreign powers again in 1854, Japan did not become a colony; rather, it soon began to compete with the Western powers in Asia, trying to create its own empire. Some scholars argue that Japan was able to escape colonization because it was quicker in "colonizing itself by itself": Yoshioka Hiroshi calls this phenomenon "internalized colonization" and argues that Japan's adoption of Western technology and ways of thought was a form of self-imposed cultural colonization that, while sharing many traits with colonial dynamics, at the same time challenges conventional ideas of power relations between colonizers and colonized.[16]

Japan's status as a non-Western imperialist power challenges any linear representation of the colonial phenomenon. Masao Miyoshi calls Japanese imperialism a "secondary colonialism," a form of "derivative" imperialism by a country formerly on the side of the colonized, and compares it to that of the United States on the North American continent and in the Philippines. However, he goes on to note that, at least at the ideological level, Japan's colonial enterprise contained a nationalist project of response to Western invasion.[17]

Interestingly, this "nationalist project" was predicated upon a type of anti-Western counter-colonialism that incorporated many elements of what it claimed to oppose. Japan represented its colonial mission as a reaction against white imperialism, and in order to do so it emphasized the presence of "common Asian values" with the countries it colonized. By doing this, it reduced the different cultures of China, Korea, Indonesia, the Philippines, and so forth to a single essential "Asianness," in a fashion similar to what the West had done with the "Orient." During the war, the Japanese government's propaganda relied heavily on the idea of a cultural continuity between Japan and other Asian countries, and on the "equality of all

Imperial subjects," be they Japanese, Chinese, Korean, or from the Philippines. Japanese domination was advocated as more "natural" than that of the white man on the basis of a supposed cultural homogeneity of Asia, the same homogeneity that Edward Said sees as an "invention of the West." The Japanese appropriated the ideology of Orientalism, turning it against the West and making it their own instrument of conquest.

On the other hand, Japan presented itself as a kind of *primus inter pares*, portraying itself as the natural leader in the "Greater East Asia Co-Prosperity Sphere" by virtue of its modernity and technological, political, economic, and military superiority. In this sense, Asia played a constitutive part in Japan's construction of national identity: the "inferior" nations of Asia embodied the "backwardness, tradition, past" that illustrated how successfully modernization had progressed in Japan. In this way, modernization was represented as a shift away from Asia, just as Western modernity was.

A firm understanding of these complex issues is essential in order to appreciate contemporary relations among Japan, the West, and Asia. At the same time, the relationship between Japanese colonialism and modernization provides an extremely useful point of comparison for a study of both colonial and postcolonial phenomena. In particular, Japanese colonialism in Asia challenges common views of the relationship between imperialism and universalistic and nationalistic stances. On the one hand, the case of Japan questions the straightforward connection often drawn by postcolonial studies between imperialism and universalism, and, on the other, it challenges the binary distinction frequently made between (Western) universalism and (non-Western, more specifically, Japanese) particularism.

American scholarship on Japan often stresses Japanese particularism, emphasizing either the country's actual uniqueness or its claim to uniqueness as the salient characteristic of Japanese culture. Many scholars describe Japan as particularistic, in contrast to supposedly "universalistic" Chinese and Western cultures. In most works, the specific articulation of

Chinese universalism is neglected, and the discussion focuses on the differences between Japan and the West.[18]

Universalism is one of the key notions of the Enlightenment, and in a broader sense, of modern Western thought. For the purposes of this study, universalism can be defined tentatively as a progressive vision of the world in which different cultures are considered different stages of a single path to civilization, and as the consequent aspiration to create a universal society based on reason. It is deeply interconnected with transcendental humanism, the idea of a universal human nature that underlies superficial cultural differences, and to an evolutionary vision of humanity, whose eventual goal is to reach a set of universally accepted values. This "universal human nature," however, ultimately coincides with specific characteristics of Western man, whose values become the basis of the "civilizing mission" that justifies colonial expansion. The West at the beginning of the modern era invests itself with the task to lead the rest of the world under the control of its own civilization, whose superiority is sanctioned by the universality of its founding values.

Particularism, on the other hand, is generally defined as a relativistic vision of the world that focuses on the uniqueness and specificity of one's own culture's values, and often borders on exceptionalism, interpreting uniqueness as superiority. Interestingly, the concept of cultural relativism and the attempt to interpret the relations among nations in terms of different cultures were prominent in the West in the postwar years, precisely when American scholars began to apply the notion of particularism to Japan. Elazar Barkan notes in *The Retreat of Scientific Racism* that one of the results of the Second World War was the discrediting of the idea of racial superiority: after the war, societies no longer interpreted differences in racial terms, but in cultural ones. Non-Western societies were not considered inferior but rather having a "different character," a different culture. The adoption of these ideas by major international organizations such as the United Nations gave them authority and legitimacy. During the same period in which such a concept of cultural relativism was forming in the West, European and particularly American scholars started applying it to Japan, arguing that Japan was "particularistic" as opposed to the universalistic West. Significantly, two of the first authoritative texts that formulated the idea of Japan's particularistic attitude both date from 1946, namely, Ruth Benedict's *The Chrysanthemum and the Sword*, which sees particularism as one of the founding values of Japanese society, and Edwin O. Reischauer's *Japan Past and Present*, which traces it back to the long isolation of the country.[19] In light of this, some critics maintain that exceptionalism is not so much an essential trait of Japanese culture as a product of American scholarship on Japan. Lynn Revell analyzes the phenomenon of *nihonjinron*, the theory of "what it means to be Japanese," generally regarded as the primary manifestation of Japan's particularist or exceptionalist attitude, arguing that "it is the commentaries on *nihonjinron* themselves that give it the semblance of a recognizable trend in Japanese society," and that "the so-called Japanese obsession with their own uniqueness exists more clearly in the eyes of the West than in Japan itself."[20]

Naoki Sakai offers a particularly nuanced and intriguing analysis of this phenomenon. He maintains that Japanese particularism does indeed exist, but that rather than being an intrinsic feature of "Japanese nature," it came into existence as an effect of policies enacted during the American occupation. Sakai asserts that Japanese particularism did not originate during the imperialistic period—during which, on the contrary, pan-Asianism was the prevailing ideology—but in the postwar years, as a result of the occupation forces' efforts to encourage Japan to distance itself from other Asian countries in order to become America's principal ally in the region against communist China.[21] During the war, Japanese leaders had promoted Pan-Asianism as the nation's answer to Western colonialism; after the war, however, the occupation forces tried to dismantle this ideological apparatus by encouraging the particularistic instances of Japanese intellectuals such as Maruyama Masao and Watsuji Tetsurō.[22]

On a theoretical level, portraying Japan as particularistic allowed America to represent itself as universalistic, while the Western image of Japan endowed Japan itself with a national identity. In Sakai's words:

> A privileged object of discourse called Japan is thus constituted in order to show *us* the supposedly concrete instance of particularism, in contrast to which *our* universalism is ascertained. Japan is defined as a specific and unitary particularity in universal terms: Japan's uniqueness and identity are provided insofar as Japan stands out as a particular object in the field of the West. Only when it is integrated into Western universalism does it gain its own identity as a particularity. In other words, Japan becomes endowed with and aware of its "self" only when it is recognized by the West.[23]

Therefore, in Sakai's opinion, universalism and particularism in the postwar era are fundamentally complicit: "Universalism and particularism endorse each other's defect in order to conceal their own; they are intimately tied to each other in their complicity. In this respect, a particularism such as nationalism can never be a serious critique of universalism, for it is an accomplice thereof."[24] Sakai calls this process a "schema of cofiguration," a system through which a culture defines itself in relation to another—an approach typical of the West in the colonial era that was subsequently adopted in Japan as well. According to Sakai, these two concepts are not only mutually dependent, but are, in a stronger sense, complicit in constituting themselves as the only possible alternatives in a binary schema that excludes a more radical otherness.[25]

The connivance between particularism and universalism attempts to conceal the internal differences of both systems: universalism and particularism both see the nation as a homogeneous entity, erasing the differences within. Although postcolonial theory exposed the involvement of Western universalism with imperialism by placing it in a binary opposition to relativism and particularism, it failed to recognize the complicity between particularism and universalism. A study of the relationship between Japanese particularism and Western/

American universalism is therefore extremely useful in order to gain a more articulated vision of (post)colonial processes.

Finally, Japan's recent "cultural colonialism" in Asia challenges visions of globalization as a Western-centered phenomenon. Lately, a number of scholars have analyzed what has been defined as the "new Asianism" of Japan in the 1990s: i.e., the diffusion of Japanese popular culture in Asia and its implications concerning Japanese nationalism and globalization.[26] On the one hand, Japan has become a significant source of cultural exports to Asia, thus questioning a simple vision of globalization as a matter of "the West imposing its culture on the rest of the world." On the other hand, in this process, Japan has been acting as a cultural mediator between Asia and the West, absorbing Western culture and "reselling" it in a domesticated, processed version to other Asian countries.

Harumi Befu argues that Japan has been a source of Western knowledge for Asian countries since the Meiji period, and that, from that time on, "Japan indigenized (creolized) the West, and . . . made it easier for other Asian countries to digest this already 'Asianized' Western culture." He calls this phenomenon the "Japanization of the West."[27]

Japanization is a key term in this context. As Koichi Iwabuchi notes, during the 1930s and early 1940s it was used to mean either "the assimilation of ethnic others into Japanese imperial citizenship under the Emperor's benevolence" or "the indigenization and domestication of foreign (Western) culture."[28] After the war, however, the second meaning tended to prevail, with a concurrent shift from the idea of "imitation" to the idea of "appropriation" of Western culture. Interestingly, since the 1990s there has been a renewed interest in Japan for "Asian values." Iwabuchi maintains that this is partly an effort to preserve an image of "traditional Asia" as backward in contrast to "modernized Japan," in the face of advancing modernization in other Asian countries. As Iwabuchi writes: "Japan's transnational cultural power is reasserted and articulated in terms of indigenized modernity."[29]

TWO

Murakami Haruki, Japan, and America

In his literary production, Murakami Haruki straddles the United States and Japan and shows how the cultural interactions between the two entities challenge dominant discourses through a "complicitous critique." With his double activity as a translator of Western literature and as a novelist widely read in Japan, in the West, and in Asia, Murakami's works cast light upon the literary side of the "Japanization of modernity" described in the previous chapter. How, then, does Murakami fit into this complex schema? Before analyzing his texts, it would be fruitful to look briefly at the ways in which he is perceived in the West, particularly in the United States, and also in Japan.

American Views of Murakami

Murakami Haruki has become enormously popular in the United States. In 1991, during his first year as a visiting scholar at Princeton University, he participated in a book-signing event that drew only fifteen people. Fourteen years later, in November 2005, he gave a reading at the Massachusetts Institute of Technology in a room that was intended to hold some five hundred people. More than thirteen hundred fans showed up, and a crowd of eight hundred people—some having come from other parts of the country just for the event—were turned away. Most American readers of Murakami today are neither specialists in Japanese studies nor particularly interested in Japanese literature: many regard him not as "a Japanese writer" but simply as "a writer."

This perception might be related in part to the reception of his works once they have been translated into English. His American translators, Alfred Birnbaum, Jay Rubin, and Philip Gabriel, tend to "domesticate" foreign elements in Murakami's fiction: culturally specific elements are often substituted with either generic or American equivalents, so that he does not sound "too Japanese" in translation. This results in a wider readership, which in turn leads to further domestication, with the logic that the wider the public, the less likely readers will understand or be interested in elements that are too culturally specific.[1] This does not mean that Murakami's novels in translation are completely transformed, of course; these are only minor changes that make his books more easily readable while preserving their distinctiveness. However, these slight adaptations play a significant role in the reception of Murakami's work in America: it is partly thanks to these modifications that his texts have acquired a special role in presenting Japanese culture to the United States. Perceived as not-too-Japanese and therefore non-threatening, these works are able to escape both the aestheticizing/feminizing stereotypes and the warrior-like, violent images through which Japanese culture has generally been represented in America.

Since the first contacts between the United States and Japan in the middle of the nineteenth century, American media, fiction, and scholarly works have dealt with Japan's radical otherness by adopting a series of representative strategies aimed at diminishing the menace of a culture so different that it questions the foundations of Western civilization and so well-structured and articulated that it threatens to undermine the myth of the undisputed superiority of the West. Such modes of representation, which render the "Other" inoffensive, have been displayed in three main ways: through critique and contempt, using Japan as a negative term of comparison to attest the superiority of American culture; through constant ridicule of difference, in which Americans affirm their own superiority and also neutralize the other, making it laughable and therefore less threatening; and lastly by an extensive aestheticization/reification, through which Japan is constituted as an object of aesthetic appreciation that is small, graceful, and harmless. Admiration for Japanese art, tradition, and beauty often conceals a mechanism of defense, an attempt to reify the ethnic Other in order to disempower it, and to project an image of backwardness against which the modernity of the West can be measured.

Depending on the state of political, economic, and military relations between the two countries, American representations of Japan have shifted toward one or the other of these strategies. As Sheila Johnson notes, such images tend to cluster around two stereotypes: that of a hypermasculine, warrior Japan, typified by samurai and swords, and that of a feminine and elegant Japan, epitomized by geisha and cherry blossoms. When relations are good, as at the beginning of the twentieth century or in the 1960s, aestheticized representations tend to prevail, whereas when relations become difficult, as during the war, or following the trade tensions of the 1980s, warrior Japan is the dominant image.[2]

Murakami's texts, however, are neither chrysanthemums nor swords. They represent a different Japan that America seems to be confronting in a less exoticizing and more understanding manner. At the same time, Murakami's works *are* the object of a certain degree of stereotyping, although of a new, different kind. Particularly in the 1990s, when Murakami first came to the attention of American readers and critics, reviews of his books always insisted on his un-Japaneseness, on his role as the symbol of a "new Japan," more technological than traditional but most of all "completely Westernized." Whereas in the 1960s American studies of Japanese literature tended to emphasize its exotic aspects, along with the aforementioned feminized and aestheticized stereotypes, domestication seems to prevail in the decades since, and in this context, Murakami Haruki's works are portrayed as a representative example of the successful modernization of a non-Western country, and a vindication of U.S. policies during the occupation.

We can find a similar approach to other authors translated in the United States in the 1990s. For instance, the anthology of short stories *Monkey Brain Sushi: New Tastes in Japanese Fiction* (1991), while on the one hand playing on some stereotypes of the "Orient" (beginning with the title and its mixture of exoticizing *clichés* on China and Japan), on the other hand it explicitly aims to give a new image of Japan: not the traditional country of kimono, geisha, and samurai, but a technologically advanced, and, most importantly, highly Americanized country. In the introduction, Alfred Birnbaum writes:

> Starting from the early 1980s, a new generation of Japanese writers has emerged to capture the electric, eclectic spirit of contemporary life in Japan's mega-cities. . . . these young authors have shunned such traditional labels as *jun bungaku*, pure literature, opting instead for the Anglicism *fuikkushon*, fiction. The choice of a Western epithet is telling: these voices bear little resemblance to Kawabata, Tanizaki, Mishima, or even Abe, Endo, and Oe—staples of the older diet. If anything, the new writers look to the American "city novel" for their style and approach. They were all born and raised in an Americanized Postwar Japan. . . . Furthermore, the Japanese language itself is changing. Trade imbalance notwithstanding, the Japanese have been enthusiastic importers of Western language.[3]

The reference to trade imbalance is significant, as it will recur in almost all reviews of Murakami's works from this period. Japanese interest in Western culture in the 1980s is interpreted as a sign that even though Japan might have become economically powerful, culturally it still looks up to the West.

Murakami's texts, too, are presented by critics and reviewers as particularly Westernized, and the most salient trait of his fiction is identified as its "un-Japaneseness." For instance, Iwamoto Yoshio in *World Literature Today* declares that in reading Murakami you should "forget everything you know about Japan" and "enter the postmodern world of Haruki Murakami's

A Wild Sheep Chase, where people sweat about their careers, drink too much, and drift through broken marriages, all without a kimono in sight."[4] Meanwhile, Herbert Mitgang writes that "Haruki Murakami, Japan's most popular novelist, writes metaphysical Far Easterns with a Western beat," and that "his rapid-fire style and American tastes seem deliberately designed to break any possible connection to traditional novelists from his own country like Kobo Abe, Yukio Mishima or Yasunari Kawabata, Japan's only Nobel laureate in literature." (Mitgang wrote these lines a few months before Ōe won the Nobel Prize in Literature.) He goes on to note that "Americanisms dance across the pages of the novel" and that the overall effect of this style is to turn the novels "into an anchored aircraft carrier for American products and culture."[5] Sarah Wright suggests in *Boston Magazine* that in Murakami's works "constant references to American cultural icons, particularly musical ones, build a baby boomer's global city while ever so quietly giggling at it from behind a painted fan," and notes that the narrator of *A Wild Sheep Chase* is "a pop-culture junkie with little concern for context or meaning," who is not interested in Japanese tradition, instead referring exclusively to Western pop icons such as Clint Eastwood, Jodie Foster, Paul McCartney, the Doors, Artie Shaw, and Steven Spielberg.[6]

This interpretation seems to be prevalent up to this day. In reviewing the new American collection of short stories by Murakami published in 2006 by Knopf, Christian Caryl lists all the references to Western culture contained in the 25 stories, from Alfred Hitchcock to Mozart to Marvin Gaye and traces the popularity of his work in America to the fact that, unlike novels by Ōe Kenzaburō and Kawabata Yasunari, that are "still populated by characters who are recognizably and distinctly Japanese, even if they are engaged in a deep and traumatic confrontation with the effects of the process we have since come to call 'globalization,'"[7] Murakami's characters have completely and successfully Westernized.

Of special interest in this regard is Elizabeth Devereaux's interview with Murakami, which she begins by writing: "Forget about cherry blossom time, the crags of Fujiyama, tea ceremonies; most especially forget about exquisitely penned haiku. Today Haruki Murakami is Japan's premier novelist, and he's earned that rank by breaking all the rules." Devereaux stresses the presence of references to Western literature in Murakami's texts as a sign of how this author is better placed in the Western than in the Japanese tradition: "The setting is just as surprising: the geography is of a modern Japan, but the heritage is Western, the prose awash in references to American and European culture. From a bottomless reservoir come allusions to The Wizard of Oz, Bogart and Bacall, Star Trek, Ma Bell and Jim Morrison, discussions of Turgenev and Stendhal, Camus and Somerset Maugham. The only thing distinctly Japanese is the food."[8]

The reference to food is particularly telling, for two reasons. First, while Devereaux claims that food in Murakami's texts is "distinctly Japanese," Japanese critics, on the contrary, note the pervasiveness in Murakami's work of Western food or so-called *katakana* food. Numano Mitsuyoshi analyzes a scene from *Kaze no uta o kike* (*Hear the Wind Sing*, 1979):

> The young protagonist is offered orange juice [*orenji jūsu*] and doughnuts [*dōnatsu*], and *katakana* [the Japanese syllabary for foreign words] highlights the fact that these are originally foreign products. Significantly, at the doctor's house, *boku* eats "coffee roll, apple pie, pancakes, croissant," all food "in *katakana*." Of course these things are common in contemporary Japan, yet to have the protagonist eat exclusively this kind of food is not a neutral choice. Furthermore, perhaps nobody does this anymore today, but until a while ago a guest was always offered green tea and *wagashi* [Japanese sweets]: Murakami voluntarily subverts this pattern. Even later in his life, the protagonist always eats "peanuts, fried potatoes, beer, whisky, wine, cheese, crackers." Even though these things are widespread in Japan today, to put them in a novel takes on a precise meaning.[9]

On the other hand, food is probably the primary Japanese cultural product that became popular in the United States in the 1990s; Devereaux's reference to the presence of Japanese food in Murakami's novels as a "last remainder of Japaneseness" expresses the desire for exoticism that makes more attractive texts otherwise entirely domesticated and Americanized. Murakami is presented as an author integrated into North American culture enough to avoid the risk of misunderstandings and not be a threat, but made appealing by a few harmless exotic elements such as food.

Jay Rubin also insists on Murakami's un-Japaneseness and contrasts him with Kawabata Yasunari's attitude during the ceremony for the Nobel Prize in Literature in 1970. Kawabata's manner corresponded fully to what Westerners would expect from a traditional Japanese novelist, he "even wore formal Japanese robes when he claimed his prize in Stockholm. He was perfect."[10] Murakami, on the contrary, seems to systematically challenge the Western reader's horizon of expectation: "What is wrong with Murakami? Is he determined to subvert all that is profound and beautiful in Japanese literature? Even his style is un-Japanese. When Murakami first turned to fiction, he could not seem to find his voice until he tried writing in English and then translating himself into Japanese."[11]

Here Rubin is referring to Murakami's statement that he was able to find his style for *Kaze no uta o kike* only by trying to write a few pages in English and then rewriting them in Japanese. In a later interview, Murakami explained that, precisely because he did not have a strong enough command of English, this operation forced him to seek a simpler language; he further commented that since he grew up reading American authors he would have liked to write like them, but he realized that he could never do so, and that he could only write in Japanese, as a Japanese.

> When I was a teen-ager, I thought how great it would be if only I could write novels in English. I had the feeling that I would be able to express my emotions so much more directly than if I wrote in Japanese. But with my limited proficiency in English, that was impossible. It took a very long time even before I could somehow write a novel in Japanese. That is why I wasn't able to write a novel until I was 29. Because I had to create, all on my own, a new Japanese language for my novels. I couldn't just borrow an already existing language. In that sense I think I'm an original.[12]

What Murakami is trying to do, rather than simply Americanizing, is to create his own style across two languages, across two cultures.

Reviews of Murakami's work, however, invariably insist on Westernization and un-Japaneseness as the defining features of his fiction.[13] Many critics stress as an instance of Murakami's Americanization the presence of references to Western literature, music, and film. Although such references are frequent in Murakami's works, they are not necessarily a simple sign of his Westernization. If we consider the insistence of American critics upon domestication in relation to the contemporaneous rhetoric urging America to rebel against the invasion of Japanese products, the underlying message of these essays appears to be that if Japan has become an economic giant, the United States still maintains its cultural hegemony—so much so that the most prominent Japanese writer disdains the Japanese tradition and finds inspiration only in the West.

This attitude is evident, for instance, in a dialogue between the writer Jay McInerney and Murakami in the *New York Times Book Review*. The introduction to the piece compares the commercial and cultural relations between Japan and the United States, and then states that "in an effort to correct this cultural trade imbalance, PEN, the writers' organization, brought Mr. McInerney together in New York with Haruki Murakami, a best-selling novelist in Japan."[14] The interview is a good example of how Murakami's novels are the object of a new exoticization of Japanese culture: they are related to the stereotype of "Japan, Inc.," the so-called mass-middle-stratum society that becomes a single enormous industrial complex. McInerney remarks that Murakami's texts are the expression of the "new Japan" of the 1980s and 1990s: "Like most Japanese, the typical Murakami protagonist believes himself to be a man of the middle, the product of, to quote from Mr. Murakami's novel *Norwegian Wood*, 'a regular workaday family, not especially rich, not especially poor. A real run-of-the-mill house, small yard, Toyota Corolla.'"[15] He notes that the protagonists of Murakami's novels are always outsiders in the conformist Japanese society, and in stressing this aspect he ends up reinforcing the idea that "groupism" is an inherent characteristic of Japanese culture. Similarly, Laura Miller, in an interview for *Salon,* maintains that "the heroes in Haruki Murakami's dazzling, addictive and rather strange novels . . . don't fit the stereotype of conformist, work-obsessed Japanese men at all."[16] The anomaly of Murakami's characters serves to reinforce the dominant cliché that Japanese are, as a rule, conformist and work-obsessed.[17]

Sometimes commentators find references to the myth of "Japan, Inc." where there is no textual trace of them. For example, in reviewing the collection *The Elephant Vanishes* for the *New York Times,* David Leavitt comments on the story "The Dancing Dwarf" ("Odoru kobito"), saying that it "takes place in one of those impressively efficient Japanese factories we're always hearing about, only in this case the factory manufactures elephants." However, although the story is actually set in an "elephant factory," there is no mention whatsoever of its "impressive efficiency." Leavitt's reading of the factory as "impressively efficient" just because it appears in a story by a Japanese writer—the story is not even set in Japan, but in an undefined, imaginary place—is telling: American commentators are so eager to find this stereotype that they see it even when it is not there.

Glynne Walley provides a deeper and more detailed analysis of Murakami's attitude toward the West by comparing Murakami Haruki and Murakami Ryū through their different relationships with American culture. Walley notes that in Haruki's works "American culture either is accepted without comment, or at most represents a fantasy world devoid of geopolitical complication," but he argues further that

> What he is doing with his constant references to cultural imports is simply to show how thoroughly they have permeated Japan. Western reviewers have tended to take this as a negative comment, as if he were trying to express disgust at how common McDonald's is in

Japan, but in reality Murakami Haruki is saying the opposite: to contemporary Japanese, McDonald's is more Japanese than American.[18]

Walley thus foregrounds Murakami Haruki's reflection on American culture and its role in contemporary Japan, rather than taking the references to Western culture simply as a sign of Haruki's infatuation with it.

Murakami's use of Western culture is in fact very complex. On the one hand, he consciously markets his works to the United States, fosters a personal relationship with his translators, travels often to America, and in lectures and interviews tends to encourage this view of himself as "Americanized." On the other hand, he "Japanizes" American culture in his texts and even resells this Asianized version of Western popular culture to China and Korea, where his novels are very successful. In this sense, his role recapitulates the Japanese government's policy of the 1980s known as *kokusaika*, internationalization, in its double meaning of "becoming more modern and progressive by attaining international standards" and of "making Japan go international by exporting its culture," putting an end to *ippō tsūkō no bunka* (one-way culture)—Japan's tendency to import foreign culture without exporting its own.[19] Most importantly, however, Murakami appropriates Western culture for its alienating effect, as a means to represent the complexity of reality. A creative use of American culture lies at the center of the narrative strategies deployed in this author's texts.

By virtue of their wide readership, Murakami's texts have begun to be considered part of American literature: his stories are regularly published in magazines such as the *New Yorker*, and apparently are no longer perceived by readers as "Japanese." In this way, they challenge a unitary and inclusive vision of American literature. Non-threatening enough to be read by everybody, they nonetheless contribute to the diffusion of certain elements of Japanese culture and worldview, while at the same time challenging Western conceptions of reality.

More recently, two critical essays have addressed Murakami's fiction from a more sophisticated perspective. Murakami Fuminobu categorizes Murakami as a "postmodernist" in the context of his analysis of contemporary critical reflections by Japanese intellectuals on Japanese modernity and modernism. He examines Murakami's work through a conceptual framework in which he defines postmodernism as the rejection of two foundational modern ideologies—"strong-is-good" and "love-is-beautiful"—that are interpreted as ways of perpetuating oppressive power structures.[20] He therefore looks at Murakami primarily in the Japanese context, avoiding the question of his Westernization and discussing instead his novels (he makes no mention of the short stories or the nonfiction) as instances of what he calls a "postmodern" vision of the world. He argues that Murakami through his fiction condemns modern rationality, sees evolution as a cause of oppression of the weak, and criticizes love as an intrinsically assimilationist and homogenizing sentiment based on the opposition between insiders and outsiders, which ultimately produces discrimination against others and inevitably turns into hatred.[21] He also finds elements of postmodernism in Murakami's use of irony and in his playful attitude that set him apart from mainstream Japanese "serious" literature. Some scholars might object to his characterization of modernity and postmodernity; however, Murakami Fuminobu defines his terms quite clearly, stating that he uses the words modern, modernity, and modernism not "as spatio-temporal concepts" but rather as terms that "specifically designate an ideology which values power, ideals, enlightenment, the future, development, progress, advancement, evolution, etc. and which has existed throughout history and which still exists in the present globalised world."[22] This approach may not be the most productive in discussing an author such as Murakami, who so heavily relies on geographical categories in his textual strategies, but without doubt the argument constitutes a significant advance beyond the stereotyping that is all too often applied to Murakami and his fiction.

Michael Fisch analyzes the use of the trope of the "other world" (*achiragawa*) in *Sputnik Sweetheart* as a means to recover an authentic language and mode of representation through "a space not colonized by modern reason and its bifurcating logic."[23] In an effort to go beyond the usual cliché about Murakami's Westernization, Fisch, like Murakami Fuminobu, avoids the question of the author's relationship with Western culture altogether, and concentrates instead on issues of fantasy and reality, trauma and dream, social responsibility and the unconscious, providing a very nuanced and intriguing reading of the novel. Given Fisch's focus on the question of language and narrative, however, it is regrettable that his analysis does not discuss any of the specific linguistic strategies employed by Murakami in this novel, as in most of his oeuvre, e.g., his reliance on the alienating effect of foreign words Japanized by means of transcription in the *katakana* syllabary, which foreground the presence of a language-within-language as another kind of *achiragawa*. The connection between foreign culture and the idea of the "other world" is briefly addressed when Fisch connects the search for identity of one of the protagonists, Miu, to her position as a *zainichi*, a Korean national born and raised in Japan, as well as to her experience of living in Europe, where her first encounter with *achiragawa* occurs. He thus hints at Murakami's creative use of foreign culture rather than mere fascination with and passive assimilation of it.

A sign of Murakami's growing success in the West is the addition of two book-length studies to this burgeoning critical literature: *Haruki Murakami and the Music of Words* by Jay Rubin and *Dances With Sheep: The Quest for Identity in the Fiction of Murakami Haruki* by Matthew Strecher, both published in 2002. Rubin's text follows Murakami's career from its beginning, tracing autobiographical elements in both novels and short stories and analyzing the influence of Western music, particularly jazz, on Murakami's style and even the structure of his texts. In contrast, Strecher concentrates on the political aspects of Murakami's work in a fashion very different from the approach of other American critics and much closer to mainstream Japanese scholarship on the author.

Japanese Views of Murakami

Whereas American critics and the reading public might share a similar image of Murakami, in Japan there is a clear gap between scholarly views of this author and the opinion of the average reader. Murakami's popularity leads a number of Japanese critics to deny him the status of *junbungaku* ("pure literature") writer; they consider him too commercial and disengaged to be a "serious intellectual." This is closely related to his new approach to Western culture, very different from that of the Japanese intellectual elite.

The question of social commitment in Japanese intellectual debate is inseparable from issues pertaining to modernity and the West. For this reason, the present discussion on Japanese views of Murakami will begin with a Japanese scholar living and working in the United States, Masao Miyoshi. While positioning himself explicitly as an American scholar, Miyoshi sets himself apart from the fascination with Murakami's literature in the United States. Miyoshi was one of the most fervent Murakami-bashers throughout the 1990s, harshly criticizing him as the symbol of a literature complicit with Japanese capitalism and Japan's worship of American culture, in contrast to the serious and politically engaged work of writers such as Ōe Kenzaburō. Despite his critical stance on American attitudes toward Japan, Miyoshi is equally unsympathetic toward Murakami; in this sense, although writing from the perspective of the American academy, he is representative of a leading trend in Japanese intellectual opinion on this author. In his influential study *Off Center* (1991), Miyoshi maintains that the forces of criticism and opposition, which were briefly vital in Japan's postwar years, have now become thoroughly vitiated, and that *junbungaku,* which he significantly calls "a self-conscious modernist enterprise," has now been "dispersed and denatured."[24]

Miyoshi regards Murakami as the prime example of this decadence, and as the leading figure of a generation of "writers acutely aware of the sterility of managed society, which they carefully nurture so that they may plausibly postulate style and snobbery as a cure." His assessment of Murakami is completely negative: he maintains that "his tales are remarkably fragmented"; they are "an entirely easy read—a smooth, popular item of consumption"; his novels *1973-nen no pinbōru, Kaze no uta o kike*, and *Hitsuji o meguru bōken* are "story-less stories of nameless characters"; and that *Noruwei no mori* "erases history, converting the 1960s to a mood, a sentiment, a style." The commercial success of this last title seems to add to his general disapproval, and he notes that the inanity of *Noruwei no mori* "must have been unapparent . . . to the more than four million people who bought the book."[25] While he is critical of the Japanese fascination with American culture, he apparently puts great trust in the American public's ability to appreciate good, serious literature, and therefore expresses his amazement at the popularity of Murakami's novels in the United States, in the typical language of the "Japan-bashing" of those years:

> He sells well and plans to expand his market to the United States. . . . Herbert Mitgang of the *New York Times* is apparently impressed with Murakami's artistic and intellectual accomplishment: he wrote two uninformed and misguided reviews for his paper, as if his assignment were to follow the U.S. administration's open-door policy in the book market. It will be an interesting test of the U.S. readership when the literary market distributes the Murakami productions, although I have my own reasons to doubt that they will ever find as many buyers here as do Honda automobiles or Sony camcorders.[26]

Once again, Murakami's success in the United States is linked to the issue of the trade imbalance—this time, though, in order to criticize his works as overly commercial, and at the same time, as being of insufficient quality.

Miyoshi contrasts Murakami's superficiality with the seriousness of writers such as Ōe, who defy a lack of interest among the general public and do not give up their political and moral commitments.[27] He calls these writers "the bearers of light into the 1990s and beyond," and regrets that they are "marginalized in such a way that no one really engages them in serious conversations."[28] Miyoshi is in step with the part of the Japanese intellectual world that sees in Murakami Haruki the anti-Ōe, the carrier of a literature of non-commitment that betrays the ideals of *kindaishugi*.

Ōe Kenzaburō himself laments the corruption of *junbungaku* in today's Japan and sees in Murakami one of the most clear examples of this degeneration:

> Serious literature and a literary readership have gone into a chronic decline, while a new tendency has emerged over the last several years. This strange new phenomenon is largely an economic one, reflected in the fact that the novels of certain young writers like Haruki Murakami and Banana Yoshimoto each sell several hundred thousand copies. It is possible that the recent sales of the books produced by these two authors alone are greater than those of all other living novelists combined. Here we see Japan's economic boom making itself felt in the literary market. In contrast to much postwar writing which fictionalized the actual experience of writers and readers who, as twenty- and thirty-year-olds, had known war, Murakami and Yoshimoto convey the experience of a youth politically uninvolved or disaffected, content to exist within a late adolescent or post-adolescent subculture.[29]

Even when they are not so harsh in their criticism of Murakami, most Japanese scholars approach his work from a political perspective, concentrating on his relationship—problematic by some accounts, nonexistent by others—with the Japanese New Left (*shinsayoku*) and the student movement of the 1960s, as well as on his complicity with "advanced capitalistic society" (*kōdo shihonshugi shakai*). There are two main reasons for these approaches: first, the fact that critical attention focused on Murakami after the great success of *Noruwei no mori*, whose protagonists are university students living in Tokyo in the years 1968–70; second, the influence of the notion of social commitment formulated by postwar *kindaishugi*.

Regarding the first motive, it is important to note the general tendency in Japanese literary studies to concentrate on the biography of authors and to investigate the ways in which their personal lives are reflected in their works. In the case of Murakami, this often means looking for instances of his relationship with the student movement of the 1960s and the transformation of this relationship during Japan's period of rapid economic growth in the 1970s and 1980s. Critics concerned with such issues tend to concentrate on identifying political symbols in his works and relating them to the writer's personal experience. One of the most notable examples from the 1980s is Kawamoto Saburō and his study *Toshi kanjusei* (Metropolitan Sensibility, 1988), which focuses on the absence of names, the obsession with numbers, and the arbitrariness of signs in *Kaze no uta o kike, 1973-nen no pinbōru,* and *Hitsuji o meguru bōken.* Kawamoto interprets these features as an expression of the new "urban conscience" and the emptiness of the capitalist society in 1980s Japan, and attributes a political meaning to the animals and surreal characters that appear in these novels, such as the Rat and the Sheep. Another example is Kuroko Kazuo and his book *Murakami Haruki: za rosuto warudo* (Murakami Haruki: The Lost World, 1989), in which he further examines the meaning of the Sheep in *Hitsuji o meguru bōken* as a symbol of the "failed revolution" of the 1960s. According to Kuroko, the death of the Sheep represents a liberation from the past, a metaphor for Murakami's distancing himself from the generation of the 1960s and, more generally, for his "refusal of history."[30]

After Murakami returned to Japan and published *Nejimakidori kuronikuru* in 1995, some critics praised what they saw as his new social commitment, especially in his book's treatment of the Japanese occupation of Manchuria; however, many of the same critics saw his subsequent novels as a "step backwards" and a return to non-commitment. Yoshida Haruo wrote an entire book on Murakami's new commitment, *Murakami Haruki tenkai suru* (Murakami Haruki Changes, 1997), but soon thereafter followed with *Murakami Haruki to Amerika* (Murakami Haruki and America, 2001), in which he interprets the themes of solitude in *Supūtoniku no koibito* (*Sputnik Sweet-*

heart, 2000) as an instance of Murakami's lamentable return to the isolation from society that characterized his works of the 1980s. Yoshida's later stance contrasts that of Michael Fisch, who sees the novel as emblematic of Murakami's attempt to transcend isolation, to find connections between individuals—and possibly a space for political action—in the domain of dreams and "other worlds." (Of these two views, Fisch's will lend greater momentum to the last chapter of this study, in which *Supūtoniku* is discussed as another example of Murakami's social engagement through the use of the fantastic genre, similar to that found in his short stories.) Yoshida is also very critical of Murakami's treatment of the Kobe earthquake of January 1995 in *Kami no kodomotachi wa mina odoru* (All God's Children Dance, 2000; *after the quake*, 2002), arguing that the decision to write about this apparently serious issue is undermined by the fact that the earthquake is always a marginal element in the stories. He therefore concludes that Murakami is once again retreating from political and social involvement.

The question of the social relevance of Murakami's literature is also at the center of Komori Yōichi's *Murakami Haruki ron* (2006), where he analyzes the novel *Umibe no Kafuka* (2002; translated as *Kafka on the Shore*, 2005) as a commentary on contemporary Japan, while also looking at the reasons for its success at home and abroad in terms of its social and political impact. After providing a psychoanalytical interpretation of the plot as a re-enactment of the myth of Oedipus, and the setting—the library, in which a significant part of the story is set—as a "maternal space" and a symbol of motherhood, Komori focuses on the novel's treatment of a number of politically charged themes: war, imperialism in Asia, comfort women, and the Emperor system.

Interestingly, Komori also devotes one section of the book to the protagonist's reading of Natsume Sōseki's novels *Kōfu* and *Gubijinsō*, which he interprets as a sort of *mise en abyme* of the textual dynamics of *Umibe no Kafuka* itself: like *Kōfu*, *Umibe* depicts the conflict between an individual and the demands of society, and embodies the search for interiority in a voyage underground.[31] In Komori's opinion, however, Murakami ultimately lacks the political engagement of Sōseki. Komori attributes the success of *Umibe* precisely to the reassurance it seems to provide readers in wealthy capitalist countries who have been traumatized by experiences such as the Tokyo subway Sarin gas attacks of March 1995 or the New York terrorist attacks of September 2001.

Komori argues that although Murakami's *Andāguraundo* encouraged readers to reflect on the experience of such trauma and its historical origins, *Umibe* simply provides escape and consolation. In this sense, he finds it telling that Kafka's murder of his father occurs inside his imagination (*sōzōryoku no naka*), since having acted "only in a dream" exempts him from any real responsibility. Komori contends that *Umibe* ultimately betrays the promises of *Andāguraundo*, and calls the former "a disappointment in the face of history as a whole [*rekishi zentai ni taisuru uragiri nano desu*]."[32] (A later part of this study will propose that Murakami's idea of imagination is, on the contrary, central to his social commitment as a writer.)

The problem of Murakami's social commitment (or lack thereof) is therefore central to his reception among Japanese critics. Their views are related to the predominance of the ideology of *kindaishugi* in the Japanese intellectual world and its image of the historically grounded, politically involved, "modernist" writer. In this regard, Murakami's choice to distance himself from the student movement and the New Left helps to clarify his specific, and quite unique, position in regard to Japanese modernisms.

Japan's New Left criticized *kindaishugi* intellectuals, and in particular Maruyama Masao, mainly for their excessive reliance on Western ideas.[33] Crucial in this sense was the work of Yoshimoto Takaaki (also known as Yoshimoto Ryūmei), a scholar of the older generation who had a very strong influence on the student movement. Yoshimoto openly rejected Maruyama's ideology of modernism, and became a celebrated advocate of postmodernism in the 1970s and 1980s.[34]

Yoshimoto became famous in the late 1950s for his study of the so-called *tenkō* (converted) intellectuals: those Japanese writers and critics who in the 1930s, under pressure from the government, had repudiated their communist beliefs and "converted" to nationalist and imperialist ideology. Yoshimoto, however, was equally critical of the works of the exponents of *puroretaria bungaku* (proletarian literature) who did not recant their socialist beliefs, and after the war harshly criticized writers such as Miyamoto Kenji and Kurahara Korehito. Yoshimoto saw them as a different kind of convert, and argued that they ultimately betrayed the cause of the Japanese people for two interrelated reasons: their excessive reliance on Western theory prevented them from understanding the concrete circumstances of Japan, and their abstract theoretical approach precluded them from reaching out to the people. Yoshimoto was most of all critical of what he saw as a widening gap in postwar Japan between the intellectuals and the people, which he traced to the futile attempt to apply Western theory to Japanese realities.

Accordingly, he also denounced Maruyama, Takeuchi Yoshimi, and Tsurumi Shunsuke for their project of founding a new modern Japanese subject. He saw their effort as a fundamentally hypocritical enterprise, a belated attempt to make up for their silence during the imperialist period; but also, more significantly, he argued that their endeavor only perpetuated the obsession with the West that had dominated Japanese politics in one way or another since the Meiji period. Yoshimoto claimed that Japanese intellectuals had either modeled their ideological stance on Western ideas—such as Christianity, Stalinism, or liberalism—or had rejected them in order to proclaim the superiority of native thought. In both cases, focusing on the West had enabled them to avoid confronting the most pressing problems of Japanese society, which he identified as the emperor system and the traditional family structure. Yoshimoto instead encouraged Japan to stop trying to either comply with or distance itself from Western modernity, and to concentrate on national matters instead.

Yoshimoto's criticism of *kindaishugi* and the New Left's subsequent rejection of Japanese modernist ideology are, however, quite different from Murakami's own attempt to transcend it. While the New Left advocated a refusal of Western ideologies, insisting on the necessity to understand "the Japanese people," Murakami goes in exactly the opposite direction, acknowledging that Western culture has pervaded Japan to such an extent that "overcoming (Western) modernity" is no longer a viable option, if it ever was. Instead he takes a different path, plunging into American popular culture, and using it to highlight the contradictions of both Japanese and Western societies through a complicitous critique that allows him to attain a new form of commitment.

For his decision to set himself apart from both *kindaishugi* and the New Left, Murakami has often been considered a "postmodernist," meaning a noninvolved, superficial, commercial writer. Toshiko Ellis notes the most significant "postmodern" features of Murakami's stories: "the namelessness of the characters, the contingent nature of the relationships that develop between them, and the pervasiveness of a vague sense of loss shared by the characters," as well as the lack of confrontation or dialogue between Murakami's characters. (Even when dialogues are present, they are "immediately turned into monologues" and "fragmented into a chain of images, which in turn is mingled with images of the exterior world.") Other "postmodernist" traits of Murakami's texts, according to Ellis, are nostalgia toward the past and a fundamental suspicion toward words.[35]

Despite Ellis's contention that these features are postmodern, I would argue that they are more reminiscent of European and American modernist writers of the 1920s and 1930s, with whom Murakami also shares a refusal of history, of the idea of linear historical progress. Ellis sees in Murakami's work "the absence of a sense of place" that sets him apart from *kindaishugi* writers, who are always preoccupied with defining their position. According to Ellis, the implication is that "the longstanding theme of conflict between West and non-West, underpinned by the conception of the West as the centre, appears to have been dismissed by Murakami as an assumption that was simply not relevant."[36]

Murakami's texts display a completely new attitude toward the West; that Western culture is simply part of the characters' everyday life, and is represented by phenomena of popular culture that Japanese readers can easily assimilate. In his works, the West is not a cultural model for Japan to emulate—a position that Japanese critics cite as another example of his lack of a critical stance. Ellis finds that in Murakami the West is "naturally de-centralised and dispersed in the text in the form of consumable images which constitute the everyday life of the characters." She does not consider this non-defensive attitude toward Western culture as "a path toward emancipation from the persistent dilemma of Japanese modernity," because "when the contradictions are suspended and dissolved into fragmented images of everyday life, literature will gradually lose its capacity to maintain a critical stance from the existing system of signs and will only contribute to inundating society with complacent discourse."[37] Through such arguments, Ellis and other critics are ultimately reproaching Murakami for his "postmodernist," non-committed attitude. The following chapters will try to demonstrate that Murakami does deal with his social role as a writer, but in a radically different manner from that of *kindaishugi* writers, and that this new and original approach to a writer's responsibility is connected to Murakami's attitude toward Western culture and the way in which he employs it in his work.

One analysis of Murakami's work takes a very different stance from the mainstream of Japanese scholarship, while still addressing the problem of Murakami's social role. The noted literary scholar Karatani Kōjin analyzes the novels *Kaze no uta o kike* and *1973-nen no pinbōru* in light of his theory of "the discovery of landscape" (discussed in the previous chapter). Karatani examines the absence of proper names and the use of numbers in these texts and interprets them as a means to foreground the arbitrariness of linguistic signs. However, he sees these elements not so much as hallmarks of "postmodernity" but as continuations of a feature typical of Japanese modernity—in this stream of argument, he claims that Murakami is the heir of Meiji-period writers, particularly Kunikida Doppo. Karatani does not consider Murakami's style to be derived from American authors; on the contrary, he argues that it is American literature that exists in Japan through the filter of Murakami: "This is not the influence of American writers. In the same way, Kunikida's *Musashino* was not born of the influence of Wordsworth. On the contrary, English romantics were read in Japan through the filter of Kunikida. In fact, American writers exist in Japan only through Murakami, through a Murakamiesque 'landscape.'"[38]

Thus, for Karatani, Murakami is the opposite of Ōe. Significantly, the title of Murakami's novel *1973-nen no pinbōru* is a parody of Ōe's *Man'en gannen no futtobōru* (Football in the First Year of the Man'en Era, 1967; *The Silent Cry*, 1994). Although *Man'en gannen* has a symbolic function and introduces in the text the reality of history, Murakami's *1973-nen* has a merely personal value, with no historical meaning. Ōe represents the stereotype of the writer grounded in history, Murakami underlines the arbitrariness of historical knowledge. This, according to Karatani, emerges in his use of dates, which are always exclusively personal, referring to moments lived only by the narrator.

Hosea Hirata relates the works of Murakami and Karatani, disclosing new perspectives on the work of both. Hirata contends that despite Karatani's criticism of Murakami, the works of the two converge on one particular point, which he calls "the search for singularity." This singularity, Hirata argues, "is neither an entity nor a unique specificity," but rather "a process of forever losing something most important and dear" that is "nothing but the subject."[39]

In another essay, Karatani defends the concept of *singularity*, distinguishing it from *particularity*. Singularity, he argues, as opposed to particularity—that is, an individuality seen from a position of generality—is an individuality no longer capable of belonging to the realm of generality. He distinguishes betweeen "I am" and "this I am": the "I" in the first case is one (a particular) of the I's in general, pertinent to any one of the I's; but the second "I," namely, "this I," is *singular*, irreplaceable by any other. Of course, he goes on to explain, this does not mean that "this I" is too distinctive to be replaced: singularity does not lead to exceptionalism.[40] Hirata comments that in distinguishing "singularity" from "particularity," Karatani is "attempting to conceive of an individuality that does not fall into essentialism," and he explains that "Karatani's notion of singularity has nothing to do with the image of a lonely, alienated, internalized modern individual popularized by modern Japanese literature."[41] Karatani finds the roots of singularity in relation to an Other that is recognized as its premise.

Karatani condemns Murakami (and Kunikida Doppo) for escaping into the transcendental ego by erasing history through the use of Romantic irony, and maintains that Murakami's transcendental ego eludes the Other and history/reality—but Karatani's own theorizations are in fact very close to what Murakami does with his fiction. In Hirata's opinion, Karatani's criticisms of Murakami are actually attacks on aspects of his own thinking that are close to Murakami's. In particular, Hirata argues, Karatani regrets not so much the loss of historicity as the loss of criticism, of a critical stance similar to that of *kindaishugi* intellectuals, a stance that he himself is unable to maintain. In fact, as subsequent chapters will show, the works of Murakami provide a new approach to the problems of individuality and particularity radically different from that of *kindaishugi* intellectuals.

Taking Hirata's contention a step further, I would argue that Murakami's characters, with their insistence on being *heibon na hito* (ordinary people) on the one hand and on their being *kojinteki na ningen* (individual human beings) on the other, are examples of the same attitude. His stories are populated by characters trying to be "singular" without falling into particularism or exceptionalism and to construct their selfhood by engaging with otherness.

Among the Japanese critics who reflect on Murakami's relationship with American culture, the first was Sengoku Hideyo, who analyzes Murakami's translations of Raymond Carver and concentrates on his use of "America as fantasy" (*sōzō to shite no Amerika*), an imaginary world strongly present in Murakami's fiction as well as in his translations. More recently, Miura Masashi has studied the influence of Murakami's (and Shibata Motoyuki's) translations on Japanese perceptions of American culture, as well as on the style of a generation of younger novelists who grew up reading Western literature through these two translators. Miura points out that while Japanese scholars are often very critical of Murakami, readers love his works and young writers look up to him as a model. He notes that Japanese readers today read more foreign fiction than Japanese works, and generally they read them in translation and not in the originals. This trend fits into the rhetoric dominant since the 1980s that laments the imbalance between translations of foreign and of Japanese literature and in general the ills of the *ippō tsūkō no bunka* tendency discussed earlier.[42]

Miura argues that modern Japanese literature today is constituted more by this translation literature than by original Japanese works, and that this situation gives a prominent role to the translators as cultural mediators. Furthermore, in Japan readers often buy a book not because of the author but because of the translator—especially in the case of Murakami. Therefore, established translators arguably have a power in shaping the system of translated literature, and, more broadly, the image of American literature and culture. Miura notes that a number of emerging authors have grown up reading Murakami and Shibata's translations of American literature. As a result, young novelists like Ono Masatsugu, Yanagi Hiroshi, and Satō Yūya often use either direct quotations or a style reminiscent not so much of Auster, Carver, Irving, and Salinger, but of Murakami and Shibata's translations of these authors. Their translational Japanese has become a lingua franca for the younger generation of Japanese readers and novelists. For this reason, Miura argues, Murakami's activity as a translator makes him even more influential and more popular among the public, which in turn often further enrages the literary establishment, which refuses to take seriously a commercially successful author.

Murakami Haruki on Murakami Haruki

The significant differences in how Murakami is perceived by American and Japanese audiences relate partly to the way in which Murakami actively presents himself to both his Japanese and foreign readerships, and to the way in which he reflects critically on his writing. For instance, in an interview with *Publisher's Weeekly* in 1993, he praises American multicultural society and the accepting attitude of the American people, referring to the *topos* of the melting pot and contrasting it with his experience in Europe: "In Europe, they are stiff, and we are always foreigners. But in America they accept us. America is a very special place, very accepting of other cultures."[43] However, in describing his arrival in the United States in *Yagate kanashiki gaikokugo* (The Ultimately Sad Foreign language), he writes that he spent his first year of his stay at Princeton in 1991 shut up in his house (which, he says, was very useful in working on his novel), fearing the xenophobic atmosphere in the country and the "Japan-bashing" that followed the First Gulf War, when Japan was accused of trying to elude its responsibilities as an American ally through its "checkbook diplomacy," i.e., sending money instead of troops, criticism that was only reinforced by the fiftieth anniversary of the attack on Pearl Harbor a few months later.[44] This seeming inconsistency serves as a clear example of a more general attitude evident in this author's way of relating to American and Japanese culture: Murakami, taking advantage of his position across cultures, presents different versions of himself to different audiences.[45]

Another significant example can be found in Murakami's comments on the question of translation: he states that he enjoys reading the English translations of his works as if they are "other books," radically different from their originals, appreciating the significant changes that his translators often make in his texts.[46] However, when discussing his own activity as translator of American writers, he maintains that he always tries to be as faithful to the original works as possible.[47] Therefore, while he shows an interest in a free circulation of meanings that goes beyond the author's intention in writing the text, coherent with his non-*kindaishugi* sense of commitment, he also reassures his Japanese readers that, through his translations, they are getting "the real thing," true American texts, as close as possible to the original in terms of rhythm, choice of words, atmosphere, and so forth. These assertions could be interpreted as attempts to please both the Japanese and the American audience in a somewhat duplicitous way, avoiding a clearly defined position. However, precisely by playing on his double positioning, Murakami is in fact able to escape any attempt to label him and his works according to binary, oppositional categories, and in this way he ends up challenging those very categories.

Murakami's position across cultures is one of the main inspirations for his literature. As he explains in the interview with Jay McInerney, he moved first to Europe and then to America because he believed that this would allow him to "write about Japanese society from the outside," and this is what defines his "identity as a writer."[48] When the interviewer notes that most of his books could be set in America without any significant change, he replies that he wanted to depict Japanese society through those aspects that could just as well occur in New York or San Francisco, and explains that "you might call it the Japanese nature that remains only after you have thrown out, one after another, all those parts that are altogether too 'Japanese.'"[49]

Not only does Murakami exploit his cultural positioning, but he often plays on the boundary between reality and fiction through a number of anti-realistic narrative techniques—and also through his commentary on his own work. For instance, the first preface to the collection *Kaiten mokuba no deddo hīto* (Dead Heat on a Merry-Go-Round, 1985) states that these stories are "sketches," stories that real people had told the author over the years. For a long time he wondered whether he could use them as material in his writing, and finally decided to publish them as they were. However, since he wrote them in the form of stories, they could also be considered fictional, in a way. The works are, he explains, something between fiction and nonfiction, real stories narrated through a literary filter. This already seems to challenge a clear-cut distinction between fiction and nonfiction, but when the collection was republished in the *Complete Works,* Murakami declared in a supplementary brochure that they were, in fact, completely fictional, and that he chose this "mock-nonfiction" format because he wanted to try a form of realistic writing in order to later write *Noruwei no mori.* Similar comments on his work ultimately lead readers to attain a more nuanced vision not only of the relationship between cultures, but also of the relationship between fact and narration, reality and fiction.

Murakami's texts, of course, are where his complex positioning yields the most challenging results. Whereas his statements in interviews and comments on his own works are sometimes illuminating on the inner dynamics of his narration, he is, first and foremost, a writer who expresses himself through stories. And his stories are often positioned on the boundary between two worlds, questioning cultural categories. In doing so, they fulfill a social function very different from that of *kindaishugi* literature, but no less significant.

THREE
Language and Culture

Writing in Japan

This chapter will analyze one of the main intercultural strategies of Murakami's texts: the use of language and writing, particularly of foreign vocabulary and of *katakana*, one of two syllabaries used along with Chinese ideograms to write in Japanese. By means of a number of strategies based on the polygraphy of Japanese, Murakami's texts highlight some crucial aspects of Japan's relationship with the West, while at the same time foregrounding the linguistically constructed nature of reality.

The creative use of writing systems is by no means exclusive to Murakami Haruki: both foreign languages and the peculiarities of the Japanese writing system have been employed in innovative ways since the early periods of the Japanese literary tradition. Throughout the Nara and Heian eras (eighth to twelfth centuries), the non-standardized use of Chinese and ideograms yielded plentiful puns and displays of erudition involving different readings of the characters, particularly in anthologies of poetry such as the *Man'yōshū* and *Kokinshū*. The use of *man'yōgana* (the *kana* syllabary in which *Man'yōshū* poems were written) soon became an art form in itself, and often the artistic value of a poem lay in its clever play with language and writing.[1] From the Kamakura era (twelfth to fourteenth centuries) onward, the phonographic use of *kanji* took on a new dimension with the use of so-called *ateji* ("attributed character"), the practice of substituting an ideogram with a homophone having a different meaning, to play on the visual aspects of the characters, which became very popular in poetry and in literature in general.[2]

A crucial shift in the relationship between literature and writing—more relevant for the purposes of this analysis of Murakami's use of language—occurred in the Meiji era, when the new government undertook reforms of the education and communication systems. Among these reforms was an effort to simplify and make "more functional" the written language, bringing it closer to the colloquial, with the famous project commonly known as *genbun itchi* (unification of speech, *gen*, and writing, *bun*). *Genbun itchi* had a strong political element that was deeply related to the need to create a national Japanese language, since there was no clearly defined or uniform standard language (*hyōjungo*), only a number of different dialects. The creation of a unitary national language (*kokugo*), based on the dialect of Tokyo, was part of a more general effort to create a sense of national identity and unity that also entailed the creation of concepts such as national polity (*kokutai*) and national subject (*kokumin*).[3] Literature played a major role in the formation and diffusion of *genbun itchi*: writers such as Futabatei Shimei, Yamada Bimyō, and Mori Ōgai, influenced by Western literary theories, decided to adopt the colloquial style in their translations of European and American literature as well as in their original fiction, thus making a significant contribution to its consolidation.

Although the adoption of *genbun itchi* is usually represented as a narrative of linear and natural progress, at the time of its formation it gave rise to controversies, and a number of alternative solutions were considered.[4] Some subsequent scholars claim that the main reason why *genbun itchi* prevailed over other solutions is not so much that it was more functional *per se*, as its advocates maintained, but that it better served the political needs of the Meiji leadership. One such scholar, Karatani Kōjin, has argued that the reform of the written language was mainly an ideological operation, part of a broader effort of the Meiji government to create a sense of national identity through the adoption of Western modes of thought. According to Karatani, *genbun itchi* was based on a Western vision of writing as derivative and secondary to speech and represented not so much a "unification of written and spoken language" as "the institution of a regime of writing as a transparent means for the transmission of ideas, based on a phonocentric ideology of writing."[5] In this new phonocentric perspective, Chinese characters came to be seen as inefficient, and the differences between written and spoken language were for the first time regarded as a problem to be overcome. Karatani, inverting this perspective, notes that the "functionality" of the Western alphabet exists only inside a phonocentric vision of language.[6]

Karatani further asserts that the *genbun itchi* ideology lies at the root of the realistic turn in Japanese literature. The two main literary movements of the Meiji era, Naturalism (*shizen-shugi*) and Romanticism (*roman-ha*), both advocated "faithful representation" in literature of external reality and interiority, which was based on this new vision of language. The written word was reinterpreted as a transposition of the oral word, which, in turn, was seen as a transposition of reality; therefore, the purpose of literature was identified with representing reality in the most transparent and accurate way. Both the idea of the written word being merely derivative of the oral word and the idea of literature being a transparent representation of reality—concepts that were alien to traditional Japanese literature and were imported from the West in the Meiji era—have been thrown into question by contemporary Japanese writers, and Murakami's work, as the subsequent pages will illustrate, is a clear example of this new attitude.

Another central element in the evolution of the Japanese language in the Meiji era was the importation of a large number of loanwords from English and other European languages.[7] This infusion of new vocabulary gave rise to a number of experiments in literature, mainly based on the creation of Chinese compounds and on the glossing of existing words with foreign equivalents—innovations that added layers of meaning to the text.[8]

Although foreign words continued to be imported throughout the twentieth century, particularly during the U.S. occupation, the biggest wave of imports from the English language since the Second World War occurred in the 1980s, interestingly, as if to compensate for the trade imbalance so feared by American commentators of those years.[9] In this latest process, loanwords were transcribed almost exclusively in the *katakana* syllabary, which consequently acquired a special role in the Japanese language. Some scholars maintain that *katakana*, by making possible the transcription of loanwords using the characters of the target language, contributes to the integration of such loanwords. On the contrary, other scholars maintain that *katakana* has the opposite effect, i.e., it prevents a real integration, keeping the foreign word separated from the text by virtue of the peculiar characters with which it is written. According to Karatani, through *katakana* the Japanese language isolates the foreign word while appropriating it, creating the paradox of a language that "lets everything in, but in fact gets by without anything getting in" (*nandemo irerareru kedo, hontō wa nanimo irezu ni sumu no desu*).[10]

Whether for its domesticating or for its alienating effect, transcription in *katakana* is central to the function of loanwords in the contemporary Japanese language. One of the most peculiar applications of *katakana* loanwords is the use of foreign equivalents of words already existing in Japanese, either as a euphemism or for their exotic or modern connotative value. A clear example are the so-called *katakana shokugyō* (*katakana* occupations), which are seen as attractive because they are associated with a modern and sophisticated lifestyle. In the case of some of these professions, such as *shisutemu anarisuto* (system analyst), the loan fills a lexical void; in most cases, however, its function is merely connotative and reflects a person's preference to be called *jānarisuto* (journalist) instead of *shinbun kisha*, *fotogurafā* (photographer) and not *shashinka*, and so forth, for the sense of cosmpolitanism and prestige that the term conveys.[11]

According to Nozumi Yukiko, the inclusion in a text of foreign words unfamiliar to the audience has an effect similar to that of *chokugo*, the special language used by the Emperor before World War II, i.e., to create in the readers a sense of inferiority caused by their inability to understand what is being said. Nozumi suggests that the use of difficult foreign words in advertising creates in the viewer a feeling of inferiority toward the message that gives the product advertised an image of superiority and therefore makes it more desirable.[12] Keiko Tanaka, on the contrary, maintains that the use of *katakana* in advertising is aimed at gratifying the reader-consumers, who, recognizing the difficult term, are pleased by their own ability, and project this positive sensation onto the product.[13]

Such use of English loanwords as euphemisms, or to connote modernity or elegance, is not peculiar to Japan. It is indeed common in many languages, and it is probably a sign of the power and prestige of Anglo-American culture in the world today. However, by transcribing such words in *katakana*, the Japanese language appropriates foreign words, modifying them sometimes to the point of rendering them impossible to recognize.[14] Phonetic adaptations and semantic shifts of loanwords also appear in other languages at times, but both their growing number and the extent of the changes are a significant feature of Japan's peculiar relationship with Western culture—a relationship that emerges very clearly in Murakami's texts.

As discussed earlier, the Japanese writing system has often been used creatively in Japanese literature: from the Heian era, when puns based on the multiple readings or graphic aspects of *kanji* were very frequent in poetry, to the Meiji era, when it was common practice to annotate ideograms with a reading different from the one usually attributed to that combination of characters to add new levels of signification to the text. However, the widespread use of *katakana* as well as the Roman alphabet in the 1970s and 1980s gave rise to a new creative use of the polygraphy of Japanese, particularly in the language of advertising. Harald Haarmann analyzes this phenomenon, noting from the 1970s onward an original use of loanwords in Japanese, such as the coining of a number of new words and the invention of peculiar language games. At the same time, the Japanese mass media created their own standard for the English language, promoting it as a symbol of modernity.[15] Foreign words are used in advertising for the sense of cosmopolitanism and modernity that they convey, and because they appeal to what Haarmann defines as the "name-fetishism" in contemporary Japanese.[16] Murakami Haruki's texts often include similar plays with *kanji*, *kana*, and the Roman alphabet, which are deeply related to his vision of language, writing, and literature.

Murakami Haruki and *Katakana*

Since the publication of Murakami's first novels, a number of reviewers and scholars have criticized his style for being too "anglicized" in its heavy reliance upon foreign, mostly English, words. The author has replied by arguing that his aim is not so much to imitate Western literature as to create his own style, his own language, using foreign vocabulary and structures in order to free himself from the constraints of Japanese mainstream literary style: "*Junbungaku*, so-called 'pure' literature, has so many dos and don'ts. Fifteen years ago, when I started to write, I threw them away and made up my own rules. Everyone says my style is influenced by Western literature, but it's not as simple as that. I made up my own language."[17]

As the following analysis of Murakami's texts will suggest, his style *was* influenced by Western literature in at least one sense: namely, the search for authenticity through experiments with language typical of Euro-American modernist writers—and, to a certain extent, of the Japanese *modanizumu* of the Taishō period. The experimental use of language is one of the many aspects that Murakami has in common with 1920s modernists, both in the West and in Japan, and is a characteristic that sets him apart from postwar *kindaishugi* authors. But this approach is not so much passive imitation as a way to exploit both the potential of foreign languages and the specific features of Japanese—particularly the polygraphy discussed in the first part of this chapter—in order to reflect on the relationship between language and reality.

While in the 1980s such widespread use of English loanwords was common mostly in advertising, in more recent years it has also become a feature of literary works. Novels by such authors as Yoshimoto Banana, Murakami Ryū, and Yamada Eimi, and even of writers of so-called *junbungaku* such as Ōe, are full of references to Western food and clothes; names such as McDonald's, Denny's, and Levi's have become common currency. Murakami Haruki can be considered a pioneer in this sense, since he introduced such elements starting from the early 1980s; more significant, however, is the fact that the presence of foreign words designating objects, brand names, and abstract words is not only quantitatively more relevant than in most of the aforementioned authors, but also has a pivotal role in the intercultural and metatextual strategies laid out in his texts.[18]

Numano Mitsuyoshi rightly notes that the great number of *katakana* words in Murakami's stories has an anti-realistic effect, making the reader aware of the presence of such words as foreign, alien elements and contributing to the general sense of estrangement created by the texts.[19] One of the instances in which this alienating effect emerges most clearly is the use of the non-abbreviated form of *katakana* words that are usually contracted, such as *rimōto kontorōrā* (remote controller) instead of *rimokon* ("Nyūyōku tankō no higeki," 1983), *aisukurīmu* (ice cream) instead of *aisu*, *sūpāmāketto* (supermarket) and not *sūpā*, *rajio kasetto* (radio cassette) instead of *rajikase* ("Kangarū biyori," 1982), *terebijon* (television) and not *terebi* ("Takushī ni notta otoko," 1985), and so forth. By using this form, slightly different from the common usage and closer to the English, the texts draw attention to the foreignness of the word, while at the same time "Japanizing" it by way of transcription into *katakana*.

The use of unabbreviated foreign terms induces an effect of estrangement in the reader: transcribed in this way, even words that are now an integral part of the Japanese vocabulary, and that have no native equivalent, stand out in their slightly unusual form, and draw attention to their existence as words. They thus undermine the naturalness and referentiality of language, distancing the reader both from the single word and from the text.

Murakami stated in an interview that his dislike of contracted forms is most of all a matter of individual taste: "I don't like abbreviations like *wāpuro* or *pasokon* (especially in the case of foreign words), and I always use *wādopurosesā*, *konpyūtā* or *Makkintosshu* instead. It is most of all a question of individual preference for the resonance of these words."[20]

It is possible to interpret this inclination as the expression of a desire to be "as Westernized as possible," and therefore be faithful to the "correct English," to an original that is perceived as superior. However, this quotation raises another important point: being faithful to the original is a means to express individual tastes and therefore to affirm individuality. In the same interview, Murakami repeatedly speaks of himself as an "individual human being" (*kojinteki na ningen*), and relates this feature to his interest in Western literature. In his texts, also, there is always a deep relationship between being an individual subject and assimilating Western culture.

Aside from this peculiar use of non-contracted forms, the sheer quantity of *katakana* words in Murakami's texts is striking. These terms often denote material objects, of which one of the categories most represented is food. Numano's observation about the novel *Kaze no uta o kike* is all the more true of the short stories, where the characters eat food "in *katakana*" almost exclusively. Furthermore, these are generally not the most stereotypical Western dishes, but special, sophisticated items such as paté de canard, spaghetti al nero di seppia, or rôti de veau. While this usage adds to the exotic appeal of the text, connoting the characters as international, modern, and stylish, it also has an effect similar to the irony and estrangement felt when readers encounter the non-abbreviated forms of foreign words.

In some stories, though, Japanese food also appears: an intriguing example is "Ōto 1979" ("Nausea 1979," from *Kaiten mokuba no deddo hīto*), where the protagonist, who scrupulously notes in his diary everything that happens to him, and is therefore able to reconstruct exactly the month in which he vomited everything he ate, recounts that, besides such Western foods as *hamu to kyūri no sandoicchi* (cucumber and ham sandwich) or *cherī pai to burakku kōhī* (cherry pie and black coffee), he also ate *unagi* (eel), *tōfu* (bean curd), *sawara no saikyōyaki* (grilled Spanish mackerel, "Saikyō" style), *sunomono* (vinegared vegetables), *misoshiru* (miso soup), and white rice, all traditional Japanese dishes. Curiously, the Japanese meal is the only one that he does not immediately vomit, although he ends up throwing it up hours later, as though Japanese tradition were only a temporary, illusory source of salvation. In the novels, the protagonists cook and eat Japanese food much more often; this might be only a coincidence, but it could also be related to the fact that the novels are more popular in the West than the short stories, and are therefore written with an eye to a Western audience that appreciates the exotic—but not too alien—element of Japanese food.[21]

Another major category in which Murakami employs a great number of *katakana* words, often as euphemisms, is sex: these range from the general *sekkusu* (sex) to the specific *penisu, vagina, masutābēshon* (masturbation), and so forth. At the same time, in some stories the author also uses old-fashioned Japanese words such as *maguwau* ("to couple"), thus confirming the fact that the use of *katakana* is aimed at introducing unusual terms for their estrangement effect, rather than being due to a simple xenophilia. Murakami uses *katakana* words in a manner similar to that of advertising, to convey a feeling of modernity, stylishness, and cosmopolitanism, but he is also very self-conscious and ironic in this respect, and in some texts he explicitly parodies the use of *katakana* words typical of advertising in the 1980s. A good example can be found in the story "Zō no shōmetsu" ("The Elephant Vanishes," from the collection *Pan'ya saishūgeki*). In the final part of the story, the narrator, who works for the advertising department of an electrical appliance manufacturer, shows a young journalist a series of kitchen appliances created by an Italian designer. He talks extensively about kitchens, and about how the most important thing in a kitchen today is "unity": unity of design, unity of color, unity of function, and so forth. His speech is clearly a parody of the language of advertisement, and is full of English words in *katakana*, such as *dezain* (design), *baransu* (balance), *konseputo* (concept), *shirīzu* (series), *shinpuru-sa* (simpleness). Furthermore, throughout the conversation, the narrator refers to the kitchen calling it *kitchin*, and when the woman asks a question using the Japanese *daidokoro*, he hastens to correct her: "We say '*kit-chin*,'—I advised her—No big deal, but the company wants us to use the English." Interestingly, the same contrast is highlighted by Mark Rebuck as an example of how English words are used in advertising to convey the idea of a modern and Western lifestyle: the word *kitchin* "is used in preference of the Japanese word *daidokoro* because it is more likely to trigger images of a place which is spacious and modern." Murakami's choice of the word is a parody of this usage of foreign words in advertising.[22]

Murakami uses *katakana* to denote not only material objects, but also abstract terms—the latter usage, however, fulfills a different function.[23] Abstract words are equally divided between common terms that do not have an equivalent in Japanese or that have replaced the Japanese word in everyday language, such as *shinfonī* (symphony), *hansamu* (handsome), or *imēji* (image), and unusual terms such as *koketisshu* (coquettish), *hisuterikku* (hysteric), or *burasshu appu* (brush up). The role of loanwords indicating abstract concepts is particularly ambiguous, and tied up with the idea of attaining individuality by engaging with foreign culture. In his interview with Jay McInerney, for instance, Murakami states that the term "identity" does not exist in Japanese, and that, therefore, Japanese have to resort to the English word:

> While living in America, I would like to write about Japanese society from the outside. I think that is what will increasingly define my

identity as a writer. By the way, do you know there is no equivalent in Japanese for the English word "identity"? That's why when we want to talk about identity we have to use the English word.[24]

Although it is true that the term *aidentitī*, in *katakana*, is often used in contemporary Japanese, it is also true that Japanese equivalents for "identity" do exist: for instance *mibun* or *dokujisei*. As in other interviews with American journalists or writers, Murakami is playing the part of the "compliant colonized," giving to America the image of Japan that Americans want it to have, i.e., a group society that does not know the freedom of American individualism, a culture to which the idea of "individual identity" is so alien that a writer needs to escape to the United States to attain such an "identity." At the same time, significantly, both on linguistic and conceptual levels, Murakami underlines how, for him, finding his own identity is related to distancing his own culture and identifying with the Western Other.

Murakami's texts reveal a similar process, which generally begins with the recognition of the presence of foreign language inside Japanese and the consequent awareness of the complexity of language, of the fact that each language contains other languages. This is the first step toward recognition of the multifaceted nature of identity and reality—which is also highlighted by other textual strategies. One aspect that clearly foregrounds the multilayered nature of language is the creative use of *furigana*: in a number of instances, Japanese words and short sentences are glossed with foreign terms in *katakana*, not only in English but also in French, German, and Greek. For example, in "Mittsu no Doitsu gensō" ("Three German Fantasies" from *Hotaru, Naya o yaku, sono ta no tanpen*), we find the word *terebitō* ("television tower") annotated with *Fuerunzētōrumu* (*Fernsehnturm*); *higashi Berurin shimin* (West Berlin citizens) with *Osuto Berurinā*; *suijō no ongaku* ("music on water," Haendel's Wassermüsik) with *Wassā mujikku*; *jitsu ni ne* ("in fact") with *yū nō* ("you know").

The glossing of *kanji* with foreign words in *katakana* has a function similar to the didactic one it had in the Meiji era, to "teach" foreign languages to readers, or at least make readers more familiar with them, and to diffuse Western culture in Japan, starting from the language. However, this creative use of the graphic potential of Japanese writing also adds layers of meaning to the text, making it richer and more complex, while at the same time raising the reader's awareness of the existence of different linguistic realities and the textual nature of the text itself, and also constructing a multifaceted vision of reality. In this sense, Murakami's *furigana* also work in a way similar to the footnotes that appear in many postmodern novels, i.e., to introduce in the text different layers of discourse—for instance, as in Burroughs's *Naked Lunch,* where the numerous footnotes do not serve the purpose of clarifying the meaning of the text, but rather of further complicating it. As Brian McHale describes this kind of phenomenon: "The effect of such glossing is not, as the text seems to pretend, helpful, but on the contrary aggressive, alienating."[25]

With his use of the polygraphy of Japanese, Murakami performs a double operation of domestication and estrangement of Western languages and cultures that reverses the ideological operation carried on in the Meiji era, when European alphabetic languages were used as an instrument to unite spoken and written language. With his wide use of *katakana,* and in some cases also of the Roman alphabet, he appropriates foreign languages that "colonize" the text but are also absorbed and deformed by it.

Far from being a unifying instrument, European languages increase the polygraphy of Japanese. With a movement contrary to that of *genbun itchi*'s repression of the visual aspect of Chinese characters, carried on in the name of a phonocentric vision of language and of the privileging of the oral word over the written, Murakami adopts linguistic strategies that exploit the specific potential of writing, comparable to those of authors such as Natsume Sōseki, who, in Karatani's words, "still sought a world beyond that of linear, phonetic speech, a world where the meaning of writing was polysemic and radial," continuing to make use of the potential of Chinese characters within the new style of writing.[26] Accordingly, although *genbun itchi* provided the basis for the realistic turn in Japanese literature, Murakami's linguistic strategies are instrumental to his rejection of traditional realism, and the alienating presence of foreign languages is central to the vision of reality that the stories construct.

In Other Words: "Rēdāhōzen," "Takushī ni notta otoko," "Tairando," "Airon no aru fūkei"

One of the texts in which the otherness of foreign language is used most effectively is "Rēdāhōzen" ("Lederhosen," from the collection *Kaiten mokuba no deddo hīto*). The story is enclosed in a double frame: there is a first narrator named "Murakami Haruki"—a feature, common to all of the stories in the collection, that will be discussed further in the next chapter—and a secondary narrator, a friend who tells him the story of how her mother divorced her father because of a pair of lederhosen. During her trip to Germany, the mother goes to buy a pair of lederhosen for her husband, but when she explains to the shop owner what she wants, to her amazement, he refuses to sell them. There follows a surreal conversation, based on a linguistic misunderstanding:

> "I mean, we cannot sell clothes to a client that does not exist."
>
> "But my husband does exist!" she said.
>
> "Of course. Your husband exists. Of course," the old man hastened to say. "Please excuse my poor English. What I mean is, um, since your husband is not here now, we cannot sell you lederhosen for your husband."
>
> "Why?" she asked, feeling confused.
>
> "It's our shop's policy. Our principle [*hōshin*, glossed with *purinshipuru* in *katakana*]. We have our clients wear the lederhosen, we adjust them meticulously, and only after we have done this we sell them. We have done business in this way for over a hundred years, and we have built a reputation on this principle."[27]

After a brief discussion, the man agrees to sell the trousers to somebody who is the same size as her husband. The woman finds a German man who agrees to help her, but when she sees her husband's Western "double" wearing the lederhosen, she realizes that she wants to divorce her husband, and does so as soon as she gets back to Japan. The daughter tells the narrator Murakami Haruki that, when she heard about this episode, she finally understood and forgave her mother, because, she says, the lederhosen are an essential part of the story. The narrator agrees with this. Neither of them, however, explain the significance of the lederhosen, which remain the sign of something unspoken and unspeakable, in which the foreignness of the term and of the object is central to its mysterious power. Marukawa Tetsushi observes that by being "constantly repeated and appropriated, the word *lederhosen* becomes a form of 'cultural consumption good.'"[28]

The use of this foreign word as the pivot of the story performs a function similar to the one that Nozumi and Tanaka describe in relation to advertising, of either flattering the readers or making them feel inferior, according to whether they recognize the "difficult word" or not, connoting the text as exotic and sophisticated and adding to its appeal. However, it also has an estranging effect that causes the reader to reflect. This is not simply the story of a woman traveling abroad and "finding herself." As both narrators say, the important point in the story is the lederhosen; the most significant fact is that the encounter with a foreign culture revolves around a "cultural consumption good," designated by a foreign word that becomes the object of a form of what Rebuck calls "name-fetishism." Both the word "lederhosen" and the surreal conversation in broken English with the shop owner are central to the protagonist's "awakening": it is foreign language and its alienating effect that allow her to attain a new perspective. Not only the name of the object, of course, but also the object itself, the pair of lederhosen, plays a central role in this story. (The next chapter will deal more extensively with the value of such "cultural consumption goods.")

Another story that focuses more specifically on a language game is "Takushī ni notta otoko" ("The Man in the Taxi," also from *Kaiten mokuba no deddo hīto*). This story also employs two levels of narration: the narrator-in-the-text is a woman whom the first narrator interviews about her work as an art buyer (another *katakana* profession). When he asks her about the most striking work of art she encountered in her career, she tells him of a strange experience she had with a painting called "The Man in the Taxi." She had bought the painting from a Czech artist in New York: it was the only picture she ever bought for herself, without the intent to resell it. It was not a particularly good picture, but she became obsessed by the man portrayed in the painting, and used to spend hours looking at it. The man in the taxi became a very important part of her life: she considered him a friend and felt for him a deep "sympathy" (in the Roman alphabet): "The sympathy I'm talking about is not a sharing of feelings or sensations, but it comes from the fact that two human beings can share the same kind of sadness."[29]

The story throws into question the boundary between reality and fiction, with foreign language playing a significant role in this process. Foreign words, both in *katakana* and in *rōmaji*, are particularly numerous, probably because the story is set partly in Japan, partly in the United States, and partly in Greece. The protagonist's clothes, described in detail, are all in *katakana*: *ribon* (ribbon), *burausu* (blouse), *gurē no tsuīdo no sukāto* (grey tweed skirt), *haihīru* (high heels), *Bābari no torenchi kōto* (Burberry's trench coat), *gurē no kashimiya no mafurā* (grey cashmere muffler). Furthermore, there are also Japanese expressions annotated with foreign *furigana*: *sore dake* (only this) is glossed with *zattsu ōru* (that's all) in one instance, and later with *dasu isuto aresu* (the German *das ist alles*); as well as *mono no mikata* (way of seeing things) glossed with *pointo obu vyū* (point of view).[30] As in other stories, the protagonist's use of foreign clothes and foreign words identifies her as a cosmopolitan and sophisticated character, similar to the one Murakami himself impersonates for his audience. However, the foreign language plays a more significant role in the second part of the story.

Years after she has gotten rid of the painting, and has almost forgotten about it, she meets the "man in the taxi" in real life, in a taxi in Athens. It is exactly the same man in the picture she had looked at for years. The boundary between reality and fiction blurs, and for a moment, she is bewildered: "She tried hard to adjust her mind. She put reality in the frame of reality, and imagination [in *katakana* in the text] in the frame of imagination. But nothing changed. She was riding a taxi in Athens, in the month of July, seated beside the man in the picture."[31] They have a short conversation, and she finds out that the painting was probably, in fact, a portrait of the man, who is a theater actor. The taxi then comes to a halt, the man gets out, and wishes the protagonist a good trip, in Japanese (*yoi go-ryokō o*; have a good trip) glossed in *furigana* with the Greek *karō takushiji* (*kalò taxidi*). The woman thanks him in Japanese, (*domo arigatō*; thank you very much) annotated with *efukarisuto poli* (*evkaristò polì*). With the expression *kalò taxidi* (have a good trip) playing on the original meaning of the word taxi, "travel," the metatextual game merges with the linguistic one to create a playful yet also meaningful estrangement. The taxi in the title of the painting, and also of the story, becomes a real object in the diegesis: the car in Athens in which the protagonist meets the man from the picture, but also a word, the Greek "taxì," travel. The whole operation is at the same time amusing and profound, making the reader aware of the multilayered nature of language, culture, and reality itself. Linguistic and metaleptic strategies merge, multiplying the possibilities of the text, destabilizing a unitary and simple vision of reality and of identity, while at the same time making the readers smile, pleased by their recognition of the game. Such playfulness is a recurring feature of Murakami's texts, which often address serious issues through laughter and irony.

Another clever use of foreign language can be found in the story "Tairando" ("Thailand," from *Kami no kodomotachi wa mina odoru*; published in English with the title *after the quake*). The title of the story itself is in *katakana*; however, interestingly, it uses a *katakana* inscription of the English word for "Thailand" (*Tairando*) instead of the one more commonly used in Japan and in Thailand, *Tai*. In a similar Anglicism, the city of Bangkok is referred to as *Bankokku*, whereas in Japanese it is normally spelled *Bankoku*, with only one "k." Strikingly, the origins of the words used are neither Japanese nor Thai, but English. This element is further strengthened by the interactions later in the story between the two protagonists, Satsuki (a Japanese physician) and Nimit (her Thai guide and chauffeur), who speak to each other in English (although this is "translated" into Japanese in the text). Again, the presence of a foreign language—English—highlights the relativity of cultural categories and the complexity of relations between Japanese and Western culture. Through the ample use of *katakana* in the story, the English language colonizes the Japanese text, while at the same time being assimilated and remolded by the Japanese syllabary. Many objects are referred to by English-*katakana* words, even where a Japanese equivalent exists, and some sentences are so full of them that they have a distancing effect on the reader.[32]

The concept of language as a filter emerges repeatedly in the text. When Satsuki—through whose consciousness almost all the story is filtered—first meets her chauffeur Nimit, she notes how he speaks very good but strangely neutral English, without any perceivable accent. She later discovers that he learned it from his former master, a Norwegian jewelry trader, and this is why his English sounds neither American nor British. When Nimit takes her to see an old Thai woman who predicts a dream that she will have, the woman speaks in Thai to Nimit, who translates into English for Satsuki, and this pattern is repeated a number of times. The old woman then tells Satsuki that she has a stone inside of her, that something is written on the stone in tiny black characters, but that she is unable to read it since it is in Japanese. Through layers of different languages, words do not disclose meaning but envelop and hide it; far from being a transparent vehicle to represent reality, language takes on a reality of its own, obscuring rather than uncovering reality.

This opacity of language is a way of calling attention to the arbitrariness and deceitfulness of the linguistic sign, in a fashion halfway between modernist and postmodernist strategies. When, at the end of the story, Satsuki tries to tell Nimit her secret—the hidden truth that she has hinted several times in the story and that the reader also is probably eager to learn—he stops her, expressing his distrust of words: "Please, doctor. Don't tell me anymore. You should have your dream, as the old woman told you to. I understand how you feel, but if you put those feelings into words, they will turn into lies. . . . Cast off mere words. Words turn into stone."

The discovery of the relativity and arbitrariness of the linguistic sign is specifically predicated upon the recognition of the existence of multiple languages. This use of different languages in the text is similar in style both to modernist writers such as Joyce and Pound, and to postmodernist or late-modernist writers such as Nabokov and Beckett, all of whom experimented with multilingualism in order to reflect on the nature of language. In Murakami, however, this multilingualism takes on a new meaning, since it involves not simply the relationship between different cultures, but the relationship between East and West, with all of its historical, political, and philosophical implications.

In other stories, Murakami also plays on linguistic differences within the Japanese language. For example, in "Airon no aru fūkei" ("Landscape with Flatiron"; also from the collection *after the quake*), one of the protagonists, Miyake, speaks in the dialect of Kansai, or western Japan, and therefore stands out as an outsider in a small town in Ibaraki Prefecture, where the language is closer to *hyōjungo*, the standard language of Tokyo and the surrounding Kantō area. The dialect is thus framed and used as a disturbing element that further problematizes the naturalness of language. In this way, the text underlines the differences within the Japanese language along with the differences between different languages. The dialect stands for the internal difference that is suppressed in what Naoki Sakai calls the "complicity between particularism and universalism" of Japan and the West, which, by postulating a binary opposition between East and West, ends up denying the differences within each of these two entities that are seen as unitary and homogeneous. Sakai argues that there is a fundamental complicity between Japanese particularism and the Western universalism it pretends to oppose: the cultural essentialism of Japan and that of the West endorse each other in order to repress the anxiety of internal diversity. By introducing the Kansai dialect along with English in his text, Murakami questions this binary opposition, proposing a more complex image of the linguistic reality of Japan, and, more broadly speaking, of the nature of language and its relation to national identity.

In this light, Murakami's interest in the history of Hokkaidō in earlier works such as *Hitsuji o meguru bōken* and *Dansu dansu dansu* is easier to understand. Hokkaidō, the northernmost island of Japan, was colonized during the Meiji period as part of the process of constituting modern Japan, and, both on the linguistic-cultural and on the institutional level, it provided a model for Japan's subsequent colonization of Asian countries. Therefore, the history of Hokkaidō is another instance of the repression of difference, and its presence in Murakami's novels represents an attempt at destabilizing "official history" through the exploration of cultural and linguistic diversity, of a plurality of languages and a plurality of stories.

However, these language games never go too far: Murakami's texts are not experimental like those of writers such as Hori Tatsuo or Yokomitsu Riichi—or, for that matter, of James Joyce and other European modernists. Murakami's fiction has always been highly readable and comprehensible, which is one of the reasons for its success, and probably also the reason why many critics dislike his writings. Kawamoto Saburō notes that one of the most salient features of Murakami's prose is precisely this readability, and relates it to his activity as a translator:

> Murakami is also a translator, and since he attributes great importance to the *readability* [written in *katakana*] of his translations, trying to make them accessible to the readers, not limiting himself to translate the English but also trying to write in a Japanese that is easy to understand, we could argue that even when he writes original fiction

he cares about this aspect. He has so many readers, after all; and that, actually, might be why he is dismissed by the critics as an "easy read."[33]

Reaching a wide audience is very important for Murakami, and the linguistic strategies he employs are at the same time a means to appeal to readers, in a way similar to that of advertising, and a way of destabilizing their vision of reality. Furthermore, this use of language and writing is one of the ways in which Murakami displays "irony through the West," an approach in which he distances himself from his own culture and presuppositions by identifying with the Western Other. Language and culture in these texts are seen not as "given" but as constantly renegotiated by the single "individual human being" (*kojinteki na ningen*), who is always on the boundary between different cultures, both on the national, internal level (the cultures of Kansai, Kantō, Hokkaidō) and on the international level (Japanese, American, European, Chinese, and so forth).

Australia as Sign: "Shidonī no gurīn sutorīto"

Linguistic strategies that foreground the complex and multilayered nature of reality are thus linked to Murakami's use of foreign cultures as alienating elements that induce reflection on cultural categories. This is particularly evident in the story "Shidonī no gurīn sutorīto," from the collection *Chūgokuyuki no surōbōto* (1983). "Shidonī" was published for the first time in 1982 in the journal *Umi*'s special issue "Kodomo no uchū" (The Universe of Children) and is one of the first short stories written by Murakami, following his first three novels, *Kaze no uta o kike*, *1973-nen no pinbōru*, and *Hitsuji o meguru bōken*. Here, as elsewhere, the presence of *katakana* words, both referring to objects and food, and to abstract concepts, is very strong.

The title of "Shidonī" is a pun on the name of Sydney Greenstreet, the actor who plays Kasper Gutman ("the Fat Man") in the movie *The Maltese Falcon* (dir. John Huston, 1941). Murakami says that often his short stories are born of a single word or sentence that strikes his imagination and develops into a whole story.[34] In this way, he underlines the fact that his fiction is not born from facts, but from words, from language. Through this insistence on self-referentiality, the stories underline their own textual nature, while at the same time hinting at the fact that language can create realities, that reality is linguistically constructed. Words become stories, and stories produce realities.

The referentiality of the "Green Street" of the title is problematized in the very first lines of the story, which begins by saying that this *midori dōri* (glossed in *katakana* with *gurīn sutorīto*) in fact has no greenery whatsoever, and is a bleak and unpleasant road: "Sydney's Green Street is not, as you may imagine from its name—or, at least, as I imagine that you might imagine—a magnificent street. First of all, in this street there are no trees to speak of. Nor are there are any lawns or fountains. God only knows why it got named 'Green Street.' Probably not even God knows."[35]

The story takes place in Sydney, and the Australian setting allows the story to play not only with *katakana* but also with *hiragana* and *kanji*, foregrounding the material and culturally constructed nature of writing and language. After describing Green Street as one of the most desolate places in Sydney, the first-person narrator *boku* ("I") reveals that this is the location of his private detective office. He then describes the office, which has a sign on the door written entirely in *hiragana*, because, he explains, not many people in Sydney can read *kanji*:

> I have my private detective office in Sydney's Green Street. That is to say, I am a private detective. On the door there is this sign:
>
> "Private Detective. Competitive prices.
> However, I only accept interesting cases."
>
> The sign is all in *hiragana*. Of course, there's a reason for that.
> The fact is that not many people in Sydney are able to read *kanji*.
>
> ("Shidonī," 258)

The passage is clearly meant to be humorous: if it is true that in Sydney not many people can read *kanji*, they certainly cannot read *hiragana* either. The reference to Japanese writing is a paradox and a joke, but it also serves to undermine the readers' horizon of expectation, making them aware of cultural difference. This feature recurs throughout the story: even though it is set in Sydney, all the characters speak Japanese, and this foregrounds the problem of language, reversing the typical feature, for instance, of Hollywood movies, where all characters speak English, no matter what their real nationality is. The references to *kanji* and *hiragana* highlight the presence of the Japanese language in the unlikely Australian setting. For instance, when the narrator visits the house of Professor Sheep (*hitsuji hakase*), the man who stole his client's ear, the man asks him whether he was unable to read the Japanese "do not disturb" sign on his door:

> There was a notice that said: "No newspaper or milk, please." [in *kanji*] . . . I rang the bell twelve times . . . the old man shouted: "What do you want? Didn't you see the notice? Can't you read kanji? Do-not-ring-for-news-pa-per-or-milk." [in *hiragana*] "Of course I can read kanji. I'm not a milk or newspaper delivery man. I'm a private detective." ("Shidonī," 274–75)

Furthermore, the name of the protagonist's client, Sheep Man (*hitsuji otoko*), is written in *hiragana* in the dialogues, but in *kanji* in the narrative sections, as though the protagonist, not knowing the *kanji* of his interlocutor's name—as often happens with Japanese names, which can be written with different combinations of ideograms having the same pronunciation—was not able to "think it" in *kanji*, and therefore had to "speak" it in *hiragana*.

> "Hello," said the little man.
>
> "Hello," I said. "You are . . ."
>
> "Please call me Sheep Man [*hiragana*]," said the Sheep Man.
>
> "Nice to meet you, *Sheep Man* [*hiragana*, italics in the text]," I said.
>
> "Nice to meet you," said the Sheep Man [*kanji*]. "You are a private detective [*hiragana*], right?"
>
> "Yes. I am a private detective [*kanji*]," I said. Then I turned off the record player, put Glenn Gould's "invention" back in the record rack, and turned toward the Sheep Man [*kanji*].
>
> "I was looking for a private detective [*kanji*]," said the Sheep Man [*kanji*]. ("Shidonī," 264–65)

The same goes for the word *shiritsu tantei* (private detective); at first, the Sheep Man says it in *kana*, maybe because he, like most citizens of Sydney, "is not able to read *kanji*," but then, after the protagonist has "said" the word in *kanji*, he picks up on it and also "says" it in ideograms. Although the dialogues are supposedly mimetic of oral speech, this use of *kana* and *kanji* makes them inseparable from their written form, thus foregrounding their textual nature, the fact that they exist only as text, have never been spoken in reality, and are not a transposition of a supposedly "real" dialogue. A similar strategy can be found in the novel *Umibe no Kafuka*, where the character Nakata-san, who is mentally retarded and unable to read, "thinks" all difficult *kanji* compounds in *katakana*.

In "Shidonī no gurīn sutorīto," this estrangement based on writing affects not only cultural categories, but also the sense of reality itself. The story is explicitly anti-realistic in many respects, starting with the already mentioned fact that it is set in Australia but all the characters are, apparently, Japanese, or at least speak Japanese. Australia itself, more than a real location described in its actual characteristics, is an imaginary place, used to introduce a vision of reality: it allows the narrator to foreground the relativity of language and culture, as well as of the categories of season and time:

> Summers are terribly cold, and winters are terribly hot. "Summers are terribly cold, and winters are terribly hot" seems a funny thing to say. Even though seasons are reversed in the South and North hemisphere, the hot one is summer, and the cold one is winter. . . . But I cannot see things in such a simple way. This involves the big problem of "what are seasons anyway?" I mean, is it winter when December comes, or is it winter when it gets cold? That is the problem. ("Shidonī," 253)

The surreal Sydney of the story, where people read and write Japanese, inhabited by Sheep Men and Sheep Doctors who want to be Sheep Men, is an "Australia as imagination" similar to the "America as imagination" (*sōzō to shite no Amerika*) that Sengoku Hideyo considers one of the main features both of Murakami's translations and of his original works. It is an imaginary place, an "Other" postulated to distance our own selves and to understand the relativity of what we take for granted, looking at the world through a distorting mirror.

As Sengoku correctly notes, it is usually America that plays this role in Murakami's fiction, as well as in his theoretical reflections. An illuminating article in this respect is "Kigō to shite no Amerika" (America as Sign) that Murakami wrote for the journal *Gunzō* in June 1982, at the beginning of his career as a professional writer. The article starts by telling the story of how, while translating a novel, he encountered the expression "you're cooking with Crisco," a phrase that he had never heard before. He could not find it in any dictionary, but he came across a similar expression, "cooking with gas," which means, he explains, *yatta ne*, "that's right, you got it." He then asks an American friend and discovers that Crisco is a brand of cooking oil, and the expression means the same thing as "cooking with gas."

This gives rise to a reflection on what America is for him. At first, being confronted with an expression he does not understand makes him feel frustrated: the word Crisco, whose meaning is immediately clear to any American, for him is an insuperable barrier. If he were to live in the United States for a while, he says, everyday objects like this would probably become familiar to him, and a word such as Crisco would enter into his vocabulary. But then, he reflects, the expression "cooking with Crisco" has a special function for him precisely because, not being immediately clear, it becomes for him just a sign (*kigō*). Murakami says he prefers the word Crisco when he does not understand its meaning: "the echo of the word [the sign] Crisco, whose meaning I don't understand, delights me immensely."[36]

This makes him realize that he is not interested in the real America as much as in his "imaginary" America: "What I'm interested in is the America I perceive inside my mind, the America I imagine. It is the America that I spy through a small window."[37] The reason for his interest in this "America as imagination" is that it allows him to distance himself from the vision of the world that society has imposed on him, and to become an individual subject: "at least that is a fixed point, to which I can relate and 'be myself.' I think everybody has a point like that. In my case, that just happened to be America."[38]

In what could be seen as a counter-orientalist mode, Murakami uses America as a means for him to be an individual, to constitute himself as a subject in relation to an "Other" outside himself, as the West has done with the "Orient" for centuries, and as Japanese intellectuals did in turn during the Meiji era. But what is peculiar in Murakami is that he considers all of this a game: he is deeply concerned with Western culture but does not necessarily take it, or himself, seriously. And this is part of a broader strategy of seriousness through irony that is deployed in his works at various levels, a strategy that is one of the most significant contributions of his fiction to the development of a new type—and a new vision—of Japanese literature.

Significantly, the whole reflection on the issue of an "imaginary" America starts from a word, Crisco. The distancing of one's own culture through the American/Western "Other," in order to question one's own cultural presuppositions and to foreground the discursive and constructed nature of individual identity and of reality itself, is directly connected to the question of the linguistic sign evoked through polygraphy, i.e., the emphasis on the opacity and arbitrariness of the sign. Both strategies, of linguistic and cultural estrangement, are situated halfway between modernism and postmodernism, or rather constitute a different way to relate to Western modernity from a geographical distance, that might be defined as para-modernist. Rather than displacing the West from a "post" position, which with its temporal implication ultimately reinforces the paradigm of modernity as progress, as postmodernist authors do, Murakami relies on the destabilizing effect of cross-cultural creative misreadings, highlighting the spatial dimension of modernity itself.

Such estrangement is pursued by Murakami to a great extent through the introduction of foreign literature in the texts, both in the form of quotations or parodies and through the presence of texts and writers within the texts, blurring the boundaries between reality and fiction and between different narrative realities.

Polygraphy and Parody

As we have seen, "Shidonī no gurīn sutorīto" is highly anti-realistic, both in its use of language, which foregrounds the textual nature of the story itself, and in the Australian setting, which becomes a means of highlighting the arbitrariness of cultural categories, and of distancing one's own culture. But the surreal aspect of the text is not limited to staging an Australia where everybody speaks Japanese. The characters and the plot are a clear example of Murakami's surrealistic streak. The story begins with the Sheep Man, a little man dressed like a sheep, asking the protagonist *boku* to get back his ear, which has been stolen by Professor Sheep. Sheep Man reveals that there are around three thousand Sheep Men in the world, in places as disparate as Alaska and Tanzania. They are not a secret society, a religious sect, or anything of that sort. They are simply Sheep Men who want to live in peace as Sheep Men ("Shidonī," 269). Their greatest enemy is Professor Sheep, who steals their ears for his collection. In fact, Professor Sheep secretly desires to be a Sheep Man, as the narrator's girlfriend Cha-Li explains to him in one of the final scenes. The girl then persuades Professor Sheep to confess that he has hidden the Sheep Man's ear under the salami, in the refrigerator of Cha-Li's pizzeria, and the protagonists retrieve it just as a customer is about to eat it on a slice of pizza.[39]

The story is narrated in a mode close to that of a fairy tale or a comic book. This is intermingled with a parodic style reminiscent of the American detective stories of the 1930s: the protagonists' language and manners clearly mimic those of characters from the hard-boiled genre. According to Giorgio Amitrano, the influence of the hard-boiled genre on Murakami's style, both through the novels of Raymond Chandler and Dashiell Hammett and through the film versions of their works, is manifest in most of his writings:

> The narrator hero of his novels is almost invariably a reincarnation of Chandler's Philip Marlowe or Hammett's Sam Spade but also of their interpretation by Humphrey Bogart, Alan Ladd, and Jack Nicholson . . . onto which the author grafted endearing elements of clumsiness and vulnerability derived from Dustin Hoffman's and Woody Allen's characters.[40]

Whereas the parodic treatment of the detective story is more remote and more serious in Murakami's novels—the narrators act *as if* they were detectives but are not actual detectives, and they often face excruciating hermeneutic and moral dilemmas—in "Shidonī no gurīn sutorīto" the parody is literal, yet entirely playful. The protagonist says that he works as a private detective as a hobby, since he has "so much money that he does not need to work" ("Shidonī," 256), and plays the part of the detective in a clearly ironic way. After saying that he is a private investigator, *boku* explains that, in fact, he has almost no clients, and he jokes both about the uselessness of detectives and about the pointlessness of the cases that he is offered. The cases his Sydney clients ask him to solve are banal and boring, and he would like something more exciting:

> I said I have a private detective's office, but, in fact, I have virtually no clients. The people of Sydney's Green Street would never pay somebody to solve a problem. They have so many problems that, rather than solving them one by one, they try to harmonize them all and go on living. In any case, Sydney's Green Street is not an easy place to live for a private detective. Sometimes a client is attracted by the "competitive prices" sign and comes in, but most of them—of course, this is only my personal opinion—are totally uninteresting cases. For example, "Why do my hens lay eggs only once a day?" or "Could you find out who steals my milk every morning?" or "A friend owes me some money, could you help me get it back?" that kind of thing. I mean, don't you agree? I did not become a private detective to take care of people's chicken or milk or loans! I'm looking for much more dramatic [*doramachikku*, in *katakana* in the text] cases. For instance, a two meter-tall butler with a blue glass eye, in

a black limousine, who asks me "Please, help me retrieve the little countess's ruby," things like that. ("Shidonī," 262–63)

However, his client in the story turns out to be a little man dressed as a sheep asking him to retrieve his stolen ear.

In many instances, the narrator appropriates and parodies features typical of the detective story. For example, this is how the Sheep Man appears onto the scene: "It was a Friday afternoon when the man dressed as a sheep entered my office. As soon as he slipped through the door, he peered outside to check that nobody was following him. Then he tried to close the door, but he could not do it. I stood up to help him, and we closed it together"("Shidonī," 264). This opening mimics that of the classic detective story, as does the client's looking back out the door, supposedly to confirm that he has not been followed. The scene turns immediately comical, however, when the small man is unable to close the door and needs to be helped by the narrator. The Sheep Man then asks the narrator to help him find his ear, which was stolen by Professor Sheep. *Boku* decides to take the case, and, again, acts as a stereotypical hard-boiled literary detective:

> "Well, Mr Sheep Man," I said. "I will get back your ear."
> "Thank you," said the Sheep Man.
> "The price is one thousand yen a day, plus five thousand when I get back the ear. Please pay three days' worth now."
> "Do I have to pay in advance?"
> "Correct," I said. ("Shidonī" 270)

Boku eventually finds Professor Sheep's house, gets hit on the head with a vase, and passes out. After remaining unconscious for several hours, he goes back to Professor Sheep's place accompanied by his girlfriend Cha-Li, and once again behaves like a hard-boiled detective, threatening to shoot the man and get the ear back. But this only results in a scolding from Cha-Li.

> "The ear belongs to the Sheep Man," I said.
> "Well, now it's mine," said Professor Sheep.

"You leave me no choice," I said, and took my automatic revolver from under my armpit. I am very short-tempered. "I will have to kill you and get the ear back."

"Calm down, you two," Cha-Li chimed in. "Sometimes you're so stupid!" she said to me. ("Shidonī," 281–82)

The case is finally solved by Cha-Li, who quotes Freud in explaining to Professor Sheep that he suffers from a "love-hate complex" and hates Sheep Men because, in fact, he would like to be a Sheep Man himself. The ear is found, and the case is closed, all thanks to psychoanalysis:

"No way! I'm never going to give back that ear. Sheep Men are my enemies. If I meet him again, I'll tear away his other ear, too!" Professor Sheep said.

"But why do you hate Sheep Men so much? They are nice people, you know?" I said.

"Do I need a reason? I just hate them! When I see them having fun in their absurd clothes, I just can't help hating them."

"Love-hate complex, huh?" Cha-Li said.

"What?" said the professor.

"Eh?" I said.

"Deep inside, you would like to be a Sheep Man. But you don't want to admit it, and instead you end up hating all Sheep Men."

"Oh, really?" the professor said. "I hadn't noticed."

"But how do you know?" I asked Cha-Li.

"You guys never read Freud or Jung?"

"No," said the professor.

"Unfortunately not," I said. ("Shidonī," 282–83)

This parody of the hard-boiled genre, transposed into a context far from its traditional setting, creates an estrangement effect similar to that produced by the language games discussed earlier in this chapter. *Boku*'s imitation of literary or cinematic detectives makes the readers aware that he is also a fictional character, and that the text being read belongs to the "other realm" of literature.

Furthermore, this use of the detective story is reminiscent of what Stefano Tani and Michael Holquist call the "anti-detective novel." Building on a term coined by William Spanos in the essay "The Detective and the Boundary," Tani investigates the use and subversion of the themes and techniques of detective fiction in postmodern literature. Both Tani and Holquist trace the history of the genre in its evolution from Edgar Allan Poe's classic rationalistic detective novel *The Murders in the Rue Morgue*, through the American hard-boiled genre, to what they define as postmodernist anti-detective fiction. Holquist notes that in the same years in which the modernist movement questioned the West's positivist ideals and looked for meaning in myth and in the unconscious, "beyond reason," the classic detective novel, beginning with *The Murders in the Rue Morgue*, recuperated reason as a means to introduce order into chaos. According to Holquist, the detective novel was born in response to a need for order, and this is particularly evident in Poe's detective stories, which constitute the rationalist counterpart to his mystery and horror tales:

> The world was a place of chaos for Poe, a vale not only of tears, but also of unspeakable horrors. . . . it is in the very depths which he experienced, and was able to capture in words, the chaos of the world, that we must search for the key to the ordered, ultra-rational world of the detective story.
>
> It was to this powerful impulse toward the irrational that he opposed the therefore necessarily potent sense of reason which finds its highest expression in *The Murders in [the] Rue Morgue* and *The Purloined Letter*. Against the metaphors for chaos, found in his other tales, he sets, in the Dupin stories, the mental metaphor for order: the detective. . . . Poe . . . lays open the world of radical rationality which is where detectives have lived ever since.[41]

The rationalistic mystery genre developed further in the works of authors such as Arthur Conan Doyle and Agatha Christie, and, in the United States, in the novels of S. S. Van Dine and Ellery Queen. In response to this hyper-rationalistic novel and its infallible detectives, American authors such as Dashiell Hammett and Raymond Chandler created a new kind of detective story, the so-called hard-boiled school, in the 1930s. They introduced into the detective novel more realistic elements, staging degraded urban environments and "human" detectives, who are liable to get personally involved in the cases they are trying to solve, or simply fail. According to Tani, in Hammett and Chandler's works,

> American city wastelands replace the idyllic countryside setting of the British detective novel, and the hard-boiled dick, a lonely hero who clings to a personal moral code, no matter how absurd his devotion to it may seem, takes the place of Dupin and Sherlock Holmes. Though the hero of hard-boiled detective fiction is normally unmarried as are Dupin and Holmes, he is far more a flesh-and-blood character. . . . the detecting process is no longer only the solution of a riddle, but a quest for truth in a reality far more complex and ambiguous than in the stereotyped "fairy tales" of the British collection.[42]

If the three main elements of every detective story are detective, detection, and solution, these novels focus on the solution, challenging the idea that the ending should reestablish order. Solutions are anticipated, annulled, negated, or parodied, frustrating the readers' expectations. The other two elements are influenced as well. In particular, the degree of involvement that was already present in the hard-boiled detective becomes even stronger, and he "gets emotionally caught in the net of his detecting effort and is torn apart between the upsurge of feelings and the necessity for rationality."[43]

Parodies of the detective genre are not unknown in modern Japanese fiction. The most famous examples are probably the pseudo-mysteries of Abe Kōbō, such as *Mikkai* (*The Secret Rendezvous*, 1977), which might be considered an instance of what Tani calls the "innovative detective novel," where the detective is "a victim of the signs he tries to interpret and of the ambiguity of reality" and "the first thing to question is no longer the mystery, but the detective."[44] On the other hand, *Moetsukita Chizu* (*The Ruined Map*, 1967) could fall into the category of the "deconstructive detective novel," where "the detective is unable to impose a meaning, an interpretation of the outside occurrences he is asked, as a sleuth, to solve and interpret."[45] Both in Euro-American anti-detective novels and in Abe's works, protagonists who find themselves caught up in the cases they try to solve are a revision of the infallible detective of the traditional mystery, which was born with

Auguste Dupin and found its consecration in Hercule Poirot and Sherlock Holmes.

This is not the case with Murakami, however: his detectives are instead a parody of the human and fallible detective of the hard-boiled school. His protagonists seemingly fit into the category of the "hard-boiled dick" protagonist of the American detective novel of the 1930s, but they are also clearly comic characters, caricatures. The protagonist of "Shidonī no gurīn sutorīto" does not simply fail; he is defeated in a ridiculous way. He finds the culprit's house simply by looking in the telephone directory, and then, when he goes to Professor Sheep's place with his hard-boiled pose, he gets hit on the head with a flowerpot and remains unconscious for hours. When he wakes up, he goes over the events of the day and concludes that he has "done enough for today": he has heard the client's case, received an advance payment, found the culprit's house, injured his ankle, and been hit on the head. The rest can wait until tomorrow, he concludes, satisfied.

Unlike postmodern anti-detective novels, which satirize the rationalistic style of Poe, the writings of Murakami consistently parody the hard-boiled genre. The choice to reference hard-boiled fiction, in contrast to postmodernist revisions of the rationalistic mystery, is once again related to his paramodernist cross-cultural use of Western pop culture for its destabilizing effect. This element is prevalent also in Murakami's longer fiction. The narrator in both *Hitsuji o meguru bōken* and its sequel *Dansu dansu dansu* shares many of the characteristics of the hard-boiled detective, and both novels feature plots loosely based on a mystery-type quest and an impossible search for meaning.

Sekai no owari to hādoboirudo wandārando presents a more complex and intriguing operation: while explicitly referencing the hard-boiled genre even in the title, it also uses the genre to create a powerful tension between the two alternate narratives that constitute the main structure of the novel, one in a partly realistic, partly science-fictional style, the other in a fantasy mode. The narrator's blasé attitude in the "hard-boiled wonderland" sections, modeled on the style of Chandler's narrators, is contrasted with the complete involvement of his alter ego in the "End of the World," the fantastic walled city in which he is trapped. The relation between the two stories is exploited in a very clever way through a number of different means in the novel, but the interplay of the different narrative voices plays a central role in building this effect, and the parody of the hard-boiled style in this novel is one of the most fascinating examples of this strategy in Murakami's oeuvre. In the short stories, however, because of their less structured plots and more experimental nature, the value of this cross-cultural parody emerges in its clearest form. Importantly, Murakami's detective-like stories are clearly ironic from the very beginning—they do not create expectations only later to frustrate them as do novels such as John Gardner's *The Sunlight Dialogues*, in which "the reader of detective fiction, a Pavlovian dog who salivates because he expects a certain food (murder) when hearing a certain sound (suspense), is going to drool in vain," since "all moments of suspense are inconsequential."[46]

Murakami's texts are close to anti-detective novels in another sense: they presuppose a prior knowledge of the stereotypes of the hard-boiled genre in order to be appreciated by the reader. Holquist notes that, just as most modernist texts require that the readers be highly familiar with myth in order to understand all references, postmodernist anti-detective fiction takes for granted the reader's knowledge of the *clichés* of traditional mystery: "Just as earlier Mann had depended on his reader's knowledge of the Faust legend, and therefore could achieve certain effects by changing the familiar story in crucial ways, so Robbe-Grillet and Borges depend on the audience's familiarity with the conventions of the detective story to provide the subtext they may then play with by defeating expectations."[47] In the same way, Murakami's stories require the reader to recognize the originals that they parody—the novels of Hammett and Chandler.

However, once again, Murakami looks at his intertexts from a distance that is not only temporal but also geographical.

In this sense, his parody of detective fiction has the same appeal as the use of foreign words, and creates similar para-modernist dynamics of cultural distancing.

Another story that explicitly satirizes the hard-boiled genre is "Sausubei sutoratto: doubi burāzazu no 'sausubei sutoratto' no tame no BGM" ("Southbay Strut: BGM for Southbay Strut by the Doobie Brothers," from the collection *Kangarū biyori*). Here also the parody takes a specifically intercultural nuance, and the text foregrounds cultural stereotypes in order to subvert them. This time, as in many of Murakami's texts, the alienating element is American culture. The story is set in California, but from the first lines the narrator, who plays the "hard-boiled dick" even more than the protagonist of "Shidonī," explains that this California does not correspond to the image that the reader might have of it:

> As in most parts of California, in Southbay it almost never rains. Even though it is in Southern California, there are no surf points, no hot rod courses and no movie star mansions. It just does not rain. There are more *yakuza* than raincoats, more syringes than umbrellas. . . . Southbay City is not the kind of South California where young people are eternally young and have eyes blue like the sea. First of all, the sea in Southbay is not blue. Its surface is covered with black oil . . . and the only ones who look eternally young are dead youths.[48]

In line with the hard-boiled genre, this text also undermines stereotypes about California and proposes a less glittering, more decadent image of America; however, in order to do so, it also makes specific use of the distance between Japan and America. This is evident, for instance, in the fact that in one of the few texts by Murakami that is set in the United States, a Japanese element such as *yakuza* is universalized and used to mean "gangster," whereas in the texts set in Japan Western elements such as orange juice and donuts are made universal.

This parody of the hard-boiled genre from a geographical distance, like the language games and the use of *katakana*, allows the text to play on the border between Japanese and

American culture. Each culture becomes an estranging factor for the other, foregrounding the relativity not only of cultural categories but also, more broadly, of both Western and Japanese categories of thought. Such an effect is even more evident in another major group of stories by Murakami, those where the protagonist is a writer, as the next chapter will explore.

FOUR

Literature and Identity

Looking for Meaning: The Writer and the Detective

In many of Murakami's texts, the narrator is a writer, a journalist, or a translator, and this writer-protagonist often plays the role of an interpreter of reality. In this sense, his texts respond to the same need to "put order into chaos," to which Euro-American modernists responded by rejecting positivist rationalism and turning to myth and the subconscious, and to which the detective novel responded by reaffirming the power of reason with the figure of the detective, the "mental metaphor for order."

Murakami is positioned halfway between these two strategies. On the one hand, the way he introduces writers and texts within the text breaks the illusion of reality and destabilizes a univocal vision of the world. The characters, and the reader with them, are made aware of the composite, stratified, and nonlinear nature of the texts, and ultimately of reality itself. On the other hand, the writers in the texts behave like detectives, using their deductive ability to reconstruct reality from traces.

An example is Murakami's story "Gogo no saigo no shibafu" (from the collection *Chūgokuyuki no surō bōto;* translated as "The Last Lawn of the Afternoon" in *The Elephant Vanishes*). In this text, the autodiegetic narrator *boku,* who is now a writer, relates an episode that occurred when he was eighteen or nineteen years old, when he cut lawns as a part-time job. It was the summer of fourteen or fifteen years ago, the year when Jim Morrison sang "Light My Fire" and Paul McCartney sang "The Long and Winding Road." (This system of characterizing dates according to references to pop culture, generally Western, is typical of Murakami's works, and will be discussed further in the next section.) The protagonist goes to the house of a 50-year-old woman to cut her lawn. When he has finished the work, the woman invites *boku* inside the house, offers him a drink, and shows him into a girl's room that is full of dust and has a calendar still on the page of the previous month. The woman asks him to look around, opening drawers and closets for him, and to tell her what he thinks of the girl who lives there. *Boku* hesitates, puzzled, but then he attempts a description of the girl, trying to guess what kind of person she is from the traces she has left behind.

> "Seems she's nice—very nice—keeps everything in order," I said. "Not too pushy, though not without character, either. Grades in the upper mid-range of her class. Goes to a women's college or junior college, doesn't have so many friends, but close ones. . . . Am I on target?"
>
> "Keep going."
>
> "I don't know what more to say. In the first place, I don't even know if what I've said so far was anywhere close."
>
> "You're pretty much on target," she said blankly, "pretty much on target."
>
> Little by little, I was beginning to get a feel for the girl; her presence hovered over everything like a hazy white shadow. . . .
>
> "She's got a boyfriend," I continued. "Or two. I don't know. I can't tell how close they are. But that's neither here nor there. What matters is . . . she hasn't really taken to anything. Her own body, the things she thinks about, what she's looking for, what others seek in her . . . the whole works."
>
> "Uh-huh," the woman said after a moment's pause. "I see what you're saying."
>
> I didn't.[1]

The nineteen-year-old protagonist is not a novelist yet, but he will become one, as we learn from the first lines of the story, and he already has the characteristics of the writer/detective. He is able to reconstruct the character of the girl based on the objects, the signs, that she has left behind, in a manner reminiscent of the semioticization of the female body through a male gaze typical of the classic "novel" of the West. As Peter Brooks has demonstrated in his study *Body Works,* the representation of a woman's body through her traces, the objects that belong to her, has been a dominant trope in Western fiction from the origins of the modern novel in the seventeenth century.[2] According to Brooks, this approach foregrounds narrative as a reconstruction from traces, particularly in the rationalist Western novel of the eighteenth and nineteenth centuries, "with its plots of education and recognition and its presentation of reality as enigmatic, requiring an inquest into the nature of its signs in order to decipher them."[3]

In Murakami's story, however, the object of the gaze and of the reconstruction is not the young woman's body, but her character, her "individual being," which is, once again, central to Murakami's reflections. The operation the narrator performs in the girl's room is a metaphor of writing: the writer interprets reality, looks for a meaning in signs with the aid of his capacity for imagination. This task is conferred upon him by the outside world—in this case, the woman who proves to be the girl's mother, who asks him to recreate her daughter. (The reader does not know if the daughter is only momentarily absent or, as some hints—the dust, the old calendar—seem to suggest, if she is dead or has left home.)

The woman asks the narrator, a stranger, to tell her the story of her own daughter, because she relies on his imagination. Imagination and deduction, skills that writers are thought to possess in greater measures than other people, are necessary in order to recreate reality, because memory alone is not sufficient. In the first pages of the story, the text presents another metaphor for writing, comparing memory to the novel.

> Memory is like fiction; or else it's fiction that's like memory. This really came to me once I started writing fiction. . . . no matter how hard you try to put everything neatly into shape, the context wan-

ders this way and that, until finally the context isn't even there anymore. You're left with this pile of kittens lolling all over one another. Warm with life, hopelessly unstable. And then to put these things together as saleable items, you call them finished products—at times it's downright embarrassing just to think of it.[4]

Memory and writing are presented as attempts to give shape and meaning to a reality that constantly eludes control. Memory, like literature, is not a faithful reproduction of events, but an interpretation—and herein lies both its fallibility and its strength. Murakami's texts are ambivalent in this respect: although they portray the writer/detective as a maker of meaning, the only character capable of finding the significance of things, of reconstructing reality through deduction and imagination, they also question the authority of the author, the reliability of the novel and of memory. As this and other stories demonstrate, Murakami's texts constantly stress the distortion of reality brought on by the attempts to represent the world "as it is," in a transparent and supposedly realistic way.

A similar operation appears in another story from *Chūgokuyuki no surō bōto*, "Tsuchi no naka no kanojo no chiisana inu" (Her Little Dog Underground, 1982; untranslated). Here the narrator, a writer and a journalist, meets a young woman in the library of the hotel where he is staying, and lends her some detective novels he has brought with him. After a short conversation, *boku* proposes to guess some things about the woman. In the style of Dupin, the narrator explains—to the reader, but not to his interlocutor—the mechanism of his deductions: from the way she moves her hands he understands that she plays the piano; from her accent, that she now lives in the Kansai region, but was originally born in Tokyo; and so forth. Again, the narrator tries to recreate an individual from a few details, and is able to do it because he is a writer. He surprises the woman by telling her the story of her life. The girl, amused, asks him whether he is a professional, and *boku* replies that, in a way, he probably is something like a professional ("puro no yō na mono desu"): he is a writer. From his job as an interviewer, he explains, he has learnt to pay attention to details. Moreover, being a writer, he is good at observing and understanding people: "I write. Interviews, reportages, things like that. Nothing special, but my job is to observe people."[5] But when the narrator, departing from strictly logical deduction, tries to guess further elements relying merely on his instinct, he inadvertently touches upon a disturbing memory, upsetting his interlocutor. At this point the game stops, and the woman becomes the narrator of her own story, even though she continues to address the first narrator, constantly asking him "What do you think happened after?" or "What do you think I should have done?"

A similar reappropriation of the story by the character-narratee, and a consequent inversion of roles between the narrator and his interlocutor/reader, is crucial in the works appearing in the collection *Kaiten mokuba no deddo hīto*, in which all the stories revolve around the relationship between a first narrator, called Murakami Haruki, and a secondary narrator, who generally has a passive attitude toward the first narrator, similar to that of the protagonist of "chiisana inu." Apparently, the author/character/narrator Murakami Haruki, as a "professional writer," is the only figure with the authority to attribute meaning to the text, and even when he lets another character speak, he does so only on the condition that the characters leave to him the role of interpreter and guarantor of the ultimate significance of the story. However, the narrator downplays his own authority and asks for the reader's sympathy, declaring that he does not have a clear and linear vision of the facts he recounts, and does not want to judge.

Writer-narrators in Murakami's texts often behave like detectives, deducing facts from clues, in an attempt to gain control over reality. Like detective-narrators, writer-narrators are exposed to failure, and in this departure from positivist detection the texts are once again reminiscent of the anti-detective novel described by Tani and Holquist, particularly in its "metanarrative" version. In the story "Naya o yaku" (from the collection *Hotaru, naya o yaku sono ta no tanpen*; "Barn Burning," in *The Elephant Vanishes*), the narrator is a novelist and a male character explicitly addresses him as such, attributing to him a superior ability to understand people. The narrator has just met the man, a friend of an ex-girlfriend, when the latter suddenly opens up to him and confesses that he sometimes burns sheds. He says that he had not told anyone about his strange hobby, but felt he could talk to the narrator because he is a writer:

> "Fact is, I've never told anyone else about this but you. I'm not the sort to go spouting off just to anyone."
>
> "So why me?"
>
> The guy extended the fingers of his left hand and stroked his cheek. The growth of beard made a dry, rasping sound. Like a bug walking over a thin, taut sheet of paper. "You're someone who writes novels, so I thought, wouldn't he be interested in patterns of human behavior and all that? And the way I see it, with novelists, before even passing judgment on something, aren't they supposed to appreciate its form? And even if they can't *appreciate* it, they should just accept it at face value, no? That's why I told you. I wanted to tell you, from my side"[6]

The man then tells him that he has already chosen the next shed he wants to burn, and that it is very close to the narrator's home. The narrator, in his writer-detective fashion, tries to analyze reality through deduction, and starts collecting evidence. He buys a detailed map of his neighborhood, and runs around with the map, marking with an X all the places where he finds a barn. He proceeds in an extremely analytical and systematic way:

> I carefully checked the conditions of each of these, and from the sixteen I eliminated all those where there were houses in the immediate proximities or greenhouses alongside. I also eliminated those in which there were farm implements or chemicals or signs that they were still in active use. I didn't imagine he would want to burn tools or fertilizer.[7]

After a long and careful process of elimination, five barns are left. Armed with a T-square, a French curve, and a divider, *boku* traces the shortest route passing all five barns. He repeatedly stresses the precision of his measurements and the rationality of his method. Then, for a month, he runs every morning along this route, reconnoitering the barns, but none of them burns down. In the meantime, the barn-burning man's girlfriend disappears, never to be seen again. The following winter, with Christmas approaching, the narrator runs into the barn-burning acquaintance, who tells him that he enacted his plan ten days after they last met. *Boku* explains to him how he checked all the sheds for a whole month, and the man comments ironically on his precision and its ineffectiveness. Evidently, he says, he must have missed that particular barn. Maybe it was too close to see it.

> "Very thorough," he gibed, obviously having his fun. "Thorough and logical. All I can say is, you must have missed it. Does happen, you know. Things too close, they don't even register."
>
> "It just doesn't make sense."
>
> He adjusted his tie, then glanced at his watch. "So very, very close," he underscored.[8]

The narrator then tells the reader that since that day he has not been able to reach the girl, and he has concluded that she must have just disappeared. He still runs past the five barns every morning, he says, and has not heard about any barns burning.

The story satirizes the narrator's "rational method." Even though he is a writer, supposedly endowed with a superior understanding of reality, he fails in his investigation, and the meaning of events remains obscure to him. The text clearly hints at a possible different reading of the events: the young man's story was a metaphor, and the "barn" that he burned is the narrator's friend, an isolated shed that can be burned with impunity because no one but the narrator will notice that it has disappeared, as the man underlines in the last dialogue: "I think I know that girl pretty well, and she absolutely hasn't got yen one [*sic*]. No real friends to speak of. An address book full of names, but that's all they are. She hasn't got anyone she can depend on. No, I take that back, she did trust you. And I'm not saying this out of courtesy."[9] The text reveals its meaning to the reader, but not to the narrator, who does not understand the barn-burning metaphor, and cannot read the clues before his eyes, possibly because they are "too close." He is blinded by his excess of rationality and fails in his search for meaning—the discovery of which is then entrusted to the reader.

The stories discussed above present the writer as a detective and narration as a form of detection. Through their deductive approach, the narrators simultaneously attribute meaning to reality and transform things and people in texts, which they treat as systems of signs to be read and interpreted. In this sense, these stories correspond to the category of the metafictional anti-detective novel, where the strictly criminal element disappears, the detective is replaced by a writer, and the focus shifts to the relationships between writer, reader, and text. According to Tani, these novels "emphasize that 'book-conscious-of-its-bookness' aspect typical also of the puzzle-like British detective fiction," since in them "the detection is present in the relation between the writer who deviously writes ('hides') his own text and the reader who wants to make sense out of it (who 'seeks' a solution)."[10] This game between author and reader was present also in earlier and more traditional versions of the detective novel. Tani remarks that the relationship between criminal-detective and writer-reader, typical of the metafictional anti-detective novel, is in fact present in any text where there is some kind of "dialogue" between reader and writer, and quotes as an example the famous Ellery Queen narrative interruptions, in which the author "challenged the reader to find the solution before the end of the novel as by that moment he had all the elements in hand."[11]

Significantly, Murakami refers to Ellery Queen's interruptions when discussing the kind of book he had always wanted to write. In an interview entitled "Making of *Nejimakidori kuronikuru*," he says that he tried to take to extremes the concept of the "open novel," since the story becomes more and more complicated and then is suddendly interrupted at the end of the second volume.[12] He then states that he has always been fascinated by Ellery Queen's "challenge to the reader." Everything that comes after, he says, is only an anticlimax. For this reason, he had always wanted to write a novel that stopped at that point, that did not come to the point of saying "you are the murderer," and this is what he has tried to do in *Nejimakidori kuronikuru*.

In 1995, however, Murakami wrote a more conventional conclusion to *Nejimakidori kuronikuru*, partly undermining this project of the "open novel." Readers were only temporarily baffled, and the deferral of the ending simply created an effect of suspense similar to the one that induces spectators to see the sequel of a movie or to buy the next issue of a comic book series. A central element in Murakami's work is the coexistence of commercial strategies that treat the book as an object to sell—as the narrator of "Gogo no saigo no shibafu" says, "It is a commercial product!" (*shōhin desu yo*)—and of literary strategies that aim at "giving meaning" to the world in a complex form that accounts for the stratified and contradictory nature of reality, and this commingling is one of the aspects most reminiscent of Western postmodernist literature.

In the anti-detective novel, too, the lack of a solution becomes one of the elements of interest of the text that not only induces the public to read it (and buy it), but also makes the reader respond more strongly to the novel's message, thus fulfilling both the commercial needs and the intellectual ambitions of the writer. Tani describes this effect:

> Any deconstructive detective novel's open-ended nonsolution, if well worked out, leaves the reader with a proliferation of clues, allowing him to fabricate one or more possible denouements. This is a way to leave the novel "alive" (nonconsumed), an object of curiosity even after the end, since a plausible solution imposed by the reader implies a rereading or rethinking, in which the artistic qualities of the novel finally stand out. Thus open-endedness proves to be a means of planting the anti-detective novel's message more firmly in the mind of the reader than a conventional detective novel would.[13]

In this sense, the suspense in the anti-detective novel is even stronger than in the traditional detective novel. Here "the tension between the reader and the novel—namely, the tension from detection to solution—is increased in comparison with traditional detective fiction, since inconsequential clues are often much more tantalizing than the ones that eventually fall into place."[14]

Absent or unsatisfying solutions are common in Murakami's works, and they often have an anti-realistic, anti-rationalistic effect. In an interview with Shibata Motoyuki in 1989, discussing the difference between short stories and novels—*tanpen shōsetsu* and *chōhen shōsetsu*—Murakami says that when he begins to write a novel, he does not know how it will develop and how long it will be; short stories, however, are different: if he decides to write 50 pages, he writes 50 pages. Does that mean, Shibata asks, that he is able to make the story end at that point? No, Murakami explains:

> It would be more correct to say that it ends naturally. I don't write stories like those of Chekov, with a clearly defined beginning and end: once I have created a situation, I develop it, then I only have to end it abruptly at a certain point [*tekitōna tokoro de putsutto kireba ii wake desu*]. Therefore, once I have decided the length, I do something like a count down [in *katakana* in the text]: when the end is near, I just finish the story where it seems most appropriate. In this sense, my favorite writer is Raymond Carver.
>
> But I cannot do this with the novels [*chōhen shōsetsu*]. My readers would never accept that they end so abruptly, and neither do I. In a long novel there has to be some sort of catharsis. It takes time to write, it takes time to read, and to interrupt it suddenly would be strange.[15]

Before *Nejimakidori kuronikuru*, the short stories were the main locus of sudden, arbitrary, and unsettling conclusions. The absence of a conclusion intertwines with the other self-reflexive strategies used by Murakami, creating a destabilized and destabilizing vision of reality. It is within this vision that the writer should attempt to give meaning to the world. Literature plays a major role in this operation, in the form of parody of literary genres and through the presence of writers in the text. The following sections will explore two other fundamental instruments in this process: the use of metatextual strategies centering on the (problematizing of the) idea of the individual subject, and the presence of literary and cultural products, fragments of Western culture, in the texts.

Many Tales

The Japanese mystery writer Norizuki Rintarō, reflecting on the relationship between Murakami and Ellery Queen, notes that Murakami's first reference to this author occurs in *Hitsuji o meguru bōken*.[16] The narrator, in his self-introduction, says that he "knows all the culprits in the novels by Ellery Queen, and owns all volumes of Proust's *À la recherche du temps perdu* but has read only half of them." Significantly, the protagonist does not say that he likes this author or that he has read his books, but that he remembers the names of all the culprits. This is a typical attitude of readers of Ellery Queen, since his novels, even more than other mysteries, center on the "whodunit" aspect of the story. Furthermore, in all of these stories the protagonist is a detective called Ellery Queen, which means that *boku* would know the names of the culprit and of the detective in every novel. Left out, Norizuki notes, are the names of the victims.

Also, in Ellery Queen's works, the name of the writer, a pseudonym that conceals two different authors, is the same as that of the protagonist-detective. Murakami uses a similar strategy: most protagonists in his novels have no name, and are defined by a generic *boku*, or "I," that has become one of the distinctive features of his fiction, a kind of single protagonist that comes back in each text and tends to coincide with the author in the reader's mind. After the success of *Noruwei no mori*, Murakami complained in an interview that readers confused him with his characters:

Murakami: After I wrote this novel [*Noruwei no mori*], I received many letters and for some reason all the readers automatically identify the "I" in the novel with me. It's true that the novel is in the first person and that the period in which it is set is the same of my adolescence, but people go too far in equating me with that character.
Shibata: But your characters have a lot in common with you in terms of interests and tastes.
Murakami: That's true, but it is only one way of seeing things. From another perspective, you could say that precisely because the text is in the first person the character ends up resembling me, having

> the same tastes that I do, and so on. . . . The fact that readers take it so literally makes me feel uneasy.[17]

Many of Murakami's texts, not only *Noruwei no mori*, seem to encourage this kind of reading. Or, rather, he is probably willfully playing on this element, foregrounding the question of what is fiction.

Language games involving proper names are very frequent in Murakami's works. For instance, in the collection *Pan'ya saishūgeki*, none of the protagonists/narrators is named, but a different character in each story bears the name "Watanabe Noboru": the elephant guardian in "Zō no shōmetsu," the protagonist's sister's boyfriend in "Famirī affea" ("A Family Affair"), *boku*'s business partner in "Futago to shizunda tairiku" ("The Twins and the Sunken Continent"), and the protagonist's cat, named after his brother-in-law, in "Nejimakidori to kayōbi no onnatachi" ("The Wind-Up Bird and Tuesday's Women"). "Watanabe Noboru" also recurs in some stories in the collection *Yoru no kumozaru*. It is, in fact, the real name of the illustrator Anzai Mizumaru, who designs the covers of most of Murakami's works and who has co-authored several nonfiction books with him. The name is both an in-joke and a way to blur the boundaries between reality and fiction.

Many critics have commented on the use of proper names in Murakami's texts.[18] Karatani Kōjin takes a particularly interesting approach to the matter by relating the absence of names in Murakami's first two novels to his vision of reality and language.[19] Starting from the observation that the title of *1973-nen no pinbōru* is a parody of Ōe Kenzaburō's *Man'en gannen no futtobōru*, Karatani notes that in Ōe's novel there is a character called "Nezumi" ("the Rat"), who shares exactly the same name as *boku*'s best friend in *Pinbōru*. But while Ōe's Nezumi bears this name because of his physical features, the name of Murakami's Nezumi is completely arbitrary and has nothing to do with his actual characteristics. Nezumi himself explains that someone once gave him this nickname and for some reason the name stuck, but he cannot remember when or why he got it in the first place. According to Karatani, Ōe's characters are unnamed because they are "types" and not individuals; in Murakami, however, this strategy takes on a different meaning. The absence of names underlines the arbitrariness of the name itself, and more generally of language. The main characters of *1973-nen no pinbōru* are the nameless narrator, *boku*, his friend Nezumi, and two twin girls who appear mysteriously in *boku*'s house one morning. The twins do not have names, and when *boku* asks what he should call them, they reply that if he really needs to give them names, he can just choose two words he likes, such as right and left, up and down, or East and West.[20] The narrator decides to call them "208" and "209," the numbers on the t-shirts the girls have received for free at the supermarket. But the girls sometimes swap shirts to tease him. Names, like clothes that can be easily taken off, are superficial accessories, without any real connection to the person. Karatani maintains that through his treatment of names Murakami sets forth the idea that language creates phenomena. Significantly, the protagonist reads again and again Kant's *Critique of Pure Reason*, which revolves around the idea that perception creates reality. According to Karatani, *boku* takes Kant's text literally.

> Names here are only a means to distinguish things that could not be differentiated otherwise. . . . This way of thinking has been typical of post-Saussurian linguistics . . . but in this case, more than of Saussure, the text is reminiscent of the *Critique of Pure Reason* that *boku* reads with such interest. According to Kant, we cannot know the world as it is . . . we can only grasp the external world through language, a system to distinguish between different options, and this is true both of time and of the self. . . . In this sense we can say that Murakami's *boku* is reading "correctly" the *Critique of Pure Reason*.[21]

The reference to Kant is certainly significant. However, the text does not really engage his philosophy, and the text is named as an object that the narrator reads but on whose content he does not comment in any way. Kant's essay stands out as an incongruous presence in a novel where the characters do nothing but eat cream cookies, take walks in an abandoned golf course, and chat and sleep all together. Kant's *Critique of Pure Reason* is a clear example of the kind of "cultural consumption goods" that abound in Murakami's texts. (Further discussion of such goods will appear later in this chapter.)

As for names, Patricia Waugh notes that an antirealistic use of proper names, willfully absent or arbitrary and absurd, is a typical feature of metafiction, aimed at highlighting the arbitrariness and non-referentiality of language and the linguistically constructed nature of reality.

> The use of names in traditional fiction is usually part of an aim to disguise the fact that there is no difference between the name and the thing named: to disguise this purely verbal existence. Metafiction, on the other hand, aims to focus attention precisely on the problem of reference. Here, proper names are often flaunted in their seeming arbitrariness or absurdity, omitted altogether . . . or placed in an overtly metaphorical or adjectival relationship with the thing they name.[22]

In the same way, Murakami's play with names is another means by which the texts foreground their own textuality and problematize the distinction between reality and fiction. In later works, the use of proper names takes on a more complex function that involves the role and responsibilities of a writer in contemporary society. This is also a distinctive theme of metafiction according to Waugh, who maintains that one of the major factors in the birth of this literary trend is the "desperate sense of the possible redundancy and irrelevance of the artist,"[23] and that authors of metafiction find a new social function for narrative precisely in the reflection on literature.

> Metafictional writers have found a solution to this by turning inwards to their own medium of expression, in order to examine the relationship between fictional form and social reality. They have come to focus on the notion that "everyday" language endorses and sustains such power structures through a continuous process of naturalization whereby forms of oppression are constructed in apparently "innocent" representations. The literary-fictional equivalent of "common sense" is the language of the traditional novel: the conventions of realism.[24]

Particularly from the 1990s onward, Murakami's metanarrative techniques have been related to his reflection on his responsibilities as a writer, a producer of meaning, not only for an elite of cultured readers but also for "common people." A means to do this is the refusal of traditional realism, which distorts reality by forcing it into rational structures, and the use of metafiction to create alternative representations of reality that contest the vision proposed by the media and by mainstream literature.

In his analysis of the relationship between Murakami and Ellery Queen, Norizuki notes that in the classic mystery novel the triangle victim-culprit-detective, in order to allow for the identification with the couple author-reader, must be reduced, through the murder, to the couple assassin-detective, between whom a game of intelligence takes place. The victims are excluded from the game, and their names do not count, so much so that they are sometimes unknown until the end. Norizuki then contrasts this classic model with a novel by Ellery Queen, *Cat of Many Tails,* in which the victims, murdered by a serial killer, have individual names and stories. The "many tails" of the title are the "many tales" of the victims, through which the author is trying to restore the individuality of the victims that is left out of the traditional detective novel. *Cat of Many Tails* also has a final note about the names of the characters, accompanied by a comment from the author: "If one of the functions of fiction is to hold a mirror up to life, its characters and places must be identified as in life; that is, through their names."[25]

Norizuki compares *Cat of Many Tails* to Murakami's *Andāguraundo* (*Underground,* 1997), a collection of interviews featuring the victims of the 1995 Sarin gas attack in the Tokyo subway system. With this book, Murakami tried to give a name and a face to the people who survived the incident, so that they would not remain simply faceless victims. After the attack, the media extensively covered the stories of the perpetrators, "extraordinary men," but not those of the victims, the common people, thus treating culprits and victims in the same way as the classic mystery novel does. Murakami tried to subvert this binary relationship between culprit and justice, author and reader, giving a voice to the multiple stories of the victims.[26]

Murakami himself discusses this concept in the paratexts of *Andāguraundo*, relating it to the idea of his responsibilities as a writer. The concept of multiple narratives here has a twofold meaning. The role of a writer for Murakami is to speak for the common people, give them a voice, tell their multiple tales. But, more importantly, a writer also has to give people stories that can compete with those of Asahara Shōkō, the leader of the Aum Shinrikyō cult. The latter operation, however, is framed by the destabilized vision of the subject and of reality that emerges from his writings. The task of the writer is to produce meaning and put order into the chaos of the contemporary world, not by giving his authoritative and univocal version of the facts, a single explanation of "how things are," as a traditional detective would do, but rather taking it upon himself to tell stories as stories, diverse, multiple, and contradictory. A writer must make sense of reality in a narrative form, but one that is made up of "many tales," which are the only way to be faithful to a reality that is complex and multilayered. In the afterword to *Andāguraundo*, Murakami refers to this manifold nature of reality as "something like Chinese boxes."

> I think that we see the structure of the world fundamentally as something like Chinese boxes. Inside a box there is another box, and inside that another one, and so on. I think that we unconsciously perceive the existence of another world one level outside the world we are seeing now, or one level inside it. . . . But the people in Aum, although they say that they are desperately looking for a "different world," in fact have a very narrow vision, and see the world as exceedingly linear and simple. . . . They are unable to see beyond one of the boxes.[27]

This inability to perceive the complexity of things is what makes both inadequate and dangerous the stories that the Aum cult proposes to people. In an article about *Yakusoku sareta basho de*, the sequel to *Andāguraundo* that contains interviews with members of the Aum cult, Murakami says that in talking to these people he realized that they are not so different from writers—both try to make sense of the world, and to offer their vision, in the form of stories, to their audience, who desire it and need it. As Murakami puts it, "When I spoke to them face-to-face, I had to realize that there are many common points between their activities as adepts and the work of novelists. There is something *strikingly similar*."[28]

In the afterword to *Yakusoku sareta basho de*, Murakami returns to this topic, explaining that between writers and Aum devotees there is, however, a fundamental difference, namely, the assumption of responsibility toward one's actions: "The point is that we take responsibility for our work, and cannot help doing so, whereas those people ultimately rely on their guru or on some religious dogma."[29]

The social role of the writer as a "maker of meaning" becomes even more significant in the face of such phenomena. Literature is a potential rival for these religious sects, and the diffusion of these cults, in Murakami's opinion, is partly to be blamed on writers of fiction, who did not realize soon enough their responsibility in this sense. As he stated in an interview,

> If I give you the right story, that story will give you a judging system, to tell what is wrong and what is right. To me, a story means to put your feet in someone else's shoes. There are so many kinds of shoes, and when you put your feet in them, you look at the world through other people's eyes. You learn something about the world through good stories, serious stories. But those people weren't given good stories. When Asahara, the Aum guru, gave them his story, they were so tied up by the power of his story. Asahara, he's got some kind of power that's turned to evil, but it's a powerful story he gave them. I feel sorry about that. What I'm saying is that we should have given them the good story.[30]

Despite criticism from some scholars of his escapism and lack of committment, Murakami's body of work is a reflection on the nature of a writer's responsibility. The problem of the social relevance of literature, which, as Waugh notes, is present in most contemporary fiction, is particularly significant in Japan because of the predominance on the literary scene of *kindaishugi* ideology and its stress on the necessity of social commitment and of a strong connection with history. As a consequence, Murakami, having reached the status of "mainstream" writer, has had to confront the issue of his own responsibility as a novelist. However, he has approached it in a way very different from conventionally "committed" writers such as Ōe.

For Murakami, if stories are not to become a false myth to which people relinquish their own individual responsibility, a dangerous simplification of the world, and a trap for fragile persons, they have to take into account the complexity and multilayeredness of reality. His texts represent this "Chinese box" structure of reality by staging other worlds and parallel realities, both in a literal and in a figurative sense. These "other boxes" are introduced in the texts through metatextual and self-reflexive strategies; fiction is presented in the texts as another world, a different level of reality.

Sincerely Speaking: *Kaiten mokuba no deddo hīto*

Self-reflexive and metafictional strategies are particularly evident in the collection *Kaiten mokuba no deddo hīto,* which seems to pave the way for *Andāguraundo* and its collection of "many tales." The book is presented as the faithful record of true stories that the protagonists have told to the author. In the preface, the author-narrator explains that he is reluctant to call this work a novel: "Usually, when I write a novel, even if it is partly based on real material [*genjitsuteki na matiriaru*]—if such a thing exists—I change it so much that it is impossible to recognize," he writes. "This is the way novels work. After all, this is the way reality [*riaritī*] itself works: the reality of a bakery is in the bread, not in the flour."[31] But the text that the reader is about to encounter, he tells us, is something different. For a long time in his life, the narrator explains, all kinds of people have come to him to tell him their stories, and he has recorded them, thinking they might be useful material for a work of fiction. "I have written these texts—let me provisionally call them sketches [*sukecchi,* in *katakana*] as a warm-up [*uōmingu appu*]; I tried to transcribe reality as it was, thinking that later these stories might come in handy. But in the end I decided to publish them as they are."[32]

The preface then explains that in these sketches there are, obviously, interventions by the author: omitting items for stylistic reasons, as well as influencing his interlocutors' stories with questions and requests for further details. He calls his work a collection of sketches because it is neither a novel nor a work of nonfiction. The material is completely real, the means completely fictional. If there are incongruities or unnatural elements, this is because it is real. If it is possible to read it without dying of boredom, this is because it is fiction.[33] Years later, however, Murakami "confessed" to his readers that the stories were completely fictional, and that he wrote the entire collection in order to experiment with a realistic mode of writing, before undertaking *Noruwei no mori*.[34]

The narrator says he prefers to listen to other people's stories than to tell his own—Murakami himself makes the same kind of argument in the collection *Tōkyō kitan*—and declares that he likes stories that are ordinary (*heibon*) more than those that are extraordinary. He also claims to have the ability to find an interesting side to other people's stories, although he says that this skill has never been very useful in his work as a novelist.[35] Furthermore, he expresses the belief that the idea that self-expression has a cathartic effect is a myth, and that writing is not socially useful and is not a form of salvation. People write, he says, because they cannot help it: "The idea that self-expression is a form of spiritual liberation is a superstition, a myth. At least self-expression in the form of writing does not liberate anyone's spirit . . . people write because they cannot help doing it. In writing there is no effect, no salvation."[36] This statement apparently negates the hermeneutic potential of writing, and suggests an idea of "writing for writing's sake," without any other purpose, a vision of writing as a primary and physiological need. This concept is reminiscent of the idea, common in postmodern theory, of narration as a primary cognitive schema.[37]

The preface is ambiguous: while it underlines the "truth" of the texts, at the same time it also highlights their textuality by discussing their half-fictional nature. The same ambivalence is evident in the structure of the text. Each story is enclosed in a double frame: a first narrator named "Murakami Haruki" listens to the story of a secondary narrator, in a dialogue interspersed with moments in which the first narrator resumes his narrative authority by commenting on the whole episode. This mechanism draws attention to the fictionality of the work, and also reinforces the role of the writer as a "maker of meaning," and the function of narrative as a way of making sense of reality.

The secondary narrators in the text tell their stories to the author because they know he is a writer, and expect him not only to "find an interesting side" to their stories, but also to give them answers that they cannot find by themselves. The characters attribute to him precisely the role of "maker of meaning" that the writers/narrators took upon themselves in other texts.

In each story the first narrator is asked by the second narrator whether he "understands," and he answers that "he thinks he understands."[38] With this peculiar narrative structure, the texts give a crucial role to the readers, through their identification with the first narrator, who is in the position of narratee of the second story, a listener rather than producer of stories. The texts both distance the readers, making them aware of their fictional nature, and bring them inside the story by creating inside it their figure *en abyme*. This element, too, is typical of Western metafiction, which often makes the reader explicitly aware of his or her role as a player. In Waugh's words, "The 'Dear Reader' is no longer quite so passive and becomes in effect an acknowledged fully active player in a new conception of literature as a collective creation rather than a monologic and authoritative version of history."[39]

The reader is also involved in the text by the repeated use of expressions such as *shōjiki ni itte* ("sincerely speaking") or *wakaranai* ("I don't know," i.e., I put myself on the same level as the reader, I deny my authorial omniscience and authority). These expressions recur in the style of almost all of Murakami's narrators, but they are particularly frequent in this collection.

The phrase "sincerely speaking" recurs in the speech of both the primary and secondary narrators, bringing them closer. When his interlocutor in "Pūru saido" ("Pool side") asks Murakami "As a novelist, what do you think of this story?" ("Shōsetsuka to shite kono hanashi o dō omou?" 75), the narrator says: "I answered sincerely and thoughtfully that I found it a story based on interesting materials" ("'Omoshiroi yōso o kunda hanashi da to omou na' to boku wa chūibukaku shōjiki ni kotaeta," 76). In "Ima wa naki ōjo no tame ni" ("For a princess now disappeared") there recurs the phrase "shōjiki na tokoro," used by the narrator (85, 89, 93, 94); in "Amayadori," it is the secondary narrator who insists on his own sincerity: "I am opening up to you because I want to speak sincerely" ("datte shōjiki ni hanashitai kara, ima kō shite Murakami-san ni uchiaketeru n desu," 138), while in "Yakyūjō" it is the first narrator who describes the secondary narrator's story as "simple and sincere" ("shinpuru de shōjiki datta," 146). This insistence on sincerity presupposes a transparence and control over one's own enunciation that denies the cognitive uncertainties that the texts build up in other ways. While the author asserts in the preface that it is impossible to know reality "as it is," the narrator in the stories repeatedly states that he is sincere and tells "things as they are." This confounds the readers and makes them doubt the reliability of the narrator himself, even more so since he insists that he is sincere, as do many unreliable narrators in the Western tradition and particularly in Euro-American modernist works. This suspicion of unreliability increases the reader's interpretive responsibility.

This involvement of the reader and the overlap between the roles of narrator and narratee further uncover the mechanisms of textual production and encourage reflection on the role of the writer. As Patricia Waugh puts it: "By breaking the conventions that separate authors from implied authors from narrators from implied readers from readers, the novel reminds us (who are 'we'?) that 'authors' do not simply 'invent' novels. 'Authors' work through linguistic, artistic and cultural conventions. They are themselves 'invented' by readers who are 'authors' working through linguistic, artistic and cultural conventions, and so on."[40]

Murakami's stories further underline their own textuality by staging other forms of writing present in the story. A particularly significant example is Murakami's use of diaries. The story "Ōto 1979," for instance, begins by saying that the protagonist "he"[41] was one of the few persons able to keep a diary for a long time without ever missing a day. For this reason he was able to say exactly how long his nausea lasted: from June 4, 1979 to July 14 of the same year. During that period, he regularly vomited everything he ate, for no apparent reason; moreover, every day he received anonymous calls from a man who said his name and then hung up. One day, both the nausea and the telephone calls suddenly stopped, and things went back to normal. The man, a colleague whom the narrator sees to exchange jazz records, tells his own story in the first person, and his narrative is sometimes interrupted by interventions of the first narrator, who recounts it in the third person, and by the Murakami character, who participates in the conversation with comments and questions.

The protagonist often refers to his diary as proof of the authenticity of his narration, and stresses the importance and usefulness of keeping a diary, his personal way of introducing order into the chaos of reality.

> To be precise . . . wait a second . . . to be precise, the last time I vomited was on July 14, at 9:00 AM. I vomited toast, a tomato salad, and a glass of milk. And I received the last phone call that night at 10:25. I was drinking some Seagram's VO that I had received as a present, and listening to Erroll Gardner's *Concert By the Sea*. It's really useful to keep a diary, don't you think?[42]

But the diary, a mere record of events, does not help him to make sense of things. The man wonders what could be the cause of these strange episodes, but is unable to find an answer. The primary narrator proposes a possible rational explanation: perhaps the husband of his lover had hired a private detective to follow him around and pursue him with telephone calls, and the nausea was the result of his own feeling of guilt toward the affair. "You are really a novelist [*sasuga shōsetsuka da*]!" the man exclaims. He then adds that his interpretation is only one of many possible hypotheses, and it is not necessarily true. But this is not important, either. What really matters, he says, is to give meaning to the story and to learn something from it. Hypotheses, like stories, do not need to be true or even realistic. Their role is to help us make sense of reality. The man, however, who keeps a diary but is not a writer, has not even thought that he might "learn" something from this incident.

> "Of course, if we are dealing with hypotheses, we can make a hundred, two hundred of them. What matters is which hypothesis you choose to believe. And, most of all, what you learn from this story."
>
> "Learn?" he asked, puzzled. "What do you mean, learn?"
>
> "What would you do if this happens again, of course. Next time it could not stop by itself in forty days. Things that begin for no reason end for no reason. But the opposite is also true."[43]

The man replies he has never thought about it in this way. However, he defends his position against the Murakami character.

> "How strange. Before talking to you, I had never thought about it. I mean, that it could happen again. Do you think it will happen again?"
>
> "I don't know," I said.
>
> "But maybe . . ." he said. "Maybe next time it will happen to someone else. For instance, it could happen to you, Murakami-san. You certainly are not completely innocent, are you?' "[44]

This is the only story in the collection in which the secondary narrator addresses the primary narrator so directly; significantly, it is also the only story in which "Murakami Haruki" expresses some sort of judgment on his interlocutor's behavior. Before giving his interpretation of this strange incident, the narrator points out to his friend that he "does not have a clear conscience," that he is sleeping with other people's wives, and he criticizes him for this. In none of the other stories does the narrator express any judgment, much less a negative judgment, toward the secondary narrator.

In "Jidai no bunsekii" (Psychoanalyst of an Era), Marukawa Tetsushi compares Murakami's attitude in *Kaiten mokuba* to that of a psychoanalyst, who listens without judging: "In these stories we find a 'Murakami' who presents himself as a listener of his generation. He always takes the same stance: he smiles, nods, if his interlocutor smiles, he smiles, he feels what his interlocutor feels, and so forth. He behaves like an analyst, neutrally and pleasantly listens and agrees."[45] The role of the psychoanalyst is similar to that of the writer as interpreter of reality: the writer/analyst Murakami Haruki is able to give meaning to the stories that people tell him because he is able to give them a narrative form. As noted by Peter Brooks, psychoanalysis was from its very beginning deeply related to this narrativization of experience:

> Psychoanalysis is necessarily narrative, and indeed, in its theoretical formulations, necessarily a "narratology": a study of how narrative works. The psychoanalyst is ever concerned with the stories told by his patients, who are patients precisely because of the weakness of the narrative discourses that they present—the incoherence, inconsistency, and lack of explanatory force in the way they tell their lives . . . the work of the analyst must in large measure be a recomposition of the narrative discourse to give a more coherent—and thus more therapeutic—representation of the patient's story.[46]

In this sense, the role of the psychoanalyst is also close to that of the detective, in that both figures search for signs and attempt to reestablish order over chaos by putting the clues together in the form of a story: "Like the detective story, the analysis is an inquest, moving back from present symptoms, clues presented to the analyst, to the signs left by earlier events. . . . The narrative chain . . . marks the victory of reason over chaos, of society and sanity over crime and neurosis."[47] And, just as the detective/narrators could get involved, fail, and be hurt by reality, so the analyst/narrator can also find a less complacent patient/secondary narrator, as occurs in "Ōto." When he abandons his role of tolerant listener, the narrator is addressed as a human being, exactly on the same level as his interlocutors and potentially subject to the same dangers. Like the detective, the writer can also get involved. Next time, the same thing could happen to him.

This process of involvement reflects the passage from the idea of the psychoanalyst as external observer to the recognition of his inevitable participation as an actor in the life of the patient—an insight already present in Freud's late works. As Peter Brooks notes, the modern psychoanalyst, like the hard-boiled detective and the modernist writer, is not an outsider anymore, but becomes part of the phenomenon he is observing:

> What comes to complicate Freud's relation with his patient is the working of transference, by which the observer/analyst/detective loses its status outside the story and becomes part of it, in a "modernist" twist on the classical tale of detection. The transferential relation in turn complicates the case history he writes, since the relation of teller to listener becomes as important as the content and structure of the tale.[48]

If the implied reader in these stories is requested to participate in the interpretation of the text and to share its responsibility, "Murakami Haruki" himself, as narrator/author of the text, is addressed as co-responsible and becomes involved in the dynamics of guilt once he takes the role of narratee. This shift would throw into question and preclude any attempt at distancing on his part; however, the text is ambiguous in this respect as well. The writer/narrator's "lack of innocence" is taken up again, and partially dismissed, in the conclusion. In the last lines, the narrator says that after their conversation he still sees the friend from time to time, although since he does not keep a diary, he is not sure exactly how often he sees him. Fortunately, neither of them have suffered from nausea so far.[49] The narrator hints that he might be subject to the same incident as the secondary narrator, but he rapidly dismisses the possibility so as to regain his superior role of writer. Significantly, he once again insists that he, unlike his friend, is not the kind of person who keeps a diary, but that he is a writer, someone who can understand the world instead of being its passive victim.

Another story from the same collection, "Yakyūjō" (Baseball Field) uses the same double narrative frame to explore the relationship between reality and literature, the concept of verisimilitude, as well as the trope of spying without being seen, another recurring element in Murakami's works that detective and writer share. The text begins with a reference to the materiality of writing and a reflection on the relationship between reality and fiction. The primary narrator recounts that he met the secondary narrator because he was fascinated by his handwriting. The protagonist is one of the many would-be novelists who send him their manuscripts asking for an opinion. He usually never reads them, but he is so struck by the handwriting of this one that he decides to read the whole story. Unfortunately, the narrative is not as good as the calligraphy. It is a true story, but so badly narrated that it lacks any verisimilitude. This is the reason why the young man will never be a novelist: since many unusual things often happen to him, he thought he would try to write about them, but "the reality of a bakery is not in the flour," and an interesting life is not enough to make a good writer. This is how the second story describes the fundamental difference between "someone who has a story to tell" and "a writer":

> "So did that really happen?" I asked, surprised.
>
> "Of course it really happened. It happened last summer. I can only write about things that really happened. This is why I only write true stories. They are all real, from beginning to end. However, when I try to read what I've written, it does not sound realistic. . . . Things like this often happen to me. This is why I thought I should try to write. If you have the right material, it should not be hard to write. But when I actually tried to put it on the page, I realized that a novel is more than this. If any person who has good material could write novels, there would be no difference between a novelist and a banker."[50]

Murakami asks the man to tell him one of the many strange incidents that have happened to him. The man narrates how when he was in college he rented an apartment from which he could see inside the house of a girl he liked, and spied on her for months with a tele lens. Spying on the woman became an obsession for him. To see a person in her everyday life, while she thinks nobody can see her, is a disturbing experience for him, and he tries to stop doing it, but is unable to quit. He loses interest in everything else, stops going to class, and forgets about washing and eating. Fortunately, the girl goes back to her home for the summer holidays and the narrator is able to get over his obsession, and resume a normal life.

This prolonged observation enhances his analytical capabilities, to the point that he becomes unable to see things without dividing them. Observing the girl for so long, he begins to see her as two separate parts, her body and her behavior, and he starts wondering which part is the real girl. The whole experience is a highly unsettling one:

> I don't really know how to explain this, but I think that spying makes you become hyperanalytical. Or maybe the cause of all this is magnification. Inside my tele lens, she is divided in two parts: her body and her behavior. Of course, in the normal world, behavior is created by the movements of the body. . . . But in the magnified world, it's different. . . . After I looked at her for a while, her body seemed to be simply there, and her behavior seemed to come from outside her. At that point, I started wondering who she really was. Was she her behavior, or her body? . . . If you look at them in this fragmented way, human beings lose any charm.[51]

Once again the story stages different levels of reality: the two windows, the one from which the protagonist spies and the one that becomes a screen on which the woman's life is projected, become two separate worlds, two different "boxes." These levels are further multiplied by the narrative structure: the life of the woman in the window is contained in the story the man tells Murakami, which in turn is framed by the story that Murakami tells the reader.

This game can be dangerous if it gets out of control; the protagonist, who "cannot write," is in fact unable to deal with this experience, and risks destruction by his desire to spy. The choice of the expression *bunsekiteki na keikō*, "analytical tendency," to describe the destructive effect of spying on the protagonist is particularly significant. Analysis is presented here as a dangerous thing that distorts reality and negatively affects the narrator. If it is not accompanied by narrative capability, the ability to recompose in story form the signs observed, analysis is not just useless but harmful. Reduced to the signs that compose it, humanity "loses any charm." However, when he describes the experience to the narrator, who in turn relays it to the reader, the incident becomes a story that takes on meaning. Even though the story the man had sent to Murakami was true, it could not become literature. Only when Murakami gives it a shape, the "real life" of the man can become a narrative.[52] "Yakyūjō" stages the mechanism of observation as its main cognitive means. In this sense, the story presents both striking similarities with, and significant differences from, the mechanisms described by Brooks in his study on scopophilia in the Western narrative tradition. Brooks relates the origin of the novel to the birth of the concept of private life. Novels, he argues, are produced and consumed individually, unlike previous literary genres such as poetry (in almost all traditions originally recited in front of a public) and theater. Furthermore, since its very beginning, the Western novel represents mainly the private lives of individuals, spied in their intimacy, when they are, so to speak, unaware of being seen. In the modern era, the idea emerges of an inviolable private sphere that automatically becomes the object of an insatiable curiosity. The interest for private life is inseparable from its violation. This desire for knowledge usually passes through the gaze: the obsession with looking (scopophilia) is deeply related to the obsession with knowing (epistemophilia), the need to control the world, to make sense of it and give order to chaos. As Brooks asserts, the visual level is therefore crucial in the realist novel: "The dominant nineteenth-century tradition, that of realism, insistently makes the visual the master relation to the world."[53]

In Murakami's text, this realist mechanism is thrown into question: if the diary in "Ōto 1979," a mere record of events, did not make sense of the world precisely because of its excessive faithfulness to reality, the act of spying in "Yakyūjō" fails to lead to objective knowledge and only distorts reality. Observation is the primary narrative mechanism that confronts the narrator, through the young man-secondary narrator, making the former a narratee-spectator of a dynamic that involves him as well. Brooks notes that this involvement of the spectator is typical of Western novels revolving around the theme of gaze, where "spectatorship is made complicit with a violation of intimate space."[54] If the novel is always a window through which the reader spies the private life of the protagonists, scenes in which the narrator spies upon a character are clearly a *mise en abyme* of this textual strategy, which duplicates the mechanism and at the same time exposes it, both involving and distancing the reader. Reality is not made simply of two levels, but of an infinite number of Chinese boxes, multiple worlds seen through multiple windows.

Interestingly, Brooks quotes as an example of the realist gaze a device from *Madame Bovary*: namely, the presence of a double window from which and into which one can look. In contrast, Murakami's double framing foregrounds the impossibility to represent a fragmented and stratified reality through the conventions of realism. Significantly, an intermediate phase between the "realist window" and Murakami's window is Henry James's idea that "the house of fiction has many windows," all of which open onto reality, but each different from the others, with a different observer in each one. This idea of windows shifts from a symbol of realistic representation in classical Western literature to an instance of epistemological doubt in the modernist tradition, to become in Murakami a sign of postmodernist ontological doubt.

The observation of an unaware woman and the idea of multiple frames are central also in Murakami's latest novel, *Afutādāku* (2004; translated by Jay Rubin as *afterdark,* 2007). Here, the question of gaze is even more clearly foregrounded and problematized. The whole text is presented through the point of view of *watashitachi,* ("we"), making the narrator and the implied reader even closer and even more complicit. The first pages of the novel revolve around the idea of looking, as "we" slowly approach the characters in a cinematographic way, first looking at a city's night scene from above, "through the eyes of a night bird flying high in the sky," and then descending into its streets and seeing the protagonists "as though we were a camera." The novel is composed of two parallel stories, taking place at the same time, during a single night. In the first chapters, we follow a young woman, Mari, as she spends the night reading in a restaurant because she does not want to go home. We then "fly" to the room where her sister, Eri, is sleeping an unnaturally deep sleep. The whole story is presented as a mystery that is slowly revealed to us mainly through the characters' conversations. As in *Sekai no owari*, the relation between the two parallel stories is at first obscure and becomes clearer as the story unfolds. Throughout the novel, "we" go backward and forward between the two scenes, to find them slightly changed each time. The limits of "our" point of view are constantly foregrounded, both by the cinematographic descriptions and by references to what "we" cannot see and therefore do not know. For instance, just as the title of Mari's book is obscured by a paper cover, the contents of her thoughts and the reasons behind her behavior cannot be divined.

The mechanism of observation through multiple frames is even more relevant in the second of the two parallel plots. Here, our role as external spectators is strongly underlined. We can look at Eri, the text says, but cannot interact with her, cannot talk to her or touch her. As though we were time-travelers, we have to obey certain rules, and we cannot interfere with the reality we are observing.[55] This narrative mechanism is a parody of the extradiegetic narrator of the traditional realist novel, the purely external observer that does not get involved with the story. It throws into question this kind of realist representation, foregrounding its limits and the fundamental complexity of the mechanisms of observation, which are never direct, linear, or transparent.

Sleeping Eri is the object of multiple acts of observation and speculation: our camera-eye looks at her, Mari and Eri's friend Takahashi talk about her, and, even more strangely, a masked man silently watches her from inside a television set in her room. All the while, she is the unaware and passive object of this spying and speculating. The television screen in Eri's room introduces another layer of reality, another frame, another limited point of view. Our camera-eye can only see what another camera, the one projecting the images on the screen, decides to show us. We wait patiently as the screen slowly reveals to us new details of the room where the masked man is. But the story goes even further: after having created this structure of multiple screens and selective gazes, the narrative goes on to break it. The next time we go back to Eri's room, we discover that her bed is empty, and she is now sleeping, in an identical bed, inside the TV screen. The masked man inside the TV disappears, and we, by an act of will, are able to go through the screen and enter that other reality. Losing our body and "allowing ourselves to become a pure point of view" (*junsui na shiten to natte*), we move from *kochiragawa,* the world on this side, to *achiragawa,* the world on the other side.

Eri then wakes up, and is for a short moment entitled to her own point of view: we now see things through her eyes, and witness her reaction to the eerie situation in which she finds herself. However, she is unable to understand what has happened, and, scared and disoriented, only desires to go back to sleep, in order to return to where she came from. In the end, we find her sleeping again in her bed, and we do not know whether she will wake up again. The idea that sleep and dreams serve as gateways to other worlds is crucial to a number of Murakami's works. This aspect, as well as the concepts of *kochiragawa* and *achiragawa,* "this side" and "that side," will be the specific object of the next chapter.

In this sense, "Yakyūjō" is more realistic than *Afutādāku,* and its problematization of reality does not center on supernatural elements but exclusively on the concepts of gaze and point of view, and on a multilayered narrative structure. Multilayeredness is created through intertextuality as well as through metatextuality; this story, too, is filled with references to classics of European and American culture. One of the intertexts is clearly Alfred Hitchcock's *Rear Window,* which Brooks quotes as an emblematic example of scopophilia in cinema.[56] The protagonist's decision to rent an apartment from which he can see his beloved's house is reminiscent of *The Great Gatsby*, a text to which Murakami refers in several occasions. Significantly, the protagonist says that, even after he overcame his obsession, from time to time he still looked at "the window on the other side of the baseball field," as Jay Gatsby looked at the light on the other side of the bay, on the front porch of Daisy's house. The reference to Fitzgerald is made explicit in Murakami's essay about this collection, where he says that he has always been fascinated by the character of Nick Carraway and by the narrative mode of *The Great Gatsby*, and this is the reason why he decided to use a similar double frame in the stories.[57] The presence of direct and indirect quotations from foreign literature and culture is another means through which Murakami's texts create an image of reality as a "Chinese box."

Fragments of Western Pop Culture

Western culture plays a major role in Murakami's attempt to introduce order into chaos, and it represents for this author an equivalent of Joyce's "myth" as described by T. S. Eliot, "a way of controlling, of ordering, of giving a shape and a significance to the immense panorama of futility and anarchy which is contemporary history."[58] While Western literature and popular culture allow the characters to distance their own culture, they also constitute a defence against the chaos of the world. Murakami gathers fragments of Western culture against the disorder of contemporary society.

The texts of Euro-American modernists were filled with quotations that referred to the cultural heritage of the West, their own tradition. They also incorporated into this tradition some elements from non-European cultures, which they were discovering through the process of colonial expansion. T. S. Eliot in "Tradition and the Individual Talent" (1919) maintains that the conscience of a twentieth-century poet is inevitably very complex and very literary, and that modern writers can only try to be creative within a given tradition, from which they cannot escape. This tradition for Eliot is not as much a rule to follow as an unconcious legacy that is constantly modified within each individual's conscience. For this reason, the most original talent not only is bound by tradition, but also ends up reinstating it.[59] Many Western modernist authors share this approach, creating a high level of intertextuality in their works. Each text is built on other texts in a dialogical dimension, through a series of constant references to the whole European literary heritage, from the Greek and Latin classics onward—a cultural foundation supposedly shared by its readers. These references turn the texts into displays of erudition, in which author and reader mutually confirm their shared cultural and artistic traditions.

Interestingly, European and American writers became interested in these ideas between the end of the nineteenth century and the beginning of the twentieth, after the intensification of contact with Japan. The relationship between modernism and the colonial enterprise has been analyzed from a number of different perspectives, but few works have dealt with the specific influences of Japanese literature on the modernist movement. Some works have analyzed, for instance, Ezra Pound's interest in *haiku*, William Butler Yeats's fascination with *nō* theater, and the interest of modernist writers in the works of Ernest Fenollosa, but they generally consider them as isolated phenomena rather than as part of a broader reliance of the modernist movement on the Japanese tradition.[60]

While a comprehensive discussion of the Japanese influences on modernist literature in relation to the wavering of the myth of original creation is beyond the scope of this work, it is worth noting the double standard that writers constantly adopted toward Western and Asian tradition. To quote a blatant example, the theories of the imagist movement on the poetic image as an expression of the tension between two opposed elements, and as the "objective correlative" of an emotion, relied heavily on Morikawa Kyoriku and Matsuo Bashō's notions of *toriawase* (juxtaposition) in poetry, but Eliot and Pound presented them as original theories, without any reference to their sources except for the occasional mention of the "charm of *haiku*." Although the Western tradition represented a legacy to confront with either respect or rebellion, Japanese tradition was seen rather as a large repertoire, unknown to most, from which it was easy to "borrow" without anyone noticing.

The relationship of Euro-American modernists to the Western tradition, on the contrary, was shaped both by a sense of belonging and respect for that cultural capital and by a need to reinstate the value of individual creativity against it. As noted by Harold Bloom, modern Western authors constantly express the need to confront the great writers that have come before them, willfully misinterpreting them in order to create something new. In Bloom's opinion, "like criticism, which is either part of literature or nothing at all, great writing is always at work strongly (or weakly) misreading other writing."[61] As a consequence, poetic history is "indistinguishable from poetic influence, since strong poets make that history by misreading one another, so as to clear imaginative space for themselves."[62] And all great literature, according to Bloom, is born of such "creative misreadings."

Murakami also stocks his works with references and quotations, but he refers to a very different cultural heritage, namely, popular culture, while at the same time collapsing the distinction between highbrow and lowbrow. In his texts, we find numerous allusions to works of "high" literature, but these—such as the reference to Kant in *1973-nen no pinbōru*—are used as cultural consumption goods rather than academic references to be taken seriously. He shares this attitude with other writers of his generation, such as Murakami Ryū, Yoshimoto Banana, and Shimada Masahiko, in whose works references to Western (usually American) music, books, movies, and other artifacts of pop culture are ubiquitous, and at the same time are presented on the same level as European classical literature and philosophy. As noted by Glynne Walley, for instance, in the novel *Shikusutinain* (1987; translated in 1993 by Ralph McCarthy under the title *69*), in order to recreate the atmosphere of the student environment of the late 1960s, Murakami Ryū relies heavily on such references:

[Murakami Ryū] engages in some intensive pop-culture name-dropping: the Beatles' White Album, the Rolling Stones' "Honky Tonky Women," kewpie dolls, French singer Adamo, the comic serial "Ken the Wolfboy," Friedrich Wilhelm Nietzsche, Cream, Arthur Rimbaud, Paul Revere and the Raiders, Luc Godard, music and arts festivals, New Music Magazine, hippies, folk music, Che Guevara and Ōe Kenzaburō all pop up by page 20.[63]

Casual juxtapositions of figures such as Nietzsche and the Stones, or Rimbaud and Cream, are also prevalent in Murakami Haruki's works. In the texts of these authors, pop culture seems to include also the works of authors generally considered to belong to "pure literature," as long as they are liable to become objects to buy or icons to quote and with whom to identify. European and American modernists had also confronted the question of the industrialization and commodification of art, the idea that modern methods of reproduction made works accessible to everyone as though they were everyday objects. They responded to this issue in various ways, ranging from the pairing of ancient greatness and contemporary banality in *The Waste Land* to the transformation of serialized consumption goods into works of art by Andy Warhol. Contemporary Japanese authors such as Murakami are different in that there is no anxiety on the part of the artist toward this commercialization of art. This attitude might be reminiscent of Fredric Jameson's definition of postmodernism as total and acritical surrender to late-capitalist consumer society. Jameson notes a common feature in all works considered to be "postmodern":

The effacement of the older (essentially high-modernist) frontier between high culture and so-called mass or commercial culture, and the emergence of new texts infused with the forms, categories and contents of that very Culture Industry so passionately denounced by all the ideologues of the modern, from [F. R.] Leavis and the American New Criticism all the way to [Theodor] Adorno and the Frankfurt School.[64]

Such commercialization of literature, according to Jameson, results in the loss of the "critical distance" that characterized art in the past, and most of all in the modernist era. This description appears to fit the case of Murakami Haruki, and Jameson would probably categorize him as a postmodernist in this sense. However, if it is true that Murakami's works display no critical distance in a traditional sense, there is undeniably a cultural distance that makes his use of Western pop culture something very different from the same usage in Europe or in the United States.

Murakami's references to pop culture lack the elitism of Eliot and Pound's complex allusions. They are, on the contrary, immediately clear to almost everyone. At the same time, Murakami looks at this cultural legacy from a significant geographical distance, and his "anxiety of influence" is intertwined with the relationship between Japan and the West and the mechanism of the "complicity of the colonized" discussed in the first chapter. While paying homage to their models, his texts reinterpret and transfigure them. Creative misreadings here become much more creative, much more misread, because they are done from a greater distance.

At the same time, Murakami Haruki's use of Western references demonstrates a constant casual and ironic attitude. In Murakami Ryū's novels, for example, America is often portrayed as a symbol of corruption and decadence. In *Kagirinaku tōmei ni chikai burū* (1976; translated by Nancy Andrew as *Almost Transparent Blue,* 1977), the soldiers from Yokota Air Base who are the protagonists of the novel's two main episodes—two parties that turn into orgies between American marines and Japanese residents of the area—are portrayed as violent and self-serving, while the Japanese characters are compliant victims of the degradation that they bring onto themselves. The novel contains a strong element of criticism of the American military presence in Japan. In Murakami Haruki, however, we find nothing of the sort: the only American soldiers that appear in one of his stories, "Hantingu naifu" ("Hunting Knife," from *Kaiten mokuba no deddo hīto*), are seen playing volleyball on the beach where the narrator is spending his holidays. In Murakami Haruki's texts, American culture is not a threatening presence; on the contrary, it is an instrument willfully and playfully used to give meaning to reality through an ironic distance, through the creation of "other worlds."

In this sense, the choice of easily understandable references to popular culture over more sophisticated references to high art takes on further significance. American culture is used as something that is familiar enough to be perceived as non-threatening, yet unfamiliar enough to make readers reflect and distance their own culture. Murakami's references to Western pop culture are reminiscent of the reassuring function that Michael Holquist finds in kitsch, always slightly alien but never too alien. As Holquist notes,

> Tourists travel from the Istanbul Hilton to the Athens Hilton, the only difference being in the quality of plumbing and the "motif" of the hotel restaurants. There is no strangeness. Our international airports are all the same; they collectively constitute a country all their own, have more in common with each other than they have with the countries in which they are actually located. And that is what kitsch is—a country all its own, unlike any other, but giving the sense of reassuring sameness. It is not real, but it is familiar.[65]

References in Murakami's texts have the same reassuring quality of international hotel chains, yet for his protagonists, they are also an instrument to distance their own culture and achieve individuality. Foreign popular culture, not too threatening and easy to digest but still alienating enough to allow the characters and the readers to distance their own culture, is a powerful instrument in Murakami's new form of social commitment. Unlike the *kindaishugi* authors, Murakami neither represents Western influence in a realistic fashion, nor depicts it as something dangerous and corrupting; on the contrary, he uses it as the basis for their play and irony, to construct a multilayered vision of reality.

A good example is Murakami's use of dates, which are often indicated by references to songs, movies, or sports happenings, in open contrast with more "serious" historical events. Karatani Kōjin notes that the dates that appear in *1973-nen no pinbōru* could seem aimed at creating an effect of nostalgia toward a historical moment shared with the readers, but in fact they are exclusively personal dates that refer to moments lived only by the narrator and are devoid of any further meaning. For instance, for the narrator 1969 is not the year of student movements, but the year when he first fell in love with a woman; 1960, which in Ōe Kenzaburō's *Man'en gannen no futtobōru* is a fundamental turning point for Japan (it is the year of the renewal of the U.S.-Japan Security Treaty) instead, becomes for Murakami "the year in which Ricky Nelson sang 'Hello Mary Lou.'" Karatani maintains that Murakami knows very well what 1960 means, but pretends to ignore it, and instead he talks about the songs—including "Hello Mary Lou," which was actually released in 1961—that were popular *around* that year. In the same fashion, the year 1934 is described as "the year in which pinball was invented, and in which Hitler started to conquer the Western world." With this use of dates, according to Karatani, Murakami performs an inversion of importance between culture and subculture.[66]

Furthermore, these dates are not simply related to popular culture, but to *Western* popular culture. For instance, in "Gogatsu no kaigansen" ("The Waterfront in May," from *Kangarū biyori*), 1976 is "the year of the Olympics and of presidential elections. Montreal? Ford?" and in "32-sai no deitorippā" ("32-Year-Old Day Tripper," from the same collection) 1963 is "the year Kennedy died and I asked a girl out for the first time. The most popular song was 'Summer Holiday' by Cliff Richard."[67] The presidential elections, lived by the protagonist mainly as a mediatic event, are in the United States, the songs are by Cliff Richards and Ricky Nelson, and so forth. American culture is a means that enables the author to refuse the official version of history and to construct an alternative version of the past. With this inversion of hierachies, the text makes the phenomenological level of individual experience—in which one perceives the contingency of songs rather than the historicity of events, whose epochal nature is borne of subsequent reconstruction—overcome the historicist level of their re-construction, making microhistory prevail over macrohistory. Once again, the individual (*kojinteki na ningen*) is at the center of the stories. And it is an individual that cannot constitute itself as a subject in a natural and unmediated way, but only through the filter of Western pop culture, which is what allows the characters to make sense of reality "in their own way" and therefore to be themselves. The prevailing of popular culture over high art, of individual stories over "History," and the alienating effect of Western culture are therefore deeply interconnected. Significantly, the characters often try to be individuals by behaving like some Western icon, be it Ellery Queen, Holden Caulfield, or Jay Gatsby. In order to be themselves, they need to play a part, to identify with a foreign and literary other. This identification is inseparable from an awareness of the fictionality of the role they are playing, of the character with whom they are identifying. The texts thus negate the original and originary nature of the individual, and foreground the constructedness of identity.

This is true not only of the use of dates but, more generally, of the presence of cultural consumption goods, such as books and records that the characters read or listen to. The examples are innumerable and have even spawned a subgenre of secondary literature on Murakami consisting of lists of references to Western pop culture in Murakami's texts.[68] This vein of research is part of a broader phenomenon of collateral products in the publishing industry that rely on the popularity of Murakami's work, such as books collecting all the recipes quoted in his stories, and other similar works. Jameson's idea that "aesthetic production today has become integrated into commodity production generally" seems particularly true here.[69]

Aside from allusions to literary texts and pop music, another major point of cultural reference in Murakami's work is jazz. Murakami himself is an expert and dedicated collector of jazz records, and often his characters are avid fans of jazz. Like the author, the characters usually claim to be particularly fond of West Coast white jazz musicians. The reference to ethnicity is significant, since jazz has always been deeply related to questions of authenticity and race. E. Taylor Atkins has noted that "Perhaps nowhere is America's cultural dominance in Japan more readily visible than in the realm of popular music. Japan's historical experience of jazz, in particular, has been strikingly intense, reflecting perhaps more than any other single art the tensions and ambivalence of Japanese-American relations in the twentieth century."[70] The case of jazz is particularly interesting because this genre has always been considered the exclusive property of African Americans, and, although this idea has been contested, it is still prevalent in the field, especially in Japan. According to Atkins,

> The idea that jazz is the exclusive cultural property of black Americans is widely accepted among musicians, fans, and jazz scholars around the world. It has crossed the Pacific to Japan largely intact. . . . Most Japanese fans, by some estimates the largest per capita jazz audience in the world, concur that jazz by black Americans is "the real thing"; at the very least many share a compulsion to categorize the music (an activity of which Japanese fans seldom weary) as "black jazz" or "white jazz."[71]

Consequently, for a Japanese being a jazz musician necessarily implies a problem of ethnic identity: if true jazz is the jazz played by African Americans, and jazz played by whites is already only imitative or derivative, what could Japanese jazz be, since it is neither "black" nor American? Some artists solve the problem by choosing a single artist and trying to imitate his style down to the finest details—for example, Nanri Fumio as the "Japanese Satchmo" or Miyazawa Akira as the "Sonny Rollins of Japan"—while others opt instead to relocate the question of ethnic authenticity by creating a national style, a "yellow jazz" that would express their own rebellion against white culture. Murakami apparently sides with the dominant American culture rather than opposing it. He considers "true jazz" to be the American version, and, like the "average Japanese fan" described by Atkins, divides it into "black jazz" and "white jazz." However, as an expression of his "individuality," he indicates as his favorite the jazz played by whites, less known and less popular. This, too, is a way to define himself as a subject in relation to Western culture.

Another interesting way Western culture references are used to make sense of the world is through metaphor. In some cases these are simply literal similitudes, like in "Takushī ni notta kyūketsuki" ("Vampire Riding a Taxi," from *Kangarū biyori*), where a sentence uttered by the vampire seems to be "a song by Donovan"; in "Kanojo no machi, kanojo no men'yō" ("Her Village, Her Sheep," from the same collection), where the documentary is "in the style of the Nouvelle Vague"; or in "Zō no shōmetsu" ("The Elephant Vanishes"), where the disappearance of the city elephant is "a story that Sherlock Holmes would have liked." In other stories, they are more complex metaphors. For instance, in "Chīzu kēki no yō na katachi o shita boku no binbō" ("My Poverty in the Shape of a Cheese Cake," from *Kangarū biyori*) the protagonist and his wife live near a railway, and when a train passes the noise is so loud that they cannot hear each other, "as in a movie by Jean-Luc Godard"; in "Supagetī no toshi ni" ("In the Year of Spaghetti," *Kangarū biyori*), while the narrator talks on the phone, the whole room turns into columns of ice, "as in a science fiction novel by J. G. Ballard." In "Ōto 1979," nausea suddenly disappears "like in Hitchcock's *The Birds*"; in "Pan'ya saishūgeki," the protagonist and his wife wake up in the middle of the night haunted by a hunger "like the tornado in *The Wizard of Oz*"; in "Futago to shizunda tairiku" ("The Twins and the Submerged Continent," from *Pan'ya saishūgeki*), the woman working next door disappears leaving only her smile, "like the Cheshire cat."

Metaphors in Murakami are often a means to interpret reality, and significantly, they are based on Western culture. A good example is the story "Rōma teikoku no hōkai, 1881-nen no Indian hōki, Hittorā no Pōrando shūnyū, soshite kyōfū no sekai" ("The Fall of the Roman Empire, the Indian Revolt of 1881, Hitler's Invasion of Poland, and the World of Strong Wind," from the collection *Pan'ya saishūgeki*). It describes one Sunday on which the narrator writes in his diary all the events of the previous week, based on the notes that he took each day. Somehow anticipating *Afutādāku*, where each chapter is introduced by the image of a clock indicating the exact time in the night during which the whole novel takes place, time in this story is very accurately delineated. In the first paragraph, the narrator says that the wind started on Sunday afternoon at 2:07, while he was writing his diary. The sudden change of weather surprises him, since in the morning the day looked calm, "like the fall of the Roman Empire." He then resumes writing the diary. On Thursday, he writes, he slept with his girlfriend. On Friday, he met a friend in a bookshop in Ginza. At 2:37, the telephone rings. He answers, but due to the strong wind he cannot hear anything, only a huge roar, like the Indian revolt of 1881, that the narrator imagines like a film with Candice Bergen.

He goes back to the diary: on Saturday, Hitler invaded Poland. Warsaw was bombed . . . but then he realizes that this happened in 1939, not this Saturday, which was when he saw it in a movie with Meryl Streep, *Sophie's Choice*. According to *boku*, in the film Meryl Streep divorces Dustin Hoffman, but then on the commuter rail she meets a civil engineer, who is Robert de Niro, and remarries. The movie he describes is a combination of *Kramer vs. Kramer* and *Falling in Love*, another example of references dropped for the readers to feel gratified when they recognize them. When he finishes writing the diary, he listens to a cello concert by Shostakovich and to an album by Sly and the Family Stone. Then his girlfriend joins him to cook *kakinabe* (oyster hotpot, one of the few Japanese dishes cooked in the short stories), and while she cuts vegetables *boku* takes notes for today's entry in next week's diary, and writes: the fall of the Roman Empire, the Indian revolt of 1881, Hitler's invasion of Poland. With these notes, he says, he is sure that next Sunday he will remember today's events.

This way of writing is radically different from the diary as mere record of facts in "Ōto 1979": here the narrator selects the relevant events of the day based on the metaphors through which he interpreted them, underlining the arbitrariness of "referential data." The effect is amplified by the story's metatextuality: the text that he will write, the page of the diary for this Sunday, is the text we have just read—which, significantly, is divided by subtitles that coincide with these three elements.

Metaphors define the title and the structure of the story, even though they are apparently external and purely decorative elements. The narrator organizes reality through metaphors (the ones in the title), and through films (*Sophie's Choice* and its two hidden intertexts, *Falling in Love* and *Kramer vs. Kramer*, and the Western with Candice Bergen). Both belong to the sphere of Western culture, and are related to important historical events of the West (the fall of the Roman Empire, the invasion of Poland), which are, however, emptied of their meaning, and transformed into mere signs. These fragments of Western culture allow the narrator to give a structure to reality, to make sense of the world.

For the protagonists of Murakami's stories, Western literature is therefore both an instrument to distance Japanese culture in order to acquire individual identity, for Japanese to "be themselves," and a way to give meaning to the outside world. In this sense, Murakami neither simply surrenders to the influence of Western culture, nor does he contest it or represent it as corrupting and dangerous. Rather, he actively uses it as a basis to make sense of reality, in the form of multiple and manifold stories. This use of Western culture is instrumental in his particular kind of commitment, very different from that of *kindaishugi* authors such as Ōe, based on the idea that the writer's task is to create meaning, but to do it through play, and in the form of stories, showing the textual, constructed, and multilayered nature of reality.

FIVE

In Other Worlds

"Nemuri": Literature as Another World

The short story "Nemuri," from the collection *TV pīpuru*—translated by Jay Rubin as "Sleep," in the collection *The Elephant Vanishes*—provides a good example of the dynamics of the formation of individual identity and the attribution of meaning to reality through the use of foreign culture/literature that have been discussed in the previous section. Literature in this text constitutes an "other world" that allows the narrator to distance the reality in which she lives, and acquire greater awareness of herself as an individual.

Literature is crucial to "Nemuri" in a number of ways: the story parodies a Western genre, it revolves around a reflection on the act of reading, and it uses a number of strategies of involvement and estrangement of the reader. In this sense, it summarizes the main intertextual and metatextual strategies present in the works of Murakami. Moreover, it deals with another central theme in this author's fiction—the relationship with other worlds in a more literal sense, realities ontologically different from the one in which we live—and it examines the dangers inherent in the attempt to attain individuality through identification with an "other world."

"Nemuri" is the story, told in the first person by one of the few female narrators in Murakami's texts (*watashi*, as opposed to the usual *boku*), of a strange insomnia experienced by a 30-year-old middle-class Japanese housewife. *Watashi* does not sleep for seventeen days in a row, but far from being upset by this, she feels more energetic every day. Thanks to her insomnia, she rediscovers the pleasures of life, and spends all her nights (and, after a while, her days as well) reading, drinking, eating sweets, and reflecting on her new condition. She continues in a state of increasing exaltation, until one night she drives to the port of Yokohama, and, while sitting in her car listening to music, she realizes that a group of men have surrounded her car and are trying to overturn it. The story ends here. The whole final scene is narrated in the present tense, which problematizes the conditions of enunciation of the text. What is the story that is being told? Is it safe to assume that the text, which begins in the present tense with the words "this is my seventeenth straight day without sleep," is a retrospective narration told by *watashi* while she is sitting in her car, being rocked by strangers? And, if that is not the case, when and how was it written? This doubt contributes to the estrangement of the reader from the text, an effect that is amplified by other literary strategies.

As previous chapters have shown, other texts by Murakami rely on (and partly subvert) the conventions of Western genres such as the detective story and the fairy tale. "Nemuri," on the other hand, is one of the few stories by Murakami with a female narrator, and, furthermore, one of the few that represents a *woman* gaining awareness of her individuality and constructing herself as a subject. As such, the story reads as a parody of Western feminist liberation narratives, such as Kate Chopin's *The Awakening* and Charlotte Perkins Gilman's "The Yellow Wallpaper." However, as is the case with Murakami's parodies of hard-boiled novels, horror movies, or fairy tales, "Nemuri" also refers to the conventions of a genre rather than to a specific text. Unlike Western postmodernist and postcolonial authors, who often rely on direct quotations, Murakami appropriates the stylistic elements of a genre; his parodies are less direct and less explicit, and refer to generic cultural capital rather than to specific works. This is related to his choice to use easily understandable references aimed at a wide public rather than erudite quotations directed to an elite. However, this use is also reminiscent of the interiorized literary imaginary that T. S. Eliot considers typical of modern writers, who live in a world made of literature and cannot write without referring to a number of intertexts. In this sense, Murakami's parody of genres is closer to the modernist use of past literature as interiorized cultural capital than to the postmodernist reappropriation and subversion of the classics of the Western canon.

At the same time, Murakami's references to Western genres from a cultural and geographical distance, within the context of the complex relationship between Japan and the West, is emblematic of what might be termed his "paramodernism." This element emerges clearly in "Nemuri," where the protagonist's "awakening" revolves around the act of reading foreign literature. Whereas for the characters in Chopin and Gilman's works the awakening coincides with becoming aware of their true selves, of something that is already inside them, that belongs to them, the protagonist of "Nemuri" constitutes herself as a subject through foreign literature. Between the protagonists in Chopin and Gilman and *watashi* there is the same difference as there is between Eliot and Murakami: while the former rediscover a legacy that is already theirs, the latter recognize that that with which they identify in order to become individual subjects is inevitably the Other.

Reading "Nemuri" against its implicit Western intertexts, looking at some of the common elements and, more importantly, at the differences between the texts, will highlight some key features both of this story and of Murakami's work in general. In particular, the story exhibits striking similarities to Chopin's *The Awakening*. Both stories revolve around the "spiritual awakening" of a young woman—the two protagonists are almost the same age, with Edna Pontellier being 28 years old and the protagonist of "Nemuri" aged 30—and have reached the same stage in life. Each has a six-year-old son and an apparently perfect husband, a successful man and a caring companion, yet both characters are fundamentally unhappy and frustrated, and the text tells the story of them "opening their eyes" to this state of affairs. For Edna as well as for *watashi,* such an awakening coincides with insomnia: the two crucial moments in Edna's refusal to comply with social conventions occur during two sleepless nights, while *watashi* does not sleep for seventeen days in a row. Both Edna and *watashi* describe their awakening as an expansion of their selves. *Watashi* realizes that by giving up sleep she has created a new space for herself, extending her waking life, and compares her state to an evolutionary leap, arguing that her insomnia is an "expansion of consciousness." Edna, too, lives her metaphorical awakening as an extension of the self: "Every step which she took toward relieving herself from obligations added to her strength and *expansion as an individual.*"[1] Furthermore, neither Edna nor *watashi* identify with the maternal role that society has imposed on them: the narrator of *The Awakening* states that Edna "was not a mother-woman,"[2] while *watashi,* looking at her sleeping child, feels that he is a total stranger to her, and is surprised at her "not very motherly thoughts" (*hahaoya rashikunai kangae*).[3]

Finally, the two texts present swimming and water as central elements in the story, as factors of regeneration and ultimately of death. A central moment in Edna's awakening is the night on which she learns to swim. Driven by her enthusiasm, she swims so far from shore that she becomes afraid that she will not be able to make it back—a scene that prefigures her eventual suicide by drowning. The act of swimming and the relationship with the sea are crucial parts of her spiritual transformation. For *watashi,* going to the local swimming pool for half an hour was part of the routine in her "life before insomnia," but when she stops sleeping, she starts swimming every day for more than an hour, fast and with total concentration, to release her unnatural excess of energies. In order to calm down when she becomes overexcited during her sleepless nights, *watashi* often drives to the Yokohama port and sits in her car looking at the ocean. *The Awakening* closes on the image of Edna swimming toward the open sea; "Nemuri" ends at the port, with the sinister scene of *watashi*'s car being rocked by strangers.

The similarity of the two final scenes foregrounds the first significant difference between the texts: whereas Edna's suicide is an extreme affirmation of her individual will, *watashi* is defeated by the conventions of the world that she had tried to oppose. There are other important differences in the way the stories treat the themes of awakening and liberation. One key distinction is that while the texts share the association between actual sleep and spiritual slumber, and between wakefulness and mental awakening, what in *The Awakening* are metaphorical correlations between the protagonist's newly acquired self-awareness and the idea of opening one's eyes or waking up from a dream, in Murakami such correlations are literalized in an insomnia as "real" on the diegetic level as it is anomalous and absurd from a biological point of view.

Edna, in a more traditional and realistic fashion, rebels against the conventions that have dominated her life by comparing them to a long sleep: "The years that have gone seem like dreams—if one might go on sleeping and dreaming—but to wake up and find—oh! Well! Perhaps it is better to wake up after all, even to suffer, rather than to remain a dupe to illusion all one's life."[4] In "Nemuri," the relation between metaphor and referent is inverted, and the protagonist is able to stop living as though she were asleep by literally giving up sleep, actively appropriating insomnia and making it into an instrument for attaining independence.

> I'm through with sleep! So what if I go mad? So what if I lose my "ground of being"? I will not be consumed by my "drives." If sleep is nothing more than a periodic repairing of the parts of me that are being worn away, I don't want it anymore. I don't need it anymore. My flesh may have to be consumed, but my mind belongs to me. I'm keeping it for myself. I will not hand it over to anyone. I don't want to be "repaired." I will not sleep. ("Sleep," 99; "Nemuri," 192)

Whereas Chopin's text approaches social commitment through a realistic mode of narration, "Nemuri" does it by surreal and metafictional means.

Literalized metaphors are another fundamental metatextual technique through which Murakami's texts represent reality as linguistically constructed. One of the best examples is the story "Binbō na obasan no hanashi" ("A Poor Aunt's Story," from the collection *Chūgokuyuki no surōbōto*), in which the protagonist, after having thought about the expression "a poor aunt" for a long time, wakes up one morning and finds that he has a poor aunt attached to his back. This sort of ghost is real enough for others to see it, although each character perceives it as something different: for one character, it is her primary school teacher; for another, it is his dog that died of cancer; and for another, his own mother.

At the end of the story, *boku* is invited to a talk show, where he explains to the public that the ghost he has on his back, like the America of "cooking with Crisco," is only a word, a sign: "What I have stuck to my back, really, is the phrase 'poor aunt' [*binbō na obasan*]—those words, without meaning, without form. If I had to give it a label, I'd call it a conceptual sign or something like that." Thus "Binbō na obasan no hanashi" narrates how a linguistic sign can take on material reality. Whereas this story is an emblematic example of the passage from epistemology to ontology on a strictly linguistic level, the literalization of the metaphor of awakening in "Nemuri" transposes the same mechanism on the level of literature and metatextuality.

The literalization of metaphors is a typical instrument of the mechanism of narrativization of the world, common to psychoanalysis and literature (as discussed in Chapter 3). Peter Brooks notes that psychoanalytical theory describes neurotic symptoms as metaphors taken literally, in a way analogous to the process of semioticization of the body central to the epistemophilia of modern Western literature. As an example, he quotes the case of one of Freud's patients, for whom the impression of having been "morally slapped in the face" results in a psychosomatic neuralgia that causes her acute pain on one cheek, as though she had really been slapped. In neurosis, according to Freud, language takes possession of the body, making it the site of the inscription of its own signs. In a similar fashion, *watashi*'s need to "wake up" results in a pathological insomnia; once again, language does not simply represent reality but produces it, and identity and reality are constructed through language and narrative.

Literalized metaphors are also a feature of the fantastic genre. According to Tzvetan Todorov, the supernatural in literature often comes from a figurative sense taken literally. Metamorphosis is a typical example: a man "strong as a lion" is transformed into a real lion.[5] The literalization of the metaphor of spiritual sleep is the first of several traits that "Nemuri" shares with the fantastic genre.

Another major difference between "Nemuri" and its Western counterparts is that although *watashi*'s insomnia and her new life are from the beginning deeply related to the act of reading, she is no Madame Bovary: she does not try to make her life resemble a novel. In her first sleepless nights, she reads *Anna Karenina* three times, but she does not identify with the novel's protagonist, nor does she try to imitate her. Literature to her is only a means to distance herself from the role of wife-mother imposed on her by society, and her "awakening" is a moment of absolute loneliness, of total alienation from human society. As she begins to feel that her husband and son are complete strangers to her, she does not try to substitute them with other human objects of affection: it is literature, swimming, chocolate, and solitary night drives that fill her new life.

This dehumanization of the contents of life—apparently lived with utter naturalness—and its literary representation, is, incidentally, one of the moments in which the text comes closest to the dynamics of postmodernism as an expression of the "civilization of goods and objects." For the narrator, chocolate takes the place of *Anna Karenina*'s Count Vronskii, a swimming pool replaces passion, books—material objects, cultural consumer goods as well as representations—replace "life."

On the first night of her insomnia, *watashi* decides to read *Anna Karenina*, simply in order to try to get to sleep, but while reading she suddenly realizes that she has become used to a life without books. She then remembers how she had always been an avid reader since her childhood, how she used to spend all her weekly allowance on books, how she decided to study literature at college, where her graduation thesis on Katherine Mansfield was so well received that all her professors recommended that she go on to graduate school. However, after marrying, she completely abandoned literature. On that first sleepless night, still identifying with her role as a wife and mother, *watashi* tells herself that she should not be up all night: "Now I am a wife. A mother. I have responsibilities. I have to make my husband's lunches and take care of my son." In the end, however, she simply cannot put the novel down, because she is completely drawn into the story, transported into its other world: "I was there with Vronsky when he spurred his horse over the obstacles. I heard the crowd cheering him on. And I was there in the stands watching his horse go down" ("Sleep," 89; "Nemuri," 173).

As is clear from this passage, this is already a moment of separation and multiplication of levels. The narrator identifies with Vronskii, but also with the spectators who watch him fall; she looks at the scene from multiple points of view and relates to the novel through a double process of identification and estrangement. Reading allows her to recognize the nature of the world as like a "Chinese box," and she finds in *Anna Karenina* precisely this multilayered structure:

> I read *Anna Karenina* three times. Each time, I made new discoveries. This enormous novel was full of revelations and riddles. Like a Chinese box, the world of the novel contained smaller worlds, and inside those were yet smaller worlds. Together, these worlds made up a single universe, and the universe waited there in the book to be discovered by the reader. ("Sleep," 100; "Nemuri," 194)

The book, which she had read when she was young, is also the material object that reconnects her to her past, to her self before marriage, to what she was and has inadvertently ceased to be.

While reading, she finds a flake of chocolate between the pages of *Anna Karenina*, and she remembers how she used to read munching on sweets, something she has completely given up now because her dentist husband does not want her to eat them. Suddenly she feels an uncontrollable desire to eat chocolate, and she immediately goes to a supermarket and buys "two of the sweetest-looking milk chocolate bars they had." This is how her new life begins: her existence before insomnia had been made up of days so identical that she kept confusing them, sometimes losing her sense of reality, but now thanks to reading she is able to enjoy life once again and give meaning to her existence, to become an individual, as opposed to simply a "mother and wife." At the same time, in typically late-capitalist fashion, she expresses her individuality by buying the things she wants, according to the logic of advertising: be yourself, drink Coca-Cola. Significantly, the new objects of her desire are all products "in *katakana*": chocolate (*chokorēto*), wine (*wain*), brandy (*burandī*).

This attempt to attain individual identity through Western literature is reminiscent of the mechanisms to which Karatani Kōjin traces the formation of modern Japanese subjectivity in the Meiji era. According to Karatani, the modernization of Japan coincides both with the adoption of a phonocentric vision of language and with the birth of an idea of literature (*bungaku*) as "realism," either as authentic expression of the self, for the romantic school (*romanha*), or as objective representation of reality, for the Naturalist movement (*shizenshugi*). Karatani sees these two phenomena as part of the same process of introduction into Japan of the dualism of subject/object, through what he calls the "discovery of landscape" (*fūkei no hakken*), which leads to the emergence of a "subject" in the Western sense of the word, an individual separated from other individuals and from the surrounding "landscape."

The constitution of a modern Japanese subject—which at the beginning of the twentieth century entailed a real obsession with the idea of "being oneself," being a free individual subject and which was to be recuperated by the ideology of *kindaishugi* in the postwar years—coincided in most cases with an imitation of the West. To be oneself meant to conform to a model, to subject oneself to it; the idea put forth by Althusser and Foucault that we can become subjects only through subjection, through identification with the cultural models that are imposed on us, seems to have been particularly true in Meiji Japan. However, those models came from the outside, from the West, and this created the conditions for more complex processes of simultaneous distancing and identification.

Tomi Suzuki analyzes the question of the formation of a modern Japanese subject from a more clearly political perspective. She notes that the idea of the subject was born in Meiji Japan within the Freedom and Popular Rights Movement (*jiyū minken undō*), but it was soon appropriated by the establishment and transformed into a more "repressive" version, into an idea of the citizen as "subject to the Emperor." The concept of the individual subject in a moral sense was then relegated to literature, where it was allowed to survive in a less threatening, more contained version. Suzuki observes that the Constitution of 1889

> . . . legally defined all individuals as "equal subject" (*subjectus*) of the Emperor, whose mythical, "sacred" power was legalized and used to unify the nation-state. The notion of the individual self as an independent ethical and moral subject (*subjectum*), a notion that played a key role in the transformation of the larger literary and cultural discourse, emerged in the late 1880s–early 1890s in reaction to this newly defined, limited political subject.[6]

Within this process, Western literature came to play a crucial role. Advocates of modernization/Westernization such as Fukuzawa Yukichi and Nakamura Keiu invited Japanese people to read and study the masterpieces of European literature in order to understand what it meant to be an individual, to be oneself. According to Suzuki, Meiji Japan's "ambitious young intellectuals . . . pursued the enigmatic 'self' by interacting with Western literature," and "the new paradigms of reality based on an enigmatic self took shape through the assimilation and naturalization of literary representation in Western literature."[7] A clear example of this "self-discovery" through Western literature is Shimazaki Tōson's reading of Rousseau. Suzuki quotes a passage from Shimazaki's diary of 1909:

In those days I was suffering from various difficulties, and I was depressed, when I encountered Rousseau. As I became involved in the book, I felt as if it brought out a self [*jibun*] that I had not been hitherto aware of . . . I felt that through this book I was beginning to understand, though vaguely, modern man's way of thinking and how to view nature directly.[8]

In a similar manner, Murakami's protagonists also find themselves and construct their individual identity through contact with Western culture. But they do not do it simply by identifying with given models and trying to reproduce them. *Watashi*, as we have seen, does not try to imitate the characters in the novels that she reads; rather, it is the act of reading in itself that becomes for her a way to enter another world, to find a space outside the rules of society. Literature for her is a means to escape from a life with which she did not even realize she was dissatisfied, since she so completely identified with the role that was imposed on her.

However, this operation is not devoid of risk. As the participants in the 1942 debate on "Overcoming the Modern" noted, to appropriate the instruments of the West inevitably implies submission to its values. For *watashi*, as for many of Murakami's characters, literature is not only a means to pursue individuality, but also a shelter, a way to escape the constraints of society, and "Nemuri" explores the dangers implicit in trying to be oneself by escaping into another world. For the narrator, reading becomes a way to shut out the world, encouraged by the kind of "individual consumption" typical of the modern novel. *Watashi*'s renewed love for reading coincides with a refusal of social interaction: she avoids her husband and son, stops seeing friends, and whenever she goes out she only wants to go back home as soon as possible to resume her reading.

On the first day of her insomnia, when her husband comes home for lunch and happily announces that he can stay home a little longer because his first patient of the afternoon has canceled his appointment, *watashi* does not even understand that at which he is hinting:

"My first afternoon patient has cancelled. I don't have to be back in the office until one-thirty." He smiled.

I couldn't figure out why this was supposed to be such a nice surprise. I wonder why I couldn't.

It was only after my husband stood up and drew me toward the bedroom that I realized what he had in mind. I wasn't in the mood for it at all. I didn't understand why I should have sex then. All I wanted was to get back to my book. I wanted to stretch out alone on the sofa and munch on chocolate while I turned the pages of *Anna Karenina*. All the time I had been washing the dishes, my only thoughts had been of Vronsky. ("Sleep," 92; "Nemuri," 189–90)

She then feigns a headache and leaves the husband listening to music until he has to go back to work. As the story progresses, not only does she refuse sex with her husband, but shuns any kind of contact with people:

If I met someone I knew, I hardly said a word—just the basic civilities. I refused all invitations. "Sorry," I'd say. "I'm going straight home today. There's something I have to do." I didn't want to get involved with anybody. I didn't want to have to waste time on endless gossiping. When I was through swimming as hard as I could, all I wanted was to hurry home and read. ("Sleep," 95; "Nemuri," 195)

If at first *watashi* feels that others do not understand her, now she actively chooses to isolate herself. Therefore when, after a while, she grows concerned about her unnatural insomnia, she does not seek people's help, but turns to books instead, going to the library and looking for texts on sleeping problems.[9] She is disappointed by most of the works on the subject, but, again, she finds a partially satisfying solution in an essay that maintains that sleep is a way to "repair" ourselves from our daily habits, which would consume us if we did not regenerate ourselves every night by sleeping. *Watashi* decides that she does not want to live like that, consumed every day by her "natural tendencies"—which, in her case, she realizes, mean mainly housekeeping—and "repairing" herself at night. She resolves to rebel against the rules of this world and stop sleeping altogether.

However, precisely when she convinces herself that she understands perfectly what is happening, *watashi* in fact loses control over reality, and ends up being overcome by it. The text is strongly based on the opposition between understanding and not understanding. In the first part of the story, the narrator constantly insists on the fact that she knows/understands (*watashi ni wa wakaru*) while others do not (*karera ni wa nani mo shiranai*). She decides not to tell anyone about her insomnia because she *knows* that they would not understand, and therefore, they know nothing about it:

Neither my husband nor my son has noticed that I'm not sleeping. And I haven't mentioned it to them. They would certainly tell me to see a doctor. But *I know*. It wouldn't do any good to go to a hospital. Therefore, I don't say anything. It's like when I suffered from insomnia before. *I just know*. This is something I have to deal with by myself. So *they don't know* anything about it. ("Nemuri," 150)[10]

She insists on the concept throughout the text: the others, her family, her friends, doctors do not and cannot understand her, and she *knows* that they would not; she is the only one who knows.

On the other hand, *her* lack of understanding of some things becomes a mark of her rejection of conventions: she refuses to understand as long as understanding means accepting, complying, and submitting. When *watashi* declares that she does not understand what her husband means when he tells her that the first patient of the afternoon has canceled his visit, she is refusing to accept his vision of things, refusing to be happy about the things with which others expect her to be satisfied.

Her relationship to the book she is reading, too, centers on the superior understanding attained by the "new self" that insomnia has given her:

The old me had been able to understand only the tiniest fragment of it, but the gaze of this new me could penetrate to the core with perfect understanding. I knew exactly what the great Tolstoy wanted to say, what he wanted the reader to get from his book; I could see how his message had organically crystallized as a novel, and what in that novel had surpassed the author himself.

After reading "Anna Karenina" as many times as I could, I read Dostoevsky. I could read book after book with utter concentration and never tire. I could understand the most difficult passages without effort. And I responded with deep emotion. I felt that I had always been meant to be like this. By abandoning sleep I had expanded myself. The power to concentrate was the most important thing. Living without this power would be like opening one's eyes without seeing anything. ("Sleep," 100–101)

Insomnia and reading give her a clearer vision of reality, a superior understanding, whereas the people around her, who sleep normally and do not read, are able to understand neither her nor reality. She is the only one who knows—or so she tells herself. In the last part of the story, the number of references to knowing and understanding increases dramatically. At the height of her insomniac euphoria, *watashi* is more self-assured than ever: she knows, she understands, she is the only one who understands. "This is how people change, I think. But *nobody knows it*. Nobody notices. *Only I know*. Even if I explained it to them, *they wouldn't understand*. They wouldn't believe me. Or if they did believe me, *they would not understand* correctly what I'm feeling" ("Nemuri," 208).[11] However, it is precisely at this point that *watashi* begins to lose control over reality. She suddenly awakens from her reverie, finds herself in her car surrounded by strangers trying to turn it over, and is completely unable to deal with the situation:

> There's something wrong. Just calm down and think, then everything will be O.K. Think. Just think. Slowly. Carefully. Something is wrong.
>
> Something is wrong.
>
> But what? *I don't know*. ("Nemuri," 209)[12]

In the end, reason betrays *watashi*, and the superior understanding she believed that she had attained through her awakening reveals itself to be illusory. At the height of her self-rediscovery, *watashi* ends up clashing against the "external world" that she had refused, and that has left her at the mercy of the inexplicable will of others. With its enigmatic and disphoric ending, the story highlights the dangers involved in the attempt to escape reality in order to become "individual subjects." Although it is necessary to distance one's own culture in order to attain individuality, reason reveals itself to be inadequate to this purpose, since it leads to a unitary vision of reality that prevents one from perceiving the existence of other worlds "one level outside, or one level inside" the one in which we live.

Confession and Deception

The opposition between "understanding" and "not understanding" is crucial also in this text's construction of its implied reader. On the one hand, the narrator's insistence on the fact that others do not understand her establishes a strong relationship with the reader, who is called upon to comprehend and support the lonely protagonist. On the other hand, her constant emphasis on the fact that nobody notices what is happening to her induces the reader to doubt her account and undermines her narrative reliability. The text thus problematizes its own conditions of enunciation, not only rendering the time of narration ambiguous and therefore breaking the illusion of reality, but also making the narrator unreliable. These mechanisms of involvement and distancing of the reader are crucial in shaping the text's vision of the construction of identity.

While repeatedly stating that nobody understands her, and that she purposefully avoids telling anyone about her new state because she knows they would not believe her, the narrator opens her heart to the page, to the reader, and in doing so she constantly underlines her sincerity. As was the case with *Kaiten mokuba,* here, too, the expression *shōjiki itte,* "honestly, sincerely speaking," is particularly frequent. This insistence on sincerity toward the page can be compared to the confessional mode that many critics consider a typical feature of the modern Japanese novel, even beyond the specific genre of the so-called I-novel (*watakushi shōsetsu*). Both Karatani Kōjin and Tomi Suzuki argue that this kind of literary confession was one of the main instruments in the formation of a modern Japanese subject through Western literature.

According to Karatani, the modern individual subject in Japan was created not only through the reading of Western literature, but also through writing, in the confessional form that Western realism came to assume in Japan. Literature and modern individual identity are inextricably related in this process, and, in Karatani's opinion, modern Japanese literature came into existence together with the confessional literary form. Such literary confession, however, should not be confused with a real act of confession, for in this case "it is the form itself that produces the 'inner life' that is confessed." These literary confessions therefore underline the mediated and textual nature of identity. In Karatani's words, "It was the literary form of the confession—confession as system—that produced the interiority that confessed, the 'true self.'"[13]

Tomi Suzuki further emphasizes the role of Western literature in this process, arguing that the *watakushi shōsetsu*, which was later to be canonized as the Japanese narrative genre *par excellence*, was always formulated along a binary axis that contrasted it with the West, in the attempt to affirm a Japanese identity different from the Western one, but that existed only in relation to the Other from which it differentiated itself.

Murakami's texts often expose similar mechanisms of identity construction through interactions with Western culture. As we have seen in the analysis of the collection *Kaiten mokuba no deddo hīto*, Murakami parodies the confessional mode in order to both highlight the fictionality of the texts and reflect on the role of the writer as a "maker of meaning." In "Nemuri," this strategy acquires a different function, and the construction of identity involves not only the narrator but also the narratee. A crucial factor in this process is the unreliability of the narrator. Although the narrator initially invites the reader's sympathy by declaring that others do not understand her, her insistence on the fact that nobody notices what is happening to her and her increasingly exaggerated self-confidence ultimately undermine her credibility.

The first time that she suffered from insomnia, when she was in college, *watashi* did not sleep for over a month; she lost six kilograms and lived the whole time as though asleep, unable to concentrate, breaking objects, bumping into things. According to her account, she gave clear signs of being unwell, but nobody noticed anything. Her second bout of insomnia is ignored by her family, too; *watashi* spends all her nights awake and even leaves the house in the middle of the night to go for solitary drives, but neither her husband nor her son notice any change in her. Adding to this the protagonist's increasing euphoria, her conviction that her insomnia is "an evolutionary leap," her repeated declarations that she is perfectly well, that she does not feel any need to rest, that she is, in fact, every day more full of energy even though she never sleeps, the reader is prompted to wonder whether her entire account should be interpreted as the expression of her progressive insanity.[14]

Whether the reader chooses to believe her or not, such doubt creates an ironic distance from the text. The narrator's unreliability increases the reader's interpretive responsibility, and leads the reader to construct his or her own version of the story, to devise a new explanation—she is mad, she is lying, she is a fictional character and this is a story, and so forth. Whereas *watashi*, having distanced the role imposed upon her by society, ultimately becomes a victim of the new world in which she has shut herself off, losing her sense of reality, the reader at first identifies with the text, but then is estranged from it, acquiring the lucidity that is denied to the narrator.

Furthermore, this estrangement of the reader from the text foregrounds the existence of an implicit omniscient author behind the autodiegetic narrator. Particularly in the case of an author such as Murakami, who often constructs a strong figure of narrator/implicit author that recurs through different texts, it is hard not to perceive an implicit author behind the unreliable narrator in "Nemuri." Through the narrator's unreliability, the text constructs a further textual level, in which the implied author, "Murakami Haruki," and the implied reader, both removed from *watashi*'s story, reserve the right to question it and interpret it. While the protagonist is confined in the world of her rational exaltation, the reader recognizes the different textual levels as many different Chinese boxes.

To Read, to Sleep, to Dream

Identity and reality in "Nemuri" are portrayed as complex, structured like Chinese boxes. The text involves the reader and encourages identification with the narrator; however, it also undermines the narrator's account, raising the suspicion that her vision of things is distorted, and that it conceals another reality, to which the reader does not have access because the whole story is filtered by her point of view. Reality is thus represented as multilayered as well as partially inaccessible.

This effect is amplified in the story by the staging of other worlds in a more literal sense. The first allusion to the idea of other realities can be found in the presence of mirrors in the text. Besides being a metaphor of textual dynamics, as is the case with many texts of metafiction, the mirrors represented in the story assume connotations tending toward the fantastic, becoming a sort of magic mirror, a surreal element entering the diegetic reality. Looking at herself in a mirror is a central component in the protagonist's self-discovery, and mirrors are another factor through which the text underlines the process of construction of individual identity.

The first time the narrator mentions a mirror is in relation to the uneasiness that she feels toward her apparently "perfect" life. When she thinks about how her existence is made of days so identical that she cannot distinguish between them, how her "footprints [are] being blown away before I ever had a chance to turn and look at them," she looks at herself in the mirror to regain a sense of reality:

> Whenever I felt like that, I would look at my face in the bathroom mirror—just look at it for fifteen minutes at a time, my mind a total blank. I'd stare at my face purely as a physical object, and gradually it would disconnect from the rest of me, becoming just some thing that happened to exist at the same time as myself. And a realization would come to me: This is happening here and now. It's got nothing to do with footprints. ("Sleep," 81; "Nemuri," 160)

In this first phase, the protagonist's sense of self comes from perceiving herself as an "other": separating mind and body and observing her face in the mirror as a thing outside herself, she is able to overcome the sense of unreality that her everyday life has caused her to have, and to regain an awareness of "being there." As in the Lacanian "mirror stage" of a child's development, for *watashi* the sense of her own identity passes through the act of seeing herself as an "other," and not through identifying with her past experience, with her traces: as she realizes, "it's got nothing to do with footprints" (*ashiato nanka kankei nai*).

The second time the narrator looks at herself in the mirror, after she has stopped sleeping, it is to admire herself, finding herself rejuvenated, beautiful, and full of life, even though she has not slept for two weeks:

> One day, after showering, I stood naked in front of the mirror. I was amazed to discover that my body appeared to be almost bursting with vitality. . . . It dawned on me that I was prettier than I had realized. I looked so much younger than before that it was almost shocking. I could probably pass for twenty-four. My skin was smooth. My eyes were bright, lips moist. The shadowed area beneath my protruding cheekbones (the one feature I really hated about myself) was no longer noticeable—at all. I sat down and looked at my face in the mirror for a good thirty minutes. I studied it from all angles, objectively. No, I had not been mistaken: I was really pretty. ("Sleep," 97; "Nemuri," 187–88)

The text is already undermining the narrator's reliability: the more she claims to have an objective view (*kyakkanteki ni nagamete mita*), the more her miraculous rejuvenation sounds suspicious. However, the story, which is based more on a postmodernist ontological doubt than on a modernist epistemological one, seems to give credence to the hypothesis that the protagonist looks in fact more beautiful and younger since she stopped sleeping, as she is every day more full of energy, swims frantically for more than an hour each day, and so forth. If in the first mirror scene it was the protagonist who separated from her self to regain a sense of reality, now it is the diegetic reality that separates from reality as we know it, becoming absurd, surreal. The mirror becomes a door onto another reality, onto other (im)possible worlds.

This aspect emerges even more clearly in the other central theme of the story: sleep. The protagonist's insomnia allows the text to reflect on the relation between reality and dream, sleep and wakefulness, mind and body.

The protagonist's first episode of insomnia, from when she was a college student, is represented as a state of separation between mind and body, and at the same time as a blurring of the boundary between sleep and wakefulness. In the description of the episode, the narrator repeats the word *ishiki*, which might be rendered in English as "consciousness" or "mind."

> The more *conscious* [*ishiki*] I was about trying to sleep, the wider awake I became. . . . My fingertips are brushing against the outermost edge of sleep. But my *mind* is wide-awake. I begin to feel sleepy. But in another room, on the other side of a transparent wall, that *mind* is awake and watching me. My physical self is drifting in the feeble morning light, but, all the while, it can feel my *mind* staring, breathing, close beside it. I am both a body on the verge of sleep and a *mind* determined to stay awake. . . . My *mind* slips away from my body. . . . The wakefulness is always there beside me. I can feel its chilling shadow. It is the shadow of myself. Weird, I think in my confusion, I'm inside my own shadow. ("Nemuri," 146–47)[15]

Her first episode of insomnia coincides with her discovery of the Chinese box-like nature of reality. Mind and body, wakefulness and sleep are represented as worlds divided by walls—worlds that are not only separate but concentric, in which *watashi* is "inside her own shadow." However, even though her first encounter with the existence of other worlds centers on the idea of "consciousness," she experiences it without adequate awareness. The mind (*ishiki*), separated from the body and unable to reach the world of sleep, is paralyzed and unable to react, and becomes a passive victim of the situation.

Her second instance of insomnia, on the contrary, is characterized by an extreme lucidity, a constant self-awareness, a thriving of the body, and a new perception of the "other worlds" of dream and death. Everything begins with a nightmare; *watashi* wakes up and tries to calm down, convince herself that "it was only a dream" (*yume dattanda, to watashi wa omotta*), and return to reality. While she is recovering from her fright, she sees someone standing beside her bed: it is a man dressed in black, who is pouring water on her feet. This, however, does not look like a dream: "This was no longer the dream, I knew. From that, I had already awakened. . . . No, this was no dream. This was reality" ("Sleep," 83; "Nemuri," 162). The man continues to pour water on her feet, which she can clearly see, but cannot feel. Paralyzed by terror, she is unable to move. At last, she manages to scream, and although she does not produce any sound, this silent cry makes the man disappear. She then gets up, drinks some brandy to calm down, and tries to make sense of what has occurred. It doesn't seem to fit either in the category of dream or reality, and she concludes that it must have been *kanashibari*, a sort of trance in which a person wakes up feeling paralyzed—a state often considered to be caused by the presence of a ghost.[16]

Kanashibari, neither dream nor reality, but "a kind of dream that doesn't feel like a dream," throws into question the existence of a clearly defined boundary between dream and reality. During the first insomnia, the narrator felt that she was living "as though in a dream"; now, though, she faces a new phenomenon that cannot be classified either as dream or as reality. Understanding *kanashibari* requires a more complex perception of the different levels of reality, and thus induces the first step of a passage from epistemological to ontological doubt.

Watashi's "new self" is amazed at how easy it is to separate mind and body and make them work independently:

> I went through the motions—shopping, cooking, playing with my son, having sex with my husband. It was easy once I got the hang of it. All I had to do was break the connection between my mind and my body. While my body went about its business, my mind floated in its own inner space. . . . After I gave up sleeping, it occurred to me what a simple thing reality is, how easy it is to make it work. It's just reality. ("Sleep," 95–96; "Nemuri," 185–86)

If during her first insomnia the narrator lived the separation between mind and body passively, as a disconcerting state in the face of which she was powerless, now she actively appropriates it, cultivating it as a resource that allows her to be herself while simultaneously continuing to play her part. To overcome the sense of alienation from her role as wife and mother, the narrator decides to distance the reality that has been imposed on her and to live in two different worlds at the same time.

However, as we have seen, the narrator is able to perceive the existence of different realities but not to connect them, and therefore those realities ultimately escape her control; what was at first an opening becomes a form of closure. In the final part of the story, *watashi* starts thinking about the ontological boundary *par excellence*, that between life and death, and she finds herself completely baffled, unable to connect these two realities. She begins to wonder whether death, far from being an "eternal sleep," might not in fact be something akin to the state of uninterrupted wakefulness that she is experiencing, and becomes terribly frightened. She sees life and death as separate worlds that are impossible to relate to each other: nobody who is still living can know what death is really like.

> Maybe death is a kind of rest, but reasoning can't tell us that. The only way to find out what death is is to die. *Death can be anything at all.* An intense terror overwhelmed me at the thought. . . . I stared at the thick darkness that stood planted in front of me, a darkness as deep and hopeless as the universe itself. I was all alone. ("Sleep," 106; "Nemuri," 204)

And this is the point where, to calm down, she drives to the Yokohama port, and then finds herself surrounded by the people trying to turn her car over. Although the act of reading had opened a new world to her, what was an "expansion of consciousness" becomes a form of segregation. *Watashi* has not acquired a new world, she has lost one: the world of sleep. She completely identifies with her waking life, becoming pure consciousness, pure rationality. The text thus warns the reader about the danger of identifying with only one of the layers of reality, becoming "unable to see beyond one of the boxes." Recognizing the existence of different levels of reality is a first step, necessary but not sufficient in itself: one must also be able to connect these different worlds. And that which provides a connection, in Murakami's texts, is imagination.

In Dreams Begins Responsibility

In other works by Murakami, the characters are able to experience different realities without being overcome by them. When they succeed, they do so with the help of imagination, which offers a valid alternative to reason. As seen in the themes of dream and death in "Nemuri," the Chinese-box structure of reality in Murakami's texts is presented not only through the use of metanarrative strategies, but also through the presence of parallel or imaginary worlds, to which the text attributes the same degree of realness as the ordinary world. It is by traveling through imaginary worlds that the characters are able to change things in the "world on this side" (*kochiragawa* or *kocchi no sekai*).

For example, in *A Wild Sheep Chase* and *Dance Dance Dance,* the access to the "other world" is provided by the Dolphin Hotel in Sapporo, which has a hidden room that exists only at certain moments, and literally belongs to another reality. This unreal place allows *boku* to communicate with other worlds, to give meaning to his experience, and to find his true self. In *The Wind-Up Bird Chronicle,* a dried-up well in the backyard of an abandoned house represents a passage to another world, halfway between dream and reality, where *boku* tries to solve the problems that concern him in "real life" and to find his wife, who disappeared at the beginning of the novel. In *Kafka on the Shore,* a mysterious forest on the island of Shikoku constitutes the entrance to a different reality, a valley inhabited by the souls of dead people, as well as the souls of persons who, having entered that dimension once, have returned to the real world, leaving there a part of their selves.

Another significant aspect of the "other world" emerges in *Dance Dance Dance.* In this novel, the parallel realities represented—the aforementioned "ghost room" in the Dolphin Hotel and another room in a building in Honolulu, where the protagonist meets his long-lost friend Kiki in "an act akin to a dream" (*yume ni rui suru kōi*)—exist only for *boku*, but are nonetheless real. The Sheep Man, who lives in the ghost room, explains to the narrator that the Dolphin Hotel has been rebuilt in the same place and with a similar name only in order for *boku* to be able to go back to it, and the same is true of the room in Honolulu, which, Kiki explains, exists only to allow *boku* to meet her. As the dates in Murakami's texts refer to events exclusive to the personal life of the narrator, so these imaginary/unreal places are deeply related to the individual subject (*kojinteki na ningen*). Like foreign culture and literature, they constitute a means through which the characters are able to "be themselves." In another work, *Hard-Boiled Wonderland and the End of the World*, the idea of the existence of parallel realities shifts toward the realm of the unconscious, and the connection between the two worlds is provided by a space inside the brain, the creation of an alternative circuit of synapses that puts the protagonist in touch with his inner self, as well as enabling him to reach toward his "others."

Some critics interpret such use of fantasy on Murakami's part as an expression of the end of the political activism of the 1960s and the passage to the consumer society of the 1980s. Matthew Strecher, on the other hand, sees the use of the supernatural in Murakami as a critique of Japan's individualism of the 1980s and 1990s. In his opinion, Murakami's characters, through their relationships with the supernatural, are constantly trying to find their own individual identities, but all the while "such attempts are hindered by a social system that encourages people to accept an identity bestowed through participation in the consumerist economic utopia of late twentieth-century Japan, rather than by seeking something unique within themselves."[17] I contend, however, that Murakami's texts do not denounce the loss of individuality of the younger generation, but, on the contrary, explore the *construction* of such individuality in contemporary Japan, in relation to the

West and to the late capitalist consumer society "imported" from it.

In this regard, it is interesting to look at Murakami's work in light of Susan Napier's analysis of the development of the fantastic genre in Japanese literature, which she considers inseparable from Western notions of modernity, individualism, and rationalism.[18] In the Meiji era, according to Napier, a number of writers reacted to new ideas imported from the West by resorting to the genres of fantasy and science fiction. In particular, the fantastic literature of this period centers on the theme of the alien and the idea of "self as outsider" as expressions of the unease experienced by intellectuals toward the Western concept of individual subject.[19] Another major concern of the fantastic genre in this period is the idea of technology as an intrinsically Western element.[20] Although a similar attitude can be found in the fantastic literature of the 1920s and 1930s, as well as in postwar authors such as Abe Kōbō and Ōe Kenzaburō, there is a significant shift of focus in Murakami. Napier writes: "Probably due to the fact that he grew up in a culture more comfortable with ideas of the Western self, Murakami depicts his other selves in a largely positive fashion, as gateways to a deeper understanding of the self as a whole."[21] The theme of the presence of other worlds and "aliens" and their connection to individual identity is central to Murakami's fiction. In this sense, his works are reminiscent of the classic fantastic genre as defined by Tzvetan Todorov, i.e., a "hesitation between real and imaginary."[22] Within this hesitation, this liminal position across different worlds, Murakami's texts find a way out of the constraints of a rationality that "cannot see beyond one of the boxes."

Furthermore, by staging alternative worlds that have a merely literary existence, the genres of fantasy and science fiction problematize the relation between reality and fiction and highlight the constructed character of both text and reality. As Rosemary Jackson notes, the fantastic is one of the most metaliterary genres:

A reluctance, or inability, to present definitive versions of "truth" or "reality" makes of the modern fantastic a literature which draws attention to its own practice as a linguistic system. . . . the fantastic raises questions of the nature of the real and unreal, foregrounding the relation between them as its central concern. It is in this sense that Todorov refers to fantasy as the most "literary" of all literary forms, as "the quintessence of literature," for it makes explicit the problems of establishing "reality" and "meaning" through a literary text.[23]

According to Jackson, this tendency to explore the relation between fiction and reality results in an interrogation of the notion of reality itself, and of its culturally constructed nature: "Fantasy has always provided a clue to the limits of a culture, by foregrounding problems of categorizing the 'real' and of the situation of the self in relation to that dominant notion of 'reality.'"[24] It is only natural, then, that an author such as Murakami, who makes frequent use of metafictional techniques, resorts to the fantastic genre to express his vision of the relationship between reality, culture, and literature.

From this perspective, it would be fruitful to analyze the collection *Kami no kodomotachi wa mina odoru* (2000; translated into English as *after the quake*), and in particular the story "Kaeru-kun, Tōkyō o sukuu" ("Superfrog Saves Tokyo"). *Kami no kodomotachi wa mina odoru* is Murakami's eighth collection of short stories and the first to be published as a series, with a specific theme linking the six narratives. All but one of the stories had first been published in the journal *Shinchō* from August to December 1999 under the title *Jishin no ato* (After the Earthquake)—the exception being "Hachimitsu pai" ("Honey Pie"), which was published for the first time in the collection. However, the common theme is presented in a problematic way; although all of the stories revolve around the Kobe earthquake of January 1995, none of them are set in Kobe, and none of the characters are directly involved in the disaster. The presence of the earthquake is always indirect, mediated by the news or by a character's narration. Murakami thus presents a sort of unofficial history of the earthquake, deliberately avoiding a faithful and realistic reconstruction, and underlining the textual and mediated nature of even such a "real" and tragic event.

The stories differ from Murakami's previous works in many respects: they are all written in the third person; their characters have names; and their protagonists differ from one another in gender, age, and profession. (Almost without exception, Murakami's other texts feature nameless characters, and an autodiegetic narrator, the ever-present *boku* ("I"), a 26- to 32-year-old male, living in Tokyo, working in advertising, or as a writer, journalist, or translator.) In this sense, the stories in *Kami no kodomotachi* seem to have inaugurated a new tendency in Murakami's fiction, and similar characteristics can be found both in *afterdark* (2007) and in *Tōkyō kitanshū* (2005).

All the stories take place in February 1995, after the January earthquake and before the Sarin gas attack by the Aum cult on the subway of Tokyo on March 20, 1995. Murakami says he purposely chose this moment, "suspended" between the two incidents, before they were linked in the public opinion to form an idea of the general decadence of the country. In fact, the gas attack and the earthquake soon became symbols of a major crisis in both Japanese and Western images of Japan. According to Yoda Tomiko, when these two events added to the post-bubble economic stagnation of the 1990s, Japan came to be perceived as "the site of an imploding national economic system, a disintegrating social order, and the virtual absence of ethical and competent leadership."[25]

Murakami has written two nonfiction books about the subway gas attack, *Andāguraundo* (*Underground*) and *Yakusoku sareta basho de – Underground 2* (*The Place That Was Promised – Underground 2*), a series of interviews with the victims of the gas attack and with members of the Aum cult respectively. He later explained that his decision to use the third-person narration in *Kami no kodomotachi* was deeply influenced by his work on these interviews and by the experience of writing other people's stories. Furthermore, *Andāguraundo*, too, proposes an "unofficial history" of the events; since the media focused mainly on the culprits, picturing them as uncommon persons, Murakami explains that he felt the need to give a face to at least some of the unnamed 5,000 victims of the accident, as well as to some of the "common people" among the cult members.

In *Andāguraundo*, the testimonies regarding the day of the attack often contradict each other, but the author intentionally leaves them as they are, underlining the fact that each story has its own dignity as a story, and abstaining from bringing them together under a single authorial point of view, into one dominant discourse, or one "reality." The same could be said of the fictional stories about the earthquake in *Kami no kodomotachi*. These stories present a variety of experiences of "common people"; the earthquake is part of their lives, yet it plays an ambiguous and problematic role.

Some critics have argued that *Kami no kodomotachi* is a reversal of Murakami's previous shift "from detachment to commitment" (*ditacchimento kara komittomento made*); that is to say, from his "postmodern" attitude of the eighties to a new *kindai-shugi*-like political commitment, as shown in the novel *The Wind-Up Bird*, which deals with Japan's activities in Manchuria during the war, and in *Andāguraundo*, where he confronts another "serious" theme, the gas attack. For instance, Yoshida Haruo, who had highly praised Murakami's new commitment in his study *Murakami Haruki tenkai suru*, wrote in 2000 that in *Kami no kodomotachi wa mina odoru* the earthquake is "only a pretext to write the collection," added to "give a bit of flavor to the stories," and not important in itself. For Yoshida, this demonstrates that Murakami, after a brief period of social commitment following his return in Japan in 1996, is now going back to the detachment and noninvolvement of the 1980s. However, it could be argued that with this book—as with his others—Murakami, rather than going backward and forward between detachment and commitment, is giving voice to a new idea of commitment, which is deeply related to his vision of reality and its representation.

For Murakami, an author's commitment is not expressed through realism, which, as the diary in "Ōto 1979," far from being faithful to reality, in fact distorts it. On the contrary, such commitment can only be achieved through metanarrative and the fantastic, which, by virtue of their ability to represent the stratified and culturally constructed nature of identity and of reality, are the only means to give sense to the world. Many texts in this collection explore the relationship between reality and perception (in a manner close to the modernist epistemological doubt), as well as the relationship between different realities, the possible existence of alternative worlds and supernatural explanations of events (thus shifting to a postmodernist ontological doubt).

In "UFO ga Kushiro ni oriru" ("An UFO lands in Kushiro"), for example, the protagonist's wife, after watching obsessively the news about the Kobe earthquake for five days, suddenly disappears; a few days later, a colleague proposes to the protagonist (named Komura) to pay his airplane ticket to Hokkaidō if he agrees to transport a mysterious parcel to his sister in Kushiro. Komura accepts, and at the airport he is greeted by the sister and another woman. The women tell him how, a few months before, the wife of an acquaintance of theirs, Saeki-san, suddenly disappeared after seeing an UFO. Komura comments that maybe the woman has not fled, but has been abducted by extraterrestrials. In one of the final scenes, Komura asks the women what is in the parcel, and one of them tells him that it contains his own soul; at his frightened reaction, she hastens to say that she is joking, but the story does not clarify what is in the box, leaving the readers in doubt.

"Airon no aru fūkei" ("Landscape with Flatiron") centers on the relationship between dream and reality. The male protagonist, Miyake, has a recurring nightmare, in which he dies inside a refrigerator. The dream is structured like a set of Chinese boxes: Miyake dreams of being trapped in a very narrow place, about to die from suffocation; he wakes up, terrified, and reaches for the refrigerator. While he opens it, he realizes that, precisely because he is afraid of refrigerators, he does not own one. At that moment, a hand comes out of the fridge, grabs him at the throat, and tries to pull him inside—this time he finally wakes up, drenched in sweat. Miyake tells Junko, the female protagonist, that Jack London, a writer they both love, throughout his life believed that he would die by drowning. In the end, he committed suicide by drinking morphine, but in a way, Miyake says, he really drowned, in a sea of alcoholism and desperation. The fundamental idea conveyed by the text is that dreams and metaphors can become real, that they can affect external reality.

In "Kami no kodomotachi wa mina odoru" ("All God's Children Dance") the mother of the protagonist is part of a religious sect, and when he was a child she always told him that his father was "O-kata," the name the cult people give to their god. When he turns seventeen, the mother finally reveals to him the secret of his birth. When she was young, she had two abortions, and then began an affair with the doctor who had performed the abortions. Even though the man took "all the necessary precautions" she became pregnant again, and when out of desperation she tried to commit suicide, she met her spiritual guide, Tabata-san, and joined his cult. Tabata-san explained to her that the fact that she had become pregnant three times, even though she was using contraceptive methods, was a sign that the baby is the son of O-kata, since three is a divine number. He then predicted to her that the baby would be a boy, and ordered her to call him Yoshiya. The mother is convinced that the child is the son of her god; Yoshiya, however, tries to find a rational explanation, and thinks that his father is the doctor, and that there must have been some problem with the contraceptive he used. But he is not completely sure either, and this story, too, wavers between a rational explanation of the facts and a supernatural one.

The protagonist of "Tairando" ("Thailand"; also discussed in Chapter 3), Satsuki, is convinced that she has caused the earthquake with her hate for a man she has not seen in many years but who still lives in Kobe. During her trip to Thailand, Satsuki and her driver Nimit travel to a remote village, where an old Thai woman reads her palm and tells her that she has a stone inside her, covered with Japanese ideograms, which causes her constant suffering. The woman then predicts that Satsuki will dream of a snake, and she will have to make it eat the stone inside her. If she does not do it, the stone will stay inside her forever, and when she dies, and her body is cremated, only the stone will remain. Once again, the story claims that dreams affect reality, and points to the possibility of actively appropriating this mechanism, using a dream for one's own spiritual salvation. The idea of using dreams and imagination as means to change reality is even more relevant in another story in the collection, "Kaeru-kun, Tōkyō o sukuu" (translated by Jay Rubin as "Superfrog Saves Tokyo").

The Power of Imagination: "Kaeru-kun, Tōkyō o sukuu"

Among the stories in *Kami no kodomotachi wa mina odoru*, "Kaeru-kun, Tōkyō o sukuu" is probably the closest to the fantastic genre as defined by Tzvetan Todorov, i.e., as an oscillation between realism and the marvelous. The story narrates how a bank employee, Katagiri, is asked by a six foot-tall frog, Kaeru-kun, to save the city of Tokyo from a terrible earthquake that might be caused by a giant worm, Mimizu-kun, who lives underground, directly below Katagiri's firm. Katagiri agrees to help Kaeru-kun, but then he is shot in the shoulder by a stranger and passes out. He wakes up in a hospital the next morning, and finds out that there is no trace of his having been shot: he just fell unconscious in the street, for no apparent reason. During the night, however, Kaeru-kun appears in Katagiri's room and tells him that he did fight Mimizu-kun, in his dreams, through imagination. Kaeru-kun then starts swelling and melts in a myriad of bugs. Katagiri wakes up screaming in his hospital bed: the frog and the bugs are gone, and he wonders whether he has dreamt the whole thing.

In some ways, the text is very realistic compared to the rest of Murakami's production: it is narrated in the third person, giving it a tone of objectivity; the protagonist, Katagiri, has a real name, in contrast with other protagonists such as *nezumi* or simply *boku*; the story's timeline is accurately delineated, with action developing over the course of three days, from the evening of February 15th to the night of February 18th, 1995; and, most importantly, the story deals with social realities of Japan never before represented in Murakami's texts, such as the economic crisis of Japan after 1989, and the streets of Kabukichō with their population of *yakuza* and Korean gangs.

We find here a realistic depiction of some very concrete underworlds: "The Kabukichō neighborhood of Shinjuku was a labyrinth of violence: old-time gangsters, Korean mobsters, Chinese Mafia, guns and drugs, money flowing beneath the surface from one murky den to another, people vanishing every now and then like puffs of smoke."[26] The text also mentions the figure of *sōkaiya*, people paid by *yakuza* or by rival companies to attend shareholder meetings to cause trouble, who often also have close connections with the political world. Katagiri has to deal with a company that went bankrupt because of a *sōkaiya* sent by the *yakuza* and now is unable to pay back a significant amount it borrowed from Tōkyō Anzen, Katagiri's firm. The company, however, is supported both by criminal organizations and by an important politician, and Katagiri despairs of ever being able to collect the payment. Here realism and the marvelous intertwine, and it is Kaeru-kun who solves the problem, threatening the managers of the insolvent company in order to prove to Katagiri that he really exists.

Through the character of Katagiri, the text also addresses the role of common people in society and in history, performing an operation similar to that of *Underground*. When Kaeru-kun asks him to save Tokyo from the earthquake, Katagiri replies that he cannot understand how an ordinary and insignificant person like him could be of any help. But Kaeru-kun replies that only a person like him could save the city, and it is for people like him that he wants to save it.

"I'm an absolutely ordinary guy. Less than ordinary. I'm going bald, I'm getting a potbelly, I turned 40 last month. My feet are flat. The doctor told me recently that I have diabetic tendencies. It's been three months or more since I last slept with a woman—and I had to pay for it. I do get some recognition within the division for my ability to collect on loans, but no real respect. I don't have a single person who likes me, either at work or in my private life. I don't know how to talk to people, and I'm bad with strangers, so I never make friends. I have no athletic ability, I'm tone-deaf, short, phimotic, nearsighted—and astigmatic. I live a horrible life. All I do is eat, sleep and shit. I don't know why I'm even living. Why should a person like me have to be the one to save Tokyo?"

"Because, Mr. Katagiri, Tokyo can only be saved by a person like you. And it's for people like you that I am trying to save Tokyo."
("Superfrog," 93; "Kaeru-kun," 144–45)

This element is clearly meant to appeal to the reader also, who is likely to be an "ordinary person" and will be flattered to see "someone like him" in the role of the hero who saves the city from destruction. As was the case with many of Murakami's narrative techniques, this is both a form of counter-history and a commercial strategy.

However, the story is also very close to the genre of the fabulous, staging talking animals, a monster living underground who wants to destroy the city, and a protagonist who shares many of the traits of the typical hero of a fairy tale: an orphan, he took care of his younger brothers and sisters, he sacrificed his personal aspirations in order to let them live their lives, and is now neglected and despised by them. He is the classic fairy tale protagonist, the "common man," small and weak, who reveals himself a hero.

Stylistic elements typical of the fairy tale, such as formulaic structures and repetitions of identical sentences, are prevalent in the text. For example, in the conversations between Katagiri and Frog, Katagiri always begins by calling his interlocutor "Kaeru-san," and Frog corrects him, with an identical formula:

"Tell me, Mr. Frog," Katagiri said.
"Please," Frog said, raising one finger again. "Call me 'Frog'."
"Tell me, Frog. . . ."[27]

The story is thus narrated in a mode halfway between realism and the marvelous. What is more important, the hesitation between a realistic/rational explanation of the events and a fantastic/supernatural one is constantly foregrounded. In the first pages, Katagiri is dumbfounded by the appearance of Frog, and he tries to find a logical explanation; he thinks this might be a joke, looks for a hidden camera, and tries to rationalize what he sees.

Frog, in another example of metatextual irony, attempts to convince Katagiri that he is neither a metaphor nor a quotation but a real frog:

> "Yes, of course, as you can see. A real frog is exactly what I am. A product neither of metaphor nor allusion nor deconstruction nor sampling nor any other such complex process, I am a genuine frog. Shall I croak for you?"
>
> Frog tilted back his head and flexed the muscles of his huge throat. Ribit, Ri-i-i-bit, Ribit ribit ribit Ribit Ribit Ri-i-i bit. His gigantic croaks rattled the pictures hanging on the walls.
>
> ("Superfrog," 85; "Kaeru-kun," 132)

In the first part of the story, the relationship between marvelous and real centers on an epistemological doubt: Katagiri faces an inexplicable event and cannot believe what he sees. The text revolves around the concepts of reality and perception: there are numerous references to the act of seeing or not seeing well, things often "look unreal" and the protagonist "can't believe his eyes."

For instance, after Frog has proved to Katagiri his authenticity by threatening some insolvent clients and making them pay their dues on the spot, he appears at his office, but nobody but Katagiri can see him. With an ambiguous move typical of the fantastic, the texts both affirms and negates the realness of Kaeru-kun, who is genuine enough to scare Katagiri's clients into paying him, yet cannot be seen by his colleagues.

Furthermore, as he explained in his unflattering description of himself, Katagiri has a bad eyesight, and when he is attacked on the street he loses his glasses, so that he cannot see what is happening. The whole scene of the aggression, which, as we later find out, might never have happened in the "real world," is narrated through the filter of Katagiri's blurred view.

> The gun was so small and so black that it hardly looked real. Katagiri stared at the object in the man's hand, not registering the fact that it was aimed at him and that the man was pulling the trigger. It all happened too quickly: it didn't make sense to him. But the gun, in fact, went off. Katagiri . . . felt an impact as though someone had struck his right shoulder with a sledgehammer. He felt no pain. . . . His glasses had flown off, and everything was a blur. He was vaguely aware that the man was approaching with the pistol pointed at him. ("Superfrog," 95; "Kaeru-kun," 147–48)

The scene is narrated twice, always underlining the fact that it is filtered by the protagonist's perception. In his hospital bed, Katagiri tries to remember what happened, and he is sure that he has been shot with a gun, but he has no injury on him. When he wakes up, he is completely disoriented; he is still without his glasses, and cannot see the clock on the wall, furthermore, the room has no windows, and therefore he is unable to tell what time it is, or whether it is day or night. His body has lost all sensation, and he cannot move. When the nurse tells him he has been found lying unconscious in the streets of Kabukichō, that he does not have any external injury, and that there has been no earthquake, he begins to question the reliability of his own memory of the events: "How much of what he remembered had actually happened and how much was hallucination? Did Frog really exist, and had Frog fought with Worm to put a stop to the earthquake? Or had that just been part of a long dream? Katagiri had no idea what was true anymore" ("Superfrog," 98; "Kaeru-kun," 151).

Up to this point, the references to the inability to see or understand underline the difficulty of knowing reality, focusing on the presence of perception as a filter—Katagiri's bad eyesight, his glasses. A similar problematic relationship between reality and perception is a typical theme of literary modernism. But when Kaeru-kun visits Katagiri in the hospital, the story shifts from an epistemological doubt to an ontological one: it is not a matter of believing what one sees anymore, the text does not question the possibility of *knowing* the world, but it questions its very realness, the existence of a unitary and clearly defined "reality."

Katagiri apologizes for having failed in his mission, but Kaeru-kun replies that he *has* helped him fight Mimizu-kun:

> "You were a great help to me in my fight, Mr. Katagiri."
> "I was?"
> "Yes, you were. You did a great job in your dreams. That's what made it possible for me to fight Worm to the finish. I have you to thank for my victory." "I don't get it," Katagiri said. "I was unconscious the whole time. They were feeding me intravenously. I don't remember doing anything in my dream."
> "That's fine, Mr. Katagiri. It's better that you don't remember. The whole terrible fight occurred in the area of imagination. That is the precise location of our battlefield." ("Superfrog," 98; "Kaeru-kun," 152)

The text supports Kaeru-kun's statement by having the nurse declare that Katagiri had slept fitfully, calling the name of Kaeru-kun, and that he "must have had many nightmares." If Satsuki in "Tairando" has the chance to save herself through a dream, Katagiri saves the whole city of Tokyo with the help of imagination.

One of the characters in *Kafka on the Shore*, Hoshino, likes to quote William Butler Yeats's idea that "in dreams begins responsibility." In this novel, dreams have inexplicable effects on reality, and the protagonist, Tamura Kafka, after falling asleep in a park, wakes up covered in blood, on the same night in which his father is assassinated many kilometers away. The connection remains blurred, but the text hints at the possibility that Tamura Kafuka, from inside a dream, might have killed his father in real life, and that he might therefore be responsible for the murder.

Significantly, in both cases, the dream is not represented in the story, and the protagonists do not remember it. Whereas Western modernists used dream as a representational strategy that, as a direct expression of the irrational mind, allowed them to escape the conventions of realism, in Murakami dreams are used as another reality, ontologically different from that of waking life. They constitute, literally, another world. For Tamura Kafuka and Katagiri, dreams are not a product of the unconscious, a creation of the mind that escapes the constraints of reason, but have a real existence of their own, and sometimes even intrude in everyday reality with significant consequences. Even more than dealing with the "other world" of foreign literature, engaging these different realities is both a necessary step in order to become individual subjects and a dangerous undertaking. In order to deal with these other worlds without being overcome by them, it is crucial to find a way to connect them rather than simply recognizing them as separate. And it is imagination that can connect "this world" and "that world," *kocchi no sekai* and *acchi no sekai*, as the means by which one can make them interact rather than simply recognize them as separate. As Kaeru-kun points out, "this is the precise location of our battlefield."

Whereas Rubin translates *sōzōryoku no naka* as "in the realm of imagination," I would translate *sōzōryoku* more emphatically as "the *power* of imagination," taking literally *chikara*—the last character in the word *sōzōryoku*—because I believe that this is the function of *sōzōryoku* in Murakami's world: a powerful and empowering instrument. Significantly, Katagiri says that during the fight he had "lost consciousness" (*ishiki o ushinatte ita*): reason, rational, conscious thinking has given way to imagination, which presides over the realm of dreams. And it is through dreams and imaginary worlds that Murakami's characters, and by extension his stories, find their form of social and political commitment, their connection to their others and to the world outside the page.

Another significant instance of the connective power of imagination can be found in the imaginary rooms in *Dance Dance Dance*. As the Sheep Man explains to *boku* when they meet on the ghost floor of the Dolphin Hotel, these parallel worlds exist in order to provide the protagonist with a way to connect to his different parts of himself, as well as to others:

> "Itallstartshere, itallendshere. Thisisyourplace. It'stheknot. It'stiedtoeverything. . . . Weconnectthings. That'swhatwedo. Likeaswitchboard, weconnectthings. . . . That'sourduty. Switchboardduty. Youseekforit, weconnect, yougotit. Getit?"[28]

Hard-Boiled Wonderland and the End of the World presents yet another version of the power of imagination. Here the protagonist of the first story is saved, while all the others who underwent the same experiment and were made into *keisanshi* ("calcutec" in Alfred Birnbaum's translation) have been destroyed, thanks to his greater imagination and his ability to construct a complex and coherent story. *Sekai no owari*, the fantastic city inside *boku*'s mind where *watashi* lives, is a creation far more structured and articulated than the other *keisanshi*'s fantasies, which are only fragments and unrelated images, and this is why *boku* is the only one who survives. Furthermore, *boku* becomes conscious of the system built inside his mind and finds out about the existence of *watashi*; he is thus able to connect the two worlds.

At the end of the novel, while *boku* dies in the real world and chooses to "become" his imaginary alter ego, *watashi* helps his shadow to flee and decides to stay in the walled city because, he says, he feels responsible for the creations of his mind. Even though the finale of *Hard-Boiled Wonderland* is often cited as an example of Murakami's escapism, I would argue that this ending is not so much a solipsistic, escapist gesture, as it is an instance of Murakami's specific idea of commitment. *Watashi*'s choice to stay in "end of the world" is a way to face up to his responsibilities toward the fantasy world that he has created, and the story thus points to the fact that we are ultimately responsible for the products of our imagination.

Whereas the narrator of "Sleep" becomes totally isolated because she retreats into the world of wakefulness and reason (she "expands her *ishiki*"), characters such as Katagiri and the protagonists of *Hard-Boiled Wonderland* and *Dance Dance Dance* are able to connect to the world because they use their dreams and their imagination. Imagination is therefore central to Murakami's definition of social commitment. It is only by descending into our inner selves and passing through "other worlds" that we can reach toward others and really "do something." Social responsibility is thus strongly situated in the realm of imagination and of interiority. Significantly, before dying—or "returning to the murk"—Kaeru-kun tells Katagiri that he has an "un-Frog" (*hi-Kaeru-kun*) inside him.

> "I am, indeed, pure Frog, but at the same time I am a thing that stands for a world of un-Frog."
>
> "Hmm, I don't get that at all."
>
> "Neither do I," Frog said, his eyes still closed. "It's just a feeling I have. What you see with your eyes is not necessarily real. My enemy is, among other things, the me inside me. Inside me is the un-me."
>
> ("Superfrog" 99–100; "Kaeru-kun," 154–55)

Not only reality, but also the self is structured "like a set of Chinese boxes": neither unitary nor linear, it always contains in itself its "anti-self," its own enemy. Therefore, for Murakami's characters, often the only way to act is by starting from the self, recognizing the other inside themselves.

In an interview from 1989 with Shibata Motoyuki, Murakami talks about the film *A Nightmare on Elm Street* (1984; dir. Wes Craven) as another example of this kind of "interiorized responsibility," which, significantly, is acted out, once again, in dreams: "I think that we are not capable of having common battles anymore. We can only fight individual wars inside ourselves. And it is from here that we should start. Just like in the movie *A Nightmare on Elm Street*: Freddy enters everybody's dreams. We have to let him in. And we have to fight him singularly, each in our own mind."[29] Tellingly, Murakami illustrates his point using an example from Western culture, while at the same time throwing into question the distinction between "high" and "low" culture, stating that he prefers the approach to social responsibility of *A Nightmare on Elm Street* to that, for instance, of Bernardo Bertolucci's film *The Conformist* (1970).[30]

Western literature is also central to "Superfrog": Kaeru-kun is a connoisseur of European literature who is forever quoting Nietzsche, Conrad, Hemingway, Tolstoy, and Dostoevsky.[31] And it is in Western literature that Kaeru-kun finds the crucial element that sustains him in his fight against Mimizu-kun. As he explains to Katagiri in the hospital the following day,

"Fyodor Dostoevsky, with unparalleled tenderness, depicted those who have been forsaken by God. He discovered the precious quality of human existence in the ghastly paradox whereby men who have invented God were forsaken by that very God. Fighting with Worm in the darkness, I found myself thinking of Dostoevsky's 'White Nights'" ("Superfrog," 99; "Kaeru-kun," 154).

For Kaeru-kun, as for the writers/narrators of Murakami's previous texts, Western literature is an instrument to bring order to chaos, to give sense to the world, and to find the strength necessary to act. As the story goes on, Katagiri, too, muses about Kaeru-kun's quotations and in the most difficult moments tries to find in them a message that can help him understand the situation he is in and to "do the right thing." At the end of the story, Katagiri decides that he will read the novels Kaeru-kun quoted, hoping that he will understand him better. The text ends with an invitation to read Western literature, as if to suggest that the readers, too, should pursue the way of self-formation through literature, distancing themselves from their own culture and becoming aware of the different layers of which reality is composed.

Imagination is therefore central to Murakami's vision of the role of literature in contemporary society. For readers, imagination allows the construction of identity through a process of separation and reconnection of the different layers of reality. For writers, who possess a greater *sōzōryoku* than most people, imagination is what they must put to the service of others, creating other worlds in the form of stories.

Like many Euro-American modernists, Murakami refuses traditional forms of realism and a unitary and authoritative representation of reality. Although modernist writers pursued a more faithful representation through the use of the unconscious and linguistic experiments, Murakami resorts to metafiction and the fantastic in order to represent the multilayered nature of reality and identity, which are constructed across different worlds, both in a geographical/cultural sense (Japan and America, Japan and the West) and in a metaphysical sense.

His works thus highlight a new social function for literature: to give people stories, not ones that distort reality by forcing it into rational structures, as linear and realistic narratives often do, but ones that allow readers to step into other worlds and make them understand, and connect, the manifold aspects of reality through imagination.

Conclusion

An indication of Murakami Haruki's rising popularity can be seen, for example, in the fact that his short stories are ever more frequently published in the *New Yorker*, which carried as many as four works by Murakami between 2005 and 2006: "Where I'm Likely to Find It," a translation of "Doko de are sore ga mitsukarisō na basho de" from the collection *Tōkyō kitanshū*, was published in May 2005; "The Kidney-Shaped Stone That Moves Every Day" ("Hibi idō suru jinzō no katachi o shita ishi") in September 2005; and "The Shinagawa Monkey" ("Shinagawazaru") in February 2006. In the meantime, the magazine also published another, older story by Murakami, "In the Year of Spaghetti" ("Supagetī no toshi ni"; 1983) in November 2005, while "Chance Traveler" ("Gūzen no tabibito"), also from *Tōkyō kitanshū*, appeared in *Harper's* in July 2005. In 2006, the *New York Times* put *Kafka on the Shore* at the top of its list of the five best novels of 2005, another clear instance of the appreciation of Murakami's fiction in North America.[1] A significant result of this trend is that Murakami is much less "orientalized" than any other Japanese writer before him, and that American readers do not buy his books looking for exoticism, but simply to enjoy them as good literature. At the same time, the spread of his work is furthering a new appreciation of Japanese literature in the United States.

Already in the 1990s, Hosea Hirata had noted that an increasing number of Americans had become interested in Japan through the works of Murakami, as reflected for instance in the fact that a high percentage of college students gave as a reason for choosing a Japanese major their fascination with Murakami's novels.[2] In the 2000s, this trend kept pace with his increasing popularity, and consequently his role as a cultural mediator introducing Japanese culture and literature to the American public was greatly enhanced.[3]

As a consequence of his growing international reputation, Murakami was asked in 2005 to write an introduction to a new volume of short stories by Akutagawa Ryūnosuke, *Rashōmon and Seventeen Other Stories*, translated by Jay Rubin and published by Penguin both in the United Kingdom and in the United States. As much as this might surprise those Japanese critics who still do not consider Murakami an author of "pure literature," the publisher clearly felt that a book by Akutagawa would appeal to a broader audience with Murakami's name on its cover. Following the success of this venture, Murakami was asked to write the introduction to a new edition of Natsume Sōseki's *Sanshirō*, also re-translated by Jay Rubin and published by Penguin.

Whereas in the 1990s Karatani Kōjin argued that American writers existed in Japan "through the filter of a Murakami-esque landscape,"[4] and Miura Masashi subsequently observed that Murakami Haruki and Shibata Motoyuki's translations had shaped the Japanese perception both of American literature and of Western culture in general since the 1980s,[5] these introductions to Akutagawa's and Sōseki's translations point to the fact that Murakami Haruki's work is also having an increasing influence on the American perceptions of Japanese literature.

In an article for the English edition of the *Asahi Shinbun*, Jay Rubin commented on the idea of Murakami introducing Akutagawa to an English-speaking audience, pointing out that while Japanese literature in the past had often been approached through an exoticizing filter, "clearly Murakami had changed everything, and now the English-speaking world was ready to accept Akutagawa as a modernist." He further contrasted this process with the recent exoticization of Japan in movies such as *Memoirs of a Geisha,* arguing that "one can only hope that the new Akutagawa is recognized as a modern master with the Murakami imprimatur rather than another example of Japanese exotica."[6]

However, in his introduction, Murakami performs operations more significant than simply presenting a major Japanese author to the American audience. The essay, very long and detailed, comes somewhat as a surprise from a writer who has often denied any interest in Japanese literature and has declared himself to be much more indebted to American fiction than to writers such as Kawabata or Mishima, whose works he claimed to have hardly ever read. But what is even more interesting is the way Murakami compares himself to Akutagawa, reflecting on what he as a novelist has learned from Akutagawa, and defining his own identity as a writer in terms of similarities with, and differences from, his predecessor.

As many of the protagonists of his fiction have done, Murakami relates to the figure of Akutagawa through a process of both identification and estrangement in order to construct himself as a subject, reinstating the concept of identity as constructed through relation with an "other." This element, as we have seen, has always been crucial to Murakami's fiction, where he explores the way in which literature provides a space for such identifications and disidentifications.

In this sense, it is worth noting that Murakami started his first novel, *Kaze no uta o kike,* with a reflection on the nature of literature, a reflection that he based on a metafictional joke. The story begins with the narrator, *boku,* commenting on the writer that has been most influential in his decision to write, a certain Derek Heartfield, an American writer of science fiction, who, he explains, committed suicide in 1938 by jumping off the Empire State Building. Although the text never states it, however, Derek Heartfield is a fictional character, a product of the author's imagination. Furthermore, this can be seen a fairly obvious reference to Kurt Vonnegut's use of the fictional alter ego Kilgore Trout, who is also a writer of science fiction and a recurring character in Vonnegut's novels. The style of *Kaze no uta o kike,* in fact, is clearly influenced, not by the imaginary Heartfield, but by Vonnegut himself. The beginning of Murakami's literary career is therefore marked by a playful yet meaningful concern with issues of intertextuality and metatextuality.

The theme of the relation between reality and fiction, identity and performance has remained central to his works ever since. In his interactions with the public, too, Murakami has often played on notions of identity, positioning himself alternatively as a Japanese writer or as a Westernized/international one, thus challenging fixed notions of cultural identity and claiming the right to a shifting, complex, and multiple subjectivity. In this perspective, his introduction to *Rashōmon* throws light on the current direction of Murakami's relationship with Japanese and American literature. In writing about Akutagawa, Murakami addresses some of the most crucial questions that recur in his own work: namely, East-West relations, the concept of literature as self-expression, the rejection of traditional realism as an inadequate means of representing the complexity of the world in which we live, the idea of identity as culturally and linguistically constructed, and the issue of a writer's social responsibility. Interestingly, the main frameworks through which Murakami develops his interpretation of Akutagawa are the concepts of interculturality and modernity. Although one is led to wonder whether Murakami here is speaking about himself rather than discussing Akutagawa, it is precisely for this reason that his interpretation sheds light on his own view of such concepts. The word "modern," with its derivates "modernism" and "modernist," recurs throughout the text, with a number of different nuances. Murakami describes Akutagawa as a writer "always pointed towards modernism,"[7] and subsequently elaborates on a number of different definitions of this idea of "modernism." He compares him to F. Scott Fitzgerald, apparently referring to an idea of literary Modernism in the Euro-American sense, and uses the term modernist as synonymous with "disengaged"—in open contrast with Maruyama's ideology of the modern (*kindaishugi*) and its idea of the intellectual as strongly rooted in history and politically committed—and associates it with the predominant representation of Akutagawa as the epitome of the disengaged *junbungaku* "pure literature" of the 1920s.

Significantly, Murakami relates this idea of "modernism" to a more general mood of the period, and describes Akutagawa as incarnating the values of "Taishō Democracy, liberalism, and modernism,"[8] thus apparently conforming to the mainstream portrayal of Akutagawa as a symbol of a certain current of Taishō literature. The references to Taishō Democracy and liberalism, however, are noteworthy. Here, Murakami is also departing from the image of Akutagawa as paradigmatically noncommitted writer, claiming for this author (and, by extension, for himself) a different kind of engagement.

Throughout the introduction, in fact, Murakami also uses the term "modernist" in a more political/sociological sense, to mean "modernized/Westernized," arguing, for instance, that Akutagawa "studied in the modern educational system," that he "was well versed in modern languages," and that "a Westernized lifestyle was, for him, entirely natural and entirely comfortable."[9] The text is particularly ambiguous in this respect. On the one hand, Murakami ostensibly espouses the Meiji intellectuals' enthusiasm for Western culture, describes Westernization as a progressive force struggling to wipe away tradition and backwardness, and criticizes the Meiji government's attitude embodied in the slogan *wakon yōsai* ("Western technology, Japanese spirit"), arguing that "they wanted to incorporate the technological progressiveness and efficiency of Western systems, but they also wanted the people to remain good, submissive Confucianists."[10] He also ultimately appears to blame Akutagawa's nervous breakdown and his subsequent suicide on the isolation of "modern" urban culture from the "backward" rest of the country. However, at the same time, he declares that Akutagawa was "by no means simply a modernist with Western affectations,"[11] and underlines the importance of this author's active appropriation and creative use of Western culture, as well as the relevance of his shifting cultural positioning, to his work as a writer.

It is even more interesting to look at the original Japanese version of the introduction, in which Murakami alternates the words *kindai*—pointing out that Akutagawa grew up at the height of *kindaika* (modernization) and was a *kindai no ko* ("child of the modern era")—with *modan*, *modanizumu*, and *modanisuto*. He also utilizes some Japanized *katakana* compound words, probably original creations, such as *modanaizu sareta* and *modanisuto-teki* (the latter cleverly translated in the English version as "modernistic"). The term *modan* and its derivates, however, are prevalent, thus once again underlining the relationship of modernity to Western language and culture, and the "Japanization" of such modernity, transformed in yet another polysemic and polymorphous *katakana* word. Through the multiple meanings attributed to the terms "modern" and "modernist," the text problematizes the category of modernity itself and underlines its geographical complexity.[12]

Significantly, another major feature of Akutagawa's work that Murakami discusses, and with which he identifies, is his writing across cultures. He describes Akutagawa as the very embodiment of the ideal of being "conversant with old and new, East and West" (*kokon tōzai ni tsūjiru*).[13] This might be an apt description of Murakami's own fiction and the way it undermines the vision of cultures as separate and unitary entities, each enclosed within its own boundaries.

Lastly, in his discussion of Akutagawa, Murakami addresses the theme of the responsibilities of a writer, and more generally of the social relevance of literature. Here, too, his interpretation of Akutagawa appears to speak for his own idea of the moral duty of a writer. His argument that Akutagawa's greatness lies partly in his having given us "popular works that appeal to a broad audience" sounds like a very good description of what Murakami himself has been trying to do by writing "popular" fiction with a wide readership both at home and abroad, in contrast to the elitist and "difficult" works of writers such as Ōe.

While presenting Akutagawa to the Western audience, Murakami also constructs a strong bond with this author and implicitly reflects on his own "modernism." In his description of Akutagawa, he repeatedly projects an image of himself as more closely related to early twentieth-century writers than to postwar authors of *junbungaku*. Furthermore, he portrays Akutagawa as an author who shunned traditional realism and fulfilled his social role as an intellectual more in the domain of the exploration of the individual self and the construction of identity than in the field of "socially committed literature." This, too, has always been Murakami's own position on the matter of social commitment, in sharp contrast to the dominant attitude in mainstream postwar literature. This introduction is therefore a particularly significant text, in that it provides us with Murakami's own reflections on some of the main themes of his work, such as his rejection of traditional realism, and his exploration of the fragmented and culturally constructed nature of identity.

Although Murakami describes Akutagawa as a quintessentially "modernist" writer, I have defined his approach, halfway between modernism and postmodernism and yet different from both, as "paramodernist." Through his fiction, Murakami approaches the idea of modernity not from a "post" position, as Western postmodernist writers have done, thus implicitly reaffirming the idea of modernity as progress and its temporal nature, but from "outside," from the vantage point offered by a foreign culture, thus foregrounding the geographical and cultural nature of modernity. In this sense, the growing importance of his role as a cultural mediator is particularly significant. Murakami is increasingly active in presenting both American culture to the Japanese audience and Japanese culture to his American readers, using it as something familiar enough to be perceived as non-threatening, yet unfamiliar enough to make his readers in both places reflect upon, and distance, their own culture.

At the same time, another crucial feature of Murakami's work is his use of what I have called the "power of imagination" and its capacity to connect different realities and different people. This element, too, is increasingly attracting the attention of both critics and readers—and I will conclude this study with one example of critical examination of Murakami's use of imagination.

The international symposium *Murakami Haruki o meguru bōken: sekai wa Murakami bungaku o dō yomu ka* (A Wild Haruki Chase: How the World Reads Murakami's Literature) took place in Tokyo, Yamanashi, Kobe, and Sapporo from March 25 to 29, 2006, and included Murakami translators and scholars from France, Brazil, Canada, Germany, Hungary, Denmark, Indonesia, Czechoslovakia, Norway, South Korea, Russia, Taiwan, Hong Kong, China, Poland, and the United States. On this occasion, the writer Richard Powers delivered the keynote speech, in which he dealt extensively with the role of imagination in the works of Murakami Haruki. The first part of Powers' speech revolved around an apparently not-so-literary topic, i.e., the discovery in neuroscience of so-called mirror neurons. Discovered in the mid-1990s by a group of Italian researchers, mirror neurons are primarily responsible for the movement of muscles; however, they are also activated, in exactly the same way as if movements were being performed, when both animal and human subjects see or imagine the same movements enacted by others.

The significance of this discovery, in Powers' view, goes beyond the realm of neuroscience, and involves the broader issue of the nature of individual identity and human relations. In his lecture, Powers connected this concept with the way in which Murakami represents parallel realities, dreams, and imagination as means to connect people through a similar process of "mirroring." He describes Murakami's writing as a "relentless exploration of estrangement from the ordinary," and notes that such estrangement is deeply related to his position across cultures. Significantly, Powers related Murakami's awareness of the fragmentary nature of identity to the new world order created by globalization, which, in his opinion, forces us "out of the old, single, unitary self" and "into a loose confederation of hundreds of brain regions." Arguing that Murakami's texts offer a relief to the angst provoked by such a sense of dispersal, Powers noted that his works make readers aware of the multilayeredness of identity and free them from the constraints of a unitary and authoritative vision of reality, providing a sense of connection through imagination. Thus, they make us aware that, in Powers' words, "We can never know the world, but in our bewilderment, we *can* know each other."[14]

The ability to provide such spaces of imagination, such mirrors that allow us both to gain an awareness of the complexity of reality and to connect to each other, is ultimately the most significant strength of literature for Murakami Haruki, and what gives it social relevance in the contemporary world. By exploiting both Japan's peculiar position vis-à-vis the West and his own positioning across cultures, Murakami in his fiction provides a very original perspective on the issue of national and international social relations in the era of globalization. Unlike most of Japanese postwar fiction, Murakami's texts do not represent Western influences as something dangerous and corrupting, but instead use Western culture as a basis to construct a multilayered image of reality. And the same might be said of the way in which he presents Japanese culture to the West. Furthermore, through their reflections on the role of literature as a "mirror" that allows readers to constitute themselves as subjects, Murakami's works situate social responsibility in the realm of interiority and imagination, and point to the fact that the basis for any kind of social interaction lies in the recognition of the "other" within ourselves. As the author himself argued in an interview with Roland Kelts, "the word 'global' is something that I can't really understand, because we do not necessarily need to be global. We already are what I call 'mutual.' If we use the connection of our world called story, I think that that's enough to keep us connected."[15]

Despite the contention of several scholars and writers that Murakami's works lack any form of commitment, I would argue that in offering such "worlds called stories," his works do perform an important social function. I am convinced that if we read Murakami's works for what they tell us about the constructed nature of identity and reality, the geographical nature of modernity, and the power of imagination to create connections between different realities and different individuals, they have the potential for having a strong social impact, and for becoming, like the space of imagination, "the precise location of our battlefield."

Reference Matter

Notes

Introduction

1. Eliot, "*Ulysses*, Order, and Myth," 480.

2. Suzuki, *Narrating the Self*, 33–36.

3. Miura, *Murakami Haruki to Shibata Motoyuki no mō hitotsu no Amerika*, 16–20.

4. Amitrano, *The New Japanese Novel*, 9.

5. Rubin, *Haruki Murakami and the Music of Words*, 37.

6. This has also created a division among his readers, who tend to be either "*Hard-Boiled Wonderland* fans" or "*Norwegian Wood* fans": the former are more likely to prefer *Dansu dansu dansu* and *Nejimaki-dori kuronikuru*, and the latter tend to like *Kokkyō no minami, taiyō no nishi* (1992; *South of the Border, West of the Sun*, 2000).

7. Edwards, *Fantastic Concepts in the Fiction of Murakami Haruki*, 7.

8. Strecher, "Magical Realism," 263.

9. Ibid., 279.

10. With his third novel, *Hitsuji o meguru bōken*, Murakami begins to portray the Japanese state as a sinister presence that seeks to promulgate a sense of collective identity, a dictatorship over the mind, among members of contemporary Japanese society. The implicit assumption here—probably a historically correct one—is that the disappearance of the student radicals after 1970 was due either to their mass-assimilation into the "system" of Japanese society or, alternatively, their destruction by that system, which is intolerant of the individual (Strecher, "Magical Realism," 279).

Chapter 1

1. Friedman, "Definitional Excursions," 495.

2. Ibid., 497.

3. Lewis, "The Roots of Muslim Rage"; Huntington, "The Clash of Civilisations." See also Wallerstein, "Culture as the Ideological Battleground of the Modern World System" and Lind, "Defending Western Culture."

4. Sakai, *Translation and Subjectivity*, 156.

5. Gray, *False Dawn*, 2.

6. For a discussion of the "overcoming the modern" debates, see, among others, Kawakami and Takeuchi, eds., *Kindai no chōkoku*; Takeuchi, "Kindai no chōkuku"; Harootunian, "Visible Discourses/ Invisible Ideologies"; Karatani, *Shinpojiumu*, 445–74; Najita and Harootunian, "Japanese Revolt against the West: Political and Cultural Criticism in the Twentieth Century," 711–14; Harootunian, *Overcome by Modernity*; Williams, "Modernity, Harootunian, and the Demands of Scholarship."

7. Maruyama, *Senchū to sengo no aida*, 189–90.

8. Bradbury and McFarlane, *Modernism*, 3.

9. Matsumoto, *Kindai no chōkoku*, 219–26.

10. Lippit, *Topographies of Japanese Modernism*, 228.

11. Karatani, *Origins of Modern Japanese Literature*, 33–34.

12. For a discussion of the birth of the I-novel and its relation to Western literature, see Suzuki, *Narrating the Self.*

13. Iwabuchi, *Recentering Globalization*, 3.

14. Minear, "Orientalism and the Study of Japan," 507–12.

15. Harris, "All the World a Melting Pot?" 35–36.

16. Yoshioka, "Samurai and Self-colonization in Japan,"101–2.

17. Miyoshi, *Off Center*, 40–43.

18. For a more detailed discussion of American scholarship on Japanese particularism, see Glazer, "From Ruth Benedict to Herman Kahn," and Revell, "*Nihonjinron*: Made in the U.S.A."

19. Particularism is considered one of the main characteristics of Japanese culture in most of the American texts from the "Japanese Miracle" debates of the 1980s. These arguments are considered to have begun with the publication of Ezra Vogel's *Japan as Number One* (1979) and William Ouchi's *Theory Z: How American Business Can Meet the Japanese Challenge* (1981). Japan apologists such as Vogel, Ouchi, and Chalmers Johnson stressed Japan's uniqueness as a positive factor that America should imitate, whereas "Japan bashers" such

as Clyde Prestowitz and Karel Van Wolferen maintained that Japan should abandon this attitude and conform to Western standards. All parties seemed to agree, however, in considering particularism or exceptionalism a founding element of "Japaneseness." For a brief bibliography on the "Japanese Miracle" debates, see among others Vogel, *Japan as Number One*; Ouchi, *Theory Z*; Chalmers Johnson, *MITI and the Japanese Miracle*; Prestowitz, *Trading Places*; Fallows, *More Like Us*; Van Wolferen, *The Enigma of Japanese Power*.

20. Revell, "*Nihonjinron*: Made in the U.S.A." 74.

21. Sakai, "You Asians," 789–818.

22. Sakai, *Translation and Subjectivity*, 72–116.

23. Ibid., 163.

24. Ibid.

25. As Naoki Sakai notes: "Neither universalism nor 'the principle of equality among modern sovereign states' allows for 'the Other.' The schema of the co-existence among nation-states serves to conceal the complicity of the West and Japan in the transferential formation of respective identities; because of this complicity, the obsession with the West warrants self-referentiality to the Japanese. An uncritical endorsement of such a schema prevents us from detecting the hidden alliance of the narcissisms of the West and of Japan. It conceals the working of the regimes in which a paranoiac impulse to identify with the West, and another with Japan, are simultaneously reproduced and mutually reinforced by one another" (Sakai, *Translation and Subjectivity*, 70–71).

26. Such studies include Moeran, "The Orient Strikes Back"; Allison, "A Challenge to Hollywood?"; Befu, "Globalization as Human Dispersal"; Befu, "Globalization Theory from the Bottom Up"; Befu and Guichard-Anguiss, *Globalizing Japan*; Iwabuchi, *Recentering Globalization*; Iwabuchi, "Complicit Exoticism"; Iwabuchi, "Marketing Japan"; Shiraishi, "Japan's Soft Power"; among others.

27. Befu, "Globalization Theory from the Bottom Up," 10.

28. Iwabuchi, *Recentering Globalization*, 9.

29. Ibid., 18.

Chapter 2

1. Another interesting case of even more extreme domestication in the translation of a Japanese author in America is the novel *Trash* (1994) by Yamada Eimi (Amy Yamada). In the English version, a note informs the reader that the text has been previously published

in Japanese in a slightly different form under the title *Torasshu*. The note also reveals that the English version also contains parts of Yamada's previous novel, *Jeshī no sebone* (Jesse's backbone), as well as some adaptations made specifically "with an American reader in mind." The final English text is therefore a "collage" of two different Japanese novels assembled for the American reader.

2. Sheila K. Johnson, *The Japanese Through American Eyes*. For example, Johnson notes that this shift was very clear in the 1960s: in the first half of the decade a great number of guidebooks and other works on Japan were published in the United States. and there was a booming interest in the country; but following the beginning of trade frictions and the tensions regarding the Vietnam war and the use of U.S. military bases in Japan, violent images of Japan, very similar to those prevalent during World War II, came to the fore again, starting with Ian Fleming's spy novel *You Only Live Twice* (1964) and the subsequent movie directed by Lewis Gilbert (1967), and most of all with such novels as James Clavell's *Shōgun* (1975), and Eric Van Lustbader's *The Ninja* (1980) and *The Miko* (1984). For a discussion of the stereotype of warrior Japan in *Shōgun* see also Smith, *Learning from Shōgun*.

3. Birnbaum, *Monkey Brain Sushi*, ii.

4. Iwamoto, "A Voice from Postmodern Japan," 295.

5. Mitgang, "Looking for America, or Is It Japan?"

6. Wright, "Dancing as Fast as He Can," 34–35.

7. Caryl, "Gods of the Mall," 33.

8. Devereaux, "PW Interviews Murakami Haruki," 7.

9. Numano, "Dōnattsu, bīru, supagetti," 150. The translation is my own.

10. Rubin, "The Other World of Murakami Haruki," 490.

11. Ibid., 491. Rubin reiterates this concept in his *Murakami Haruki and the Music of Words* (2002), where he goes on to note that the works of Murakami, "a novelist whose writing has been heavily influenced by his reading of American literature," strike his Japanese readers as fresh and new because they often read "like a translation from English" (Ibid., 288). At the same time, he also comments on Murakami's "return to Japan" and increased interest in Japanese history in *Nejimakidori kuronikuru*, which he defines "Murakami's most ambitious novel" because of the way it deals with "Japan's dark and violent recent past" (Ibid., 213).

12. McInerney, "Roll over Bashō," 4.

13. In his review of the short story collection *The Elephant Vanishes*, David Leavitt writes that Murakami's characters "listen to Wagner and Herbie Hancock, but disdain 'stupid Japanese rock music. Love songs sweet enough to rot your teeth.' They read Len Deighton novels and *War and Peace* and not Kobo Abe and *The Tale of Genji*. Their universe is Japanese, but their cultural reference points are almost exclusively Western" (Leavitt, "As Japanese as Burt Bacharach," 8). Jean-Christophe Castelli, on the other hand, notes that references to Western culture are not unique to Murakami Haruki, and that "Junichiro Tanizaki learned his craft from reading Edgar Allan Poe; Yukio Mishima drew inspiration from Jean Genet; and Kobo Abe's spooky parables are nothing if not Kafkaesque." However, he argues, "their style and substance have remained recognizably Japanese," while Murakami is "so translatable that he is, paradoxically, the most *un*translatable of Japanese writers; everything in his fiction can be conveyed to an American reader except the shock of prose that reads so, well, *American*. His writing injects the rock 'n' roll of everyday language into exquisite silences of Japanese literary prose" (Castelli, "Tokyo Prose," 278–79). Pico Iyer in 1997 writes that "Murakami—a cool 48-year-old who once ran a jazz bar, has translated John Irving, Truman Capote and Raymond Carver into Japanese and recently taught at Princeton—has been perfectly positioned to serve as the voice of hip, Westernized Japan. His *Norwegian Wood* (note the Beatles reference) sold more than 2 million copies around the globe" (Iyer, "Tales of the Living Dead," 114). Jamie James, in the same year, writes in the *New York Times* an article titled "East Meets West," whose subtitle reads: "In Haruki Murakami's latest novel, postwar Japan is adrift, eating fast food and wearing Van Halen T-shirts" (James, "East Meets West," 8). There he relates Murakami's work to the phenomenon of *nihonjinron*, taking him as an example of the end of Japanese exceptionalism and of its final surrender to the West: "One of the preoccupying themes of Japanese literature in this century has been the question of what it means to be Japanese, especially in an era that has seen the rise and fall of militarism and the decline of traditional culture. But from reading the books of Haruki Murakami, one of the country's most celebrated novelists, you'd never know he was Japanese at all: his characters read Turgenev and Jack London, listen to Rossini and Bob Dylan, eat pate de foie gras and spaghetti, and know how to make a proper salty dog. . . . The novels that have been published in English—*A Wild Sheep Chase, Hard-Boiled Wonderland and the*

End of the World—occupy a shadowland between cyberpunk sci-fi, gumshoe detective fiction and hip social satire. Western critics searching for parallels have variously likened him to Raymond Carver, Raymond Chandler, Arthur C. Clarke, Don DeLillo, Philip K. Dick, Bret Easton Ellis and Thomas Pynchon—a roster so ill assorted as to suggest that Murakami may in fact be an original" (James, "East Meets West," 8). James has his own personal selection of Western writers to whom Murakami might be compared: "Parts of *The Wind-Up Bird Chronicle* have the bluntness of Hemingway. . . . Yet the novel's biggest debt is to Kafka, whose influence may have filtered down to Murakami by way of Kobo Abe, Murakami's great category-smashing predecessor," while the conclusion of the novel contains "an almost Joycean range of literary forms: flashbacks, dreams, letters, newspaper stories and transcripts of internet chats" (James, "East Meets West," 8).

14. McInerney, "Roll over Bashō," 1.

15. Ibid., 8.

16. Miller, "The Salon Interview—Haruki Murakami," 4.

17. Examples of this attitude abound: to note a few more, Jean-Christophe Castelli in *Harper's Bazaar* maintains that Murakami's stories are "allegories for a nation sleepwalking through prosperity, bumping into the shrouded furniture of its history on the way to the gleaming electronic future" (Castelli, "Tokyo Prose," 278); Sam North comments that "Alienation is key to Murakami's books and from them one comes to understand Japan a little better. Externally we see a nation conforming in dress and look and attitudes. We see pictures of teen girls with crazes, buying millions of copies of one object or another. [Scenes that could not be found, by the way, in any of Murakami's texts.] There appears to us to be a national will to conform and that is why Murakami's characters seem to be so strange and yet so popular with the Japanese. They are about people who cannot fit in, or make sense of the society they live in. They struggle to obey the rules and reject normal life, even when claiming to be ordinary" (North, "Haruki Murakami—Outside Looking In," accessed January 28, 2008).

18. Walley, "Two Murakamis and Their American Influence," 41–42.

19. The issue of *kokusaika* is central to Japan's relations with the West and with modernity in the 1980s. In a famous speech given in 1980 entitled "Bunka no jidai no keizai un'ei" (Economic Administration in the Age of Culture), then-Prime Minister Ōhira Masayoshi maintained that Japan, in the postwar years and up to the 1970s, had

concentrated exclusively on the economic recovery, obtaining extraordinary results, but the time had come to transcend modern industrialization and to enter into a new age with a greater focus on culture. He argued: "In the era of modernization and economic growth, Japanese have looked only at the West and neglected their own traditional culture, adopting standards decided by others," but it is now time to put an end to this attitude. (*Ōhira sōri no seisaku kenkyūkai hokōkusho,* 21; quoted in Harootunian, "Visible Discourses/Invisible Ideologies," 80.) Ōhira therefore advocated the reconstitution of an authentic and organic "Japanese culture." This concept was taken up by the media and by the following administrations, that insisted on a "return to Japanese tradition" in opposition to the excessive Westernization of the country. The concept of *kokusaika* thus became very popular in the official rhetoric of the period. In this ideological framework there emerged institutions such as the Japan Foundation, which finances foreign research on Japan in order to "diffuse knowledge of Japanese language and culture in the world." *Kokusaika* is a fundamentally ambiguous concept: on the one hand it hints at the necessity for Japan to comply with international standards, which seems to lead to further Westernization, but on the other hand it stresses the need to export Japanese culture in order to make up for the "cultural trade imbalance" between Japan and the West, and the consequent necessity of valuing more Japanese culture "against" Westernization.

20. Murakami Fuminobu, *Postmodernist, Feminist and Postcolonial Currents,* 7.

21. Ibid., 21–44.

22. Ibid., 9.

23. Fisch, "In Search of the Real," 363.

24. Miyoshi, *Off Center,* 233.

25. Ibid., 235–36.

26. Ibid., 236.

27. Miyoshi writes further: "If there is anyone now in Japan whose work deserves full-scale studies, it is Ōe Kenzaburō" (Ibid., 236).

28. Ibid., 237.

29. Ōe, *Japan, the Ambiguous and Myself,* 51. Ōe reiterates his criticism in "Japan's Dual Identity: A Writer's Dilemma," where he argues: "Lack of activity in the field of *junbungaku* can be substantiated objectively when we compare the volume of its publications with that of other types of literature, such as popular historical novels, science

fiction, mysteries, and various nonfiction genres. Although the prewar and war years provide no basis for comparison, never have there been so many publications in Japan as in the past forty years. The number of serious literary works, however, has decreased as the number of other publications has continued to grow. Moreover, there is not one work of *junbungaku* to be found in the 1985 list of the ten best-selling Japanese books in either fiction or nonfiction. Amidst this trend, Haruki Murakami, a writer born after the war, is said to be attracting new readers to *junbungaku*. It is clear, however, that Murakami's target lies outside this sphere, and deliberately so. There is nothing that directly links Murakami with postwar literature of the 1946–1970 period. If I may be allowed a possibly hasty comment here, I believe that no revival of *junbungaku* will be possible unless ways are found to fill the wide gap that exists between him and pre-1970 writing" (Ōe, *Japan, the Ambiguous and Myself*, 78–79).

30. Kuroko, *Murakami Haruki*. Another example is Morimoto Takako, who maintains that the most recurring theme in Murakami's works is the sense of loss of the generation of the 1960s and interprets his stories as a commentary on Japan's capitalistic society. She quotes the funeral of the answering machine in *1973-nen no pinbōru* as a symbol of the death of communication in the 1970s, and the disturbed and surreal telephone calls in *Pan'ya saishūgeki* as a symbol of the "discommunication" of the 1980s (Morimoto, 92). Nagahara Takamichi also interprets the collection *Hotaru, Naya o yaku, sono ta no tanpen* ("Firefly," "Barn Burning," and Other Stories, 1986) as a commentary on the sense of loss of the "failed revolution" of the 1960s, the Cold War, and the shift to the *baburu jidai*, the era of the bubble economy (Nagahara, "*Hotaru, Naya o yaku, sono ta no tanpen*," 112–13).

31. Komori, *Murakami Haruki ron*, 117–30.

32. Ibid., 277.

33. The New Left's approach to Western culture was itself ambivalent: calling themselves *shinsayoku*, the New Left, in reference to the British and American movements of the 1960s, at the same time radical students rejected the "modernist" approach of the Japanese left of the older generation, rediscovering anti-modern figures as Yanagita Kunio and Kuki Shūzō.

34. For a discussion of Yoshimoto Takaaki's early thought and his influence on the Japanese New Left, see Shirakawa, *Yoshimoto Takaaki ron*; Nakamura, *Yoshimoto Takaaki*; and Olson, "Intellectuals and 'The People.'" For an analysis of Yoshimoto's more recent "postmodern

turn," see Murakami Fuminobu, *Postmodernist, Feminist and Postcolonial Currents*, 95–135.

35. Ellis, "Questioning Modernism and Postmodernism in Japanese Literature," 144.

36. Ibid., 147.

37. Ibid., 151.

38. Karatani, "Murakami Haruki no fūkei," 98. The translation is my own.

39. Hirata, *Discourses of Seduction*, 70.

40. Karatani, *Tankyū II*, 10.

41. Hirata, *Discourses of Seduction*, 72–73.

42. Sengoku, *Airon o kakeru seinen*; Miura, *Murakami Haruki to Shibata Motoyuki no mō hitotsu no Amerika*.

43. Devereaux, "PW Interviews Murakami Haruki."

44. Murakami wrote of this experience: "Once the war ended, when I had started thinking the worst was over, the fiftieth anniversary of Pearl Harbor came, and throughout America the 'anti-Japan' sentiment began to grow again. . . . It was not nice to find oneself in that situation. . . . In particular, since the beginning of December, except for the most basic grocery shopping, I spent most of my time locked up in my house, without ever going out. And I was not alone in feeling like this: most Japanese around me felt exactly the same" (Murakami, *Yagate kanashiki gaikokugo*, 17–18; my translation).

45. In a similar way, Murakami presents himself primarily as a novelist in America because his novels are better known in the United States, but as a writer of short stories in Japan because he is recognized there as such. Accordingly, he is more willing to discuss his short stories when he is in Japan.

46. Murakami Haruki, *Hon'yaku yawa*, 28.

47. Ibid., 88–89, 108.

48. McInerney, "Roll over Bashō," 4.

49. Ibid., 6.

Chapter 3

1. As is well known, writing was imported to Japan from China around the fifth century CE. Since Chinese is structurally and phonetically very different from Japanese, a number of adaptations were necessary in order to use Chinese logograms to write the Japanese language. In an early stage, Chinese characters were used both for their semantic value (to transcribe the corresponding Japanese words)

and for their phonetic value. The latter ideograms, called *kana* (from *kari-na*, "borrowed words"), could be read with a Chinese reading, i.e., as sounds close to the original Chinese pronunciation of the character (*jion*), or with a Japanese reading, using the Japanese pronunciation of the word represented by the character for its phonetic value (*jikun*). The two types of character were called *ongana* and *kungana* respectively. In this first phase, there was no standard reading for characters, and in each instance it was not clear whether they were used for their phonetic or for their semantic value, nor whether they should be read with their *on* reading or with their *kun* one, and this gave rise to a number of language games in the literature of the time. For a history of the Japanese writing system, see Seeley, *A History of Writing in Japan*; Twine, *Language and the Modern State*; and Yamamoto, *Genbun itchi no rekishi ronkō*.

2. During the Heian era (794–1192), a new system of simplified characters began to develop, leading to the creation of the two syllabaries known today as *hiragana* (flat *kana*) and *katakana* (square *kana*). In general, *hiragana* characters derive from a graphic simplification through cursivization of the Chinese characters, while *katakana* characters are obtained by isolating a part of the original ideogram. The process of formation of these two syllabaries was completed around the ninth century. The *katakana* syllabary was originally used mainly to annotate religious texts, to indicate the order in which the words should be read (the texts were written in Chinese and then annotated so that the sentences could be read in the Japanese order) and later also as phonograms to facilitate the reading of the characters (in a manner similar to contemporary *furigana* glosses). The *hiragana* syllabary, on the other hand, was used mainly in private writings and in women's literature, both poetry and prose (*monogatari, nikki,* and *sōshi*). Literature written by men (mainly poetry), historiography, and official documents were in Chinese, which became the literary language of Japan, in a manner similar to Latin in medieval Europe.

3. This emphasis on language education was also related to Japan's imperial enterprise in Asia: the newly reformed national language later became the basis for educational policies in occupied territories from Korea and Taiwan to Southeast Asia, and the teaching of the Japanese language was a powerful instrument in the Japanization of Asian colonies. See, among others, Miyawaki, "Maraya, Shingapōru no kōminka"; Miyawaki, "Nihon no 'Manshūkoku'"; and Tsurumi, *Japanese Colonial Education in Taiwan*.

4. For instance, Meiji scholars such as Yano Fumio, Suematsu Kenchō, and Ochiai Naobumi maintained that colloquial Japanese was not suited for use as a written language, because of its verbosity and the complexity of its honorific system, as well as for the importance of the relative positions of speaker and listener, which could not be easily translated in a written text. Instead they advocated the adoption of a "normal style," or *futsūbun*, obtained by combining the best elements of the four main written styles in use at the time, *kanbun* (Chinese style), *wabun* (Japanese style), *sōrōbun* (characterized by the use of the verb *sōrō* as copula), and *wakan konkōbun* (a combination of *wabun* and *kanbun*), with a simplified vocabulary and the introduction of a number of foreign words. Mori Ōgai himself, at first an enthusiastic advocate of the use of the colloquial in literature, from 1890 abandoned *genbun itchi* and promoted the use of a "new national written language," or *shin kokubun*, a modernized version of *wabun*. However, thanks to the support of leading intellectuals and scholars of Western studies such as Fukuzawa Yukichi, *genbun itchi* prevailed in the end, and it was adopted for school textbooks, newspapers, and literature—although official documents and government decrees were still written in *kanbun*, or Sino-Japanese, until the 1940s. For further discussion of the reform of spoken and written Japanese, see Twine, *Language and the Modern State* and Yamamoto, *Genbun itchi no rekishi ronkō*.

5. Karatani, *Origins of Modern Japanese Literature*, 44–54.

6. The concept of alphabetic writing as the mark of Western civilization has had its supporters also in the West: for instance, Jack Goody and Ian Watt in "The Consequences of Literacy" state that alphabetic writing is superior to every other writing system because it enables the birth of history, taxonomy, logic, creativity, individualism, and democracy, whereas "all non-Western societies including India and China are cognitively mythical, pre-logical, and irrational as well as collective, theocratic, and undemocratic, that is, anterior to full maturity as a civilization" (Goody and Watt, "The Consequences of Literacy," 52).

7. Following the opening of Japanese ports to foreign trade in 1854 and renewed contacts with the West, a large number of new material objects and abstract concepts entered Japan, and it became necessary to create new words to designate them. Chinese writing played a major role in this process. One main strategy to create new words was the adoption of Chinese equivalents of Western words, which were mainly derived from Chinese-English dictionaries, particularly

W. Lobscheid's *English and Chinese Dictionary, with Punti and Mandarin Pronunciation* (Hong Kong, 1866–69), whose Chinese terms were adopted with their Japanese pronunciation, e.g., *sūgaku* (数学, mathematics), *denki* (電気, electricity), *rippō* (立法, legislation), and *gasshūkoku* (合衆国, United States). Another means was the creation of original Japanese words through the combination of two or more morphemes of Chinese origin. Examples of this type are *bigaku* (美学: *bi*, beauty and *gaku*, study; aesthetics) and *atsuryoku* (圧力: *atsu*, press and *ryoku*, force; pressure). The other major way to designate new objects and concepts was to borrow words from Western languages, mainly from English. These were generally transcribed in *katakana* and accompanied by a Japanese equivalent in *kanji*, in parentheses: for example, *furī torēdo* (free trade) is annotated with *jiyū shōbai* (自由商売), "free commerce"; *minisutoru* (minister) with *daijin* (大臣), "minister"; but these were also sometimes transcribed with *kanji* used phonetically (*ateji*), accompanied by small *hiragana* written on the right side of the character (*furigana*), with typical examples being country names such as 伊太利 (*Itari*, Italy) and 独逸 (*Doitsu*, Germany). Because of the fascination with all things Western in Meiji Japan, it also became common to annotate existing Japanese words written in *katakana* or *hiragana* with loanwords with a similar meaning, for example glossing *shinri* (truth) with *torūsu*, or *shokubun* (obligation) with *oburigēshon* (Seeley, *A History of Writing in Japan*, 136–39).

8. A famous example can be found in Tsubouchi Shōyō's translations of the works of William Shakespeare, in which he discovered an effective way to translate the complex and subtle use of language in the originals through a creative use of *furigana*. In Tsubouchi's translations, glosses often indicate that the *kanji* should not be read in the usual way, and sometimes even require a reading that is not possible for that group of characters. According to David Rycroft, this traditional practice "gives a richness and subtlety to the eye as multiple shades of meaning can be communicated and co-exist in the mind of the reader," and constitutes an effective equivalent to Shakespeare's puns (Rycroft, "Tsubouchi Shōyō's Translation of *Hamlet*," 198).

9. This increase is evident in the number of foreign words present in major Japanese dictionaries. For example, in 1967 Kadokawa' *Gairaigo jiten* (Dictionary of Foreign Words) listed 25,000 loanwords; in 1991, Sanseidō's *Gairaigo jiten* contained 33,500; and in 2000 the number in the Sanseidō dictionary rose to 45,000. Among these loan-

words, terms derived from English are the great majority (Rebuck, "The Function of English Loanwords in Japanese," 53).

10. Karatani, "Nihongo no kanōsei ni tsuite," 42; quoted in Rebuck, "The Function of English Loanwords in Japanese," 54.

11. In some cases, the use of loanwords to indicate abstract concepts has also resulted in giving recognition to an existing social problem, as in the case of the word *sekuhara* (*sekushuaru harasumento;* sexual harassment), the introduction of which, according to Rebuck, has brought to public attention the existence of the phenomenon. Other examples of this function of loanwords are *domesuchikku baiorensu* (domestic violence) and *sutōkā* (stalker). Rebuck, "The Function of English Loanwords in Japanese," 55.

12. Nozumi, *Nihon shakai ni afureru katakanago,* 78.

13. Tanaka, *Advertising Language,* 56.

14. Many loanwords undergo not only phonetic transformations that make it possible to write them and read them using the Japanese phonology, but also abbreviations and contractions that alter them in a significant way. For example, the term *pāsonaru konpyūtā* (personal computer) becomes *pasokon, rimōto kontorōrā* (remote controller) becomes *rimokon,* and *rajio kasetto* (radio cassette player) becomes *rajikase.* In some cases, these loanwords end up designating objects or concepts very far from the foreign original: the term *purinto kurabu* ("print club") becomes *purikura,* the small picture stickers made in game arcades, and the expression *mazā konpurekkusu* (mother complex) becomes *mazakon,* the excessive attachment of adult males to their mothers. There is also a class of composite words that unite foreign and Japanese words or parts of words: such as *asashan* (from *asa,* morning, and *shanpū,* shampoo), the habit of washing one's hair in the morning; and *kogyaru* (from *ko,* child, and *gyaru,* girl), a type of fashion popular among Japanese teenagers in the 1990s.

15. Haarmann, *Symbolic Values of Foreign Language Use,* 16. Haarmann quotes as an example the names of magazines created by putting together words from different foreign languages, like *Elleteen,* from the French *elle* and the English *teen;* or *Puchisebun,* from *puchi* (*petit*) and *sebun* (seven), standing for seventeen, as specified by the subtitle, *brilliant magazine for teens* (Haarmann, *Symbolic Values of Foreign Language Use,* 24). Sometimes the polygraphy of Japanese is amplified by introducing, together with *kanji, hiragana,* and *katakana* foreign words written in the Roman alphabet. Haarmann quotes the following examples: *This is ōbun renji* (THIS IS オーブンレンジ),

where *this is* in the alphabet and *ōbun* (oven) and *renji* (range), common words in contemporary Japanese, are in *katakana; Enjoy tezukuri raifu* (Enjoy 手作りライフ), where *enjoy* in the Roman alphabet, *tezukuri* (handmade) is in *kanji* and *hiragana*, and *raifu* (life) is in *katakana;* and *Mō hitotsu no eregansu and sometimes casual* (もう一つのエレガンス and sometimes casual), with *mō hitotsu no* (one more) in *hiragana* and *kanji, eregansu* (elegance) in *katakana*, and "and sometimes casual" in English.

16. Haarmann, *Symbolic Values of Foreign Language Use*, 126.

17. Interview with Murakami in Parry, "Haruki Murakami," 174.

18. For example, among the novels, eight out of eleven have *katakana* in their titles (*katakana* and corresponding English in brackets):

1973-nen no [pinbōru] ([Pinball], 1973)
Sekai no owari to [hādoboirudo wandārando] ([Hard-Boiled Wonderland] and the End of the World)
[Noruwei] no mori ([Norwegian] Wood)
[Dansu dansu dansu] ([Dance Dance Dance])
Nejimakidori [kuronikuru] (The Wind-Up Bird [Chronicle])
[Supūtoniku] no koibito (The [Sputnik] Sweetheart)
Umibe no [Kafuka] ([Kafka] on the Shore)
[Afutadāku] ([afterdark])

Another title, although in Japanese, is the translation of an American song: *Kokkyō no minami, taiyō no nishi* (*South of the Border, West of the Sun*). Among the collections of short stories, five out of nine have *katakana* words in their titles:

Chūgokuyuki no [surō bōto] (A [Slow Boat] to China; a quotation from the song with the same title)
[Kangarū] biyori (A Perfect Day for [Kangaroos]; a reference to J. D. Salinger's "A Perfect Day for Bananafish")
Kaiten mokuba no [deddo hīto] (The [Dead Heat] of the Merry-Go-Round)
TV [pīpuru] (TV [People])
[Rekishinton] no yūrei (The Ghost of [Lexington])

A great number of the short stories themselves have titles containing *katakana*:

"[Nyūyōku] tankō no higeki" ("[New York] Mining Disaster")
"[Shidonī] no [gurīn sutorīto]" ("[Sydney]'s [Green Street]")
"[Bāto Bakarakku] wa osuki?" ("Do You Like [Burt Bacharach]?")
"32-sai no [dē torippā]" ("A 32-Year-Old [Day Tripper]")
"[Chīzu kēki] no yōna katachi o shita boku no binbō" ("My Poverty in the Shape of a [Cheese Cake]")
"[Supagetī] no toshi ni" ("The Year of [Spaghetti]")

"[Sausubei sutoratto—Dūbī Burazāzu'sausubei sutoratto'] no tame no BGM" ("[Southbay Strutt]—BGM for [Southbay Strutt by the Doobie Brothers]")

The following short stories have titles entirely in *katakana*:

"Rēdāhōzen" ("Lederhosen")
"Pūru saido" ("Pool Side")
"Hantingu naifu" ("Hunting Knife")
"Zonbi" ("Zombie")
"Tairando" ("Thailand")

19. Numano, "Dōnattsu, bīru, supagetti," 150.

20. Ōga, "E-mēru intabyū," 24. Translation mine.

21. A significant example is the story "Supagetī no toshi ni" "("The Year of Spaghetti")," where the narrator cooks exclusively spaghetti for a whole year, and goes into the details of the kinds of pasta sauces he prepares, before launching into a surreal description of a phone call from his girlfriend. The story was originally published in Japanese in 1981, but it was only translated in the *New Yorker* in 2005—possibly a sign that Murakami was finally famous enough that his stories might be appreciated even without "distinctly Japanese food."

22. Rebuck, "The Function of English Loanwords in Japanese," 57. Another intriguing use of the word *kitchin* can be found in Yoshimoto Banana's debut novel by the same name, where the transformation of the kitchen from a place of patriarchal oppression and confinement of women in conventional gender roles to the central site of the protagonist's process of growth and acquisition of agency is deeply related to the use of the "modern" and "foreign" word *kitchin* in opposition to the "traditional" *daidokoro*. For a discussion of Yoshimoto's use of the word *kitchin*, and more broadly of foreign language and culture, see Sherif, "Japanese Without Apology."

23. There are numerous examples of Murakami's use of *katakana* for abstract terms. For instance, in "Ima naki ōjo no tame ni" ("For a Princess Who Is Not Here Anymore"), from *Kaiten mokuba no deddo hīto*: *imēji* (image), *baitaritī* (vitality), *koketisshu* (coquettish), *enerugī* (energy), *furēzu* (phrase), *supoiru* (spoil), *puro pianisuto* (pro[fessional] pianist), *hisuterikku* (hysteric), *senshibiritī* (sensibility), and *anbaransu* (unbalance); in "Warera no jidai no fōkuroa—kōdo shihonshugi zenshi" ("The Folklore of Our Age—Prehistory of Late Capitalism," from *TV pīpuru*): *tafu* (tough), *uairudo* (wild), *etosetora etosetora* (etcetera etcetera), *sairento na majoritī* (silent majority), *riberaru* (liberal), *konsābatibu* (conservative), *pīsu* (peace), *rīdashippu* (leadership), *kurasu disukasshon* (class discussion), *doroppu auto* (dropout), *misu kurīn to*

misutā kurīn (Miss Clean and Mister Clean), *baitaru na* (vital), *hai* (*high*), *a rōsuto* (arrosto), *pettingu* (petting), *radikaru* (radical), *yunīku na* (unique), *moraru* (moral), *purakutikaru* (practical), *fearī tēru* (fairy tale).

24. McInerney, "Roll over Bashō," 10.

25. McHale, *Postmodernist Fiction*, 169.

26. Karatani, *Origins of Modern Japanese Literature*, 76.

27. The original Japanese reads:

> "Tsumari wareware wa sonzai shinai okyakusama ni wa shinamono o uru koto wa dekinai no desu."
>
> "Shujin wa sonzai shimasu," to kanojo wa itta.
>
> "Sore wa sō desu. Shujin wa sonzai shite irassharu. Mochiron desu," to rōjin wa awatete itta. "Eigo ga umaku shaberen no de mōshiwake nai desu. Watashi no iwan to suru koto wa, umu, goshujin ga koko ni orarenai no de areba, goshujin no tame no rēdāhōzen o o-uri suru koto wa dekin to iu koto desu."
>
> "Dōshite?" to kanojo wa konran shita atama de tazuneta.
>
> "Mise no hōshin nan desu. Hōshin [glossed with *purinshipuru*]. Wareware wa omie ni natta okyakusama no taikei ni atta rēdāhōzen o jissai ni haiteitadaki, komakai chōsei o shi, sono ue de hajimete o-uri suru no desu. Hyakunen ijō no aida, wareware wa sono yō ni shite shōbai shite orimasu. Sono yō na hōshin no yue ni wareware wa shinrai o kizuite maitta no desu." ("Lederhosen," 29–30)

My own translation appears here because it better serves the purpose of my analysis; however, it is instructive also to consider Alfred Birnbaum's clever rendering of the foreignness of the German clerk's speech in his translation of "Lederhosen" in Murakami Haruki, *The Elephant Vanishes*.

28. Marukawa, "Jidai no bunsekii," 124. Translation mine.

29. "Takushī ni notta otoko," in Murakami Haruki, *Kaiten mokuba no deddo hīto*, 48. Translation mine.

30. Ibid., 45–46.

31. Ibid., 52–53.

32. "Thailand," trans. Jay Rubin, *after the quake*, 78. A particularly heavy concentration of *katakana* can be found when Satsuki and Nimit are heading toward the highway, and he puts on a jazz tape in the car stereo: "He took a cassette tape [*kasetto teepu*] from the glove compartment [*gurōbu konpātomento*] and put it into the car stereo [*kā sutereo*] at a low volume. It was jazz [*jazu*]. A melody [*merodī*] she seemed to remember, full of nostalgia. 'May I ask you to you raise the volume a little?' said Satsuki. 'With pleasure, madam' said Nimit and raised the volume [*boriūmu*] of the car stereo [*kā sutereo*]. The song was

'I can't get started'" (104, my translation). The corresponding excerpt appears in *after the quake*, 66. The words "I can't get started" in the Japanese text are not in *katakana* but in the Roman alphabet.

33. Kawamoto, *Toshi kanjusei*, 32. Translation mine.

34. An interesting example is the latest collection of short stories, *Tōkyō kitanshū* (2005), in which Murakami says that he experimented with a new method of composition, putting down a list of words, picking groups of three words from the list, and making up five stories that contained three elements each.

35. "Shidonī no gurīn sutorīto," in Murakami Haruki, *Chūgokuyuki no surōbōto*, 125. All subsequent references to this source will appear in the text. All translations are mine.

36. Murakami Haruki, "Kigō to shite no Amerika" 246. Translation mine.

37. Ibid.

38. Ibid., 247.

39. Other surreal elements include the fact that the narrator eats pizza three times a day, and that the detective finds the name and address of *hitsuji hakase*, the man he is asked to find, simply by looking in the telephone directory.

40. Amitrano, *The New Japanese Novel*, 15.

41. Holquist, "Whodunit and Other Questions," 141.

42. Tani, *The Doomed Detective*, 22. By the 1960s, however, when authors such as Jorge Luis Borges and Vladimir Nabokov chose to use some techniques of detective fiction in their novels, they did not turn to the hard-boiled genre, but to the classic British detective story, in order to subvert its basic elements.

43. Tani, *The Doomed Detective*, 200.

44. Ibid., 58.

45. Ibid., 76.

46. Ibid., 68.

47. Holquist, "Whodunit and Other Questions," 155.

48. "Sausubei sutoratto," in Murakami Haruki, *Kangarū biyori*, 189–90. Translation mine.

Chapter 4

1. "The Last Lawn of the Afternoon," trans. Alfred Birnbaum, in Murakami Haruki, *The Elephant Vanishes*, 287–88.

2. Brooks analyzes in particular the novel *Julie, ou la nouvelle Heloïse* by Jean-Jacques Rousseau—interestingly, an author that has

been crucial to the process of creation of an individual subject through the Western Other in Japan—in which, in his words, "Julie's body becomes the obsessive project of a massive writing project originating from its presentation by way of its impress or imprint, so that it becomes a kind of allegory of the relation of representation to desire and its objects" (Brooks, *Body Work*, 47).

3. Ibid., 48.

4. "The Last Lawn of the Afternoon," trans. Alfred Birnbaum, in Murakami Haruki, *The Elephant Vanishes*, 269.

5. "Chiisana inu," in Murakami Haruki, *Chūgokuyuki no surō bōto*, 217.

6. "Barn Burning," trans. Alfred Birnbaum, in Murakami Haruki, *The Elephant Vanishes*, 141–42.

7. Ibid., 145.

8. Ibid., 148.

9. Ibid., 149.

10. Tani, *The Doomed Detective*, 200.

11. Ibid., 202.

12. The novel *Nejimakidori kuronikuru* (*The Wind-Up Bird Chronicle*) was published in Japan in three volumes, the first two in 1994, and the third in 1995. At the time of this interview, only the first two had come out.

13. Tani, *The Doomed Detective*, 85.

14. Ibid., 96.

15. Shibata, "Murakami Haruki rongu intabyū," 11. Translation mine.

16. Norizuki, "Andāguraundo," 187.

17. Shibata, "Murakami Haruki rongu intabyū," 20. Translation mine.

18. An essay dedicated entirely to the issue is Hatanaka, "Murakami Haruki no namae o meguru bōken."

19. Karatani, "Murakami Haruki no fūkei."

20. Murakami Haruki, *1973-nen no pinbōru*, 13.

21. Karatani, "Murakami Haruki no fūkei," 91–93. Translation mine.

22. Waugh, *Metafiction*, 93.

23. Ibid., 8.

24. Ibid., 11.

25. Ellery Queen, *Cat of Many Tails*, 287.

26. Paul Auster performed a similar operation in the United States with the victims of the New York terrorist attacks of September 11th,

2001, in *I Thought My Father Was God*, a book based on a radio program, as if to prove that influence does not necessarily go from West to East. Interestingly, the American translation of the other "socially committed" work by Murakami, the collection of short stories *Kami no kodomotachi wa mina odoru* (dealing with the Kobe earthquake of 1995, one month before the Sarin incident), which came out in the United States in 2002, was advertised as "Murakami's heartfelt *get well* to the United States after September 11th." The operation was doubly effective since it enabled the American publishers to get better sales for the collection, riding the wave of the 9/11 phenomenon, and it allowed the country to regain its dominant role: even when a Japanese author (writing in 1999) narrates the devastating earthquake of 1995, he somehow does so having in mind the tragedy of New York in 2001.

27. Murakami Haruki, *Yakusoku sareta basho de*, 295–96. Translation mine.

28. Ibid., 293. Italics in original.

29. Ibid., 295.

30. Murakami Haruki, in Miller, "The Salon Interview," 10.

31. Murakami Haruki, *Kaiten mokuba*, 9.

32. Ibid., 10.

33. Ibid., 14.

34. "Jisaku o kataru," in Murakami Haruki, *Murakami Haruki zensakuhin 1979–89*, vol. 5, 9–12.

35. Murakami Haruki, *Kaiten mokuba*, 11.

36. Ibid., 13.

37. See, among others, Lyotard, *La condition postmoderne*.

38. Some examples of such exchanges are: "'Wakaru deshō?' 'Wakaru to omou' to boku wa dōi shita." ("Ōto 1979," in Murakami Haruki, *Kaiten mokuba*, 115); "'Watashi no itteiru imi wa wakatte itadakeru kashira?' Wakaru yō na ki ga suru, to boku wa itta." ("Amayadori," in ibid., 131); "'O-wakari ni narimasuka?' Wakaru to omou, to boku wa itta." ("Yakyūjō," in ibid., 155); "'Wakarimasuka?' Wakaru to omou, to boku wa itta." ("Hantingu naifu," in ibid., 189).

39. Waugh, *Metafiction*, 43.

40. Ibid., 120.

41. As in most texts by Murakami, the protagonist does not have a name; in this collection, in particular, the narrator, *boku*, is sometimes called "Murakami Haruki" by the characters, but his interlocutors are only *boku* or *watashi* in their own speech and *kare* or *kanojo* in the narrator's account.

42. "Ōto 1979," in Murakami Haruki, *Kaiten mokuba*, 117.

43. Ibid., 119.

44. Ibid., 120.

45. Marukawa, "Jidai no bunsekii," 122.

46. Brooks, *Body Work*, 231–32.

47. Ibid., 233.

48. Ibid., *Body Work*, 241–42.

49. "Ōto 1979," in Murakami Haruki, *Kaiten mokuba*, 120.

50. "Yakyūjō," in Murakami Haruki, *Kaiten mokuba*, 149–51.

51. Ibid., 159–60.

52. Interestingly, the first story quoted in the text, about a man eating crabs during a trip with his girlfriend, was later developed by Murakami himself and became the short story "Kani" (2003; translated into English as "Crabs," in the 2006 collection *Blind Willow, Sleeping Woman*).

53. Brooks, *Body Work*, 88.

54. Ibid., 35.

55. Murakami Haruki, *Afutādāku*, 38–39.

56. Brooks, *Body Work*, 122.

57. "Jisaku o kataru," in Murakami Haruki, *Murakami Haruki zensakuhin*, vol. 3, 10.

58. Eliot, "*Ulysses*, Order and Myth," 480.

59. Eliot, "Tradition and the Individual Talent,"13–22.

60. See, for instance, Flanagan, "The Orient as Pretext for Aesthetic and Cultural Revolution in Modern American Poetry"; Qian, *Orientalism and Modernism*; Kodama, *America no japonisme*; Kern, *Orientalism, Modernism, and the American Poem*.

61. Bloom, *The Anxiety of Influence*, xix.

62. Ibid., 5.

63. Walley, "Two Murakamis and Their American Influence," 45.

64. Jameson, "Postmodernism," 55.

65. Holquist, "Whodunit and Other Questions," 159.

66. Karatani, "Murakami Haruki no fūkei," 102.

67. "Gogatsu no kaigansen," in Murakami Haruki, *Kangarū biyori*, 119, 133.

68. See, for example, Konishi, *Murakami Haruki no ongaku zukan*.

69. Jameson, "Postmodernism," 56.

70. Atkins, "Can Japanese Sing the Blues?" 29.

71. Ibid., 35.

Chapter 5

1. Chopin, *The Awakening*, 151. Italics mine.

2. Ibid., 51.

3. "Sleep," in Murakami Haruki, *The Elephant Vanishes*, 105; "Nemuri," in Murakami Haruki, *TV pīpuru*, 201–2. For this story, I will be providing citations for both the English translation and Japanese originals. All subsequent citations will appear in the text.

4. Chopin, *The Awakening*, 171.

5. Todorov, *Introduction à la littérature fantastique*, 82.

6. Suzuki, *Narrating the Self*, 33.

7. Ibid., 41.

8. Shimazaki Tōson, 1909, quoted in Suzuki, *Narrating the Self*, 41.

9. Interestingly, libraries are a typical refuge for Murakami's characters. The protagonist of *Umibe no Kafuka*, a fifteen-year-old boy who flees from home, ends up living in a little room inside a public library in Shikoku; both *boku* and *watashi* in *Sekai no owari to hādoboirudo wandārando* spend a great part of their time in a library; the story "Toshokan kitan" (from the collection *Kangarū biyori*) on the other hand, explores the unsettling side of a library, which conceals an underground world in which the protagonist is locked in a dark room and made to memorize books while waiting to be eaten.

10. I have provided here my own translation of the passage in order to highlight some of the specific features of the original. The italics are also mine.

11. Translation and italics mine.

12. Translation and italics mine.

13. Karatani, *Origins of Modern Japanese Literature*, 76–77.

14. The text slowly builds the unreliability of the narrator from the first pages. Her whole description of her married life, apparently perfect yet subtly unsettling, is highly suspicious. The protagonist constantly writes that she "cannot complain" (*monku wa ienai*) about her situation—something she repeats three times in the space of ten lines ("Nemuri," 150–51), and her account is interspersed with *excusationes non petitae*; she says that her husband is a good man, that everybody likes him, except, strangely, herself; she explains that he goes home for lunch everyday, but really, cooking for him is no trouble at all, in fact, she is happy to have someone to eat with ("Nemuri," 155). When she says that at the beginning of their marriage they were very happy, she hastens to add that, of course, they are still happy now ("Nemuri," 156), and so forth. The text is there-

fore from the beginning narrated in a mode that hints at the possibility of the narrator's self-deception.

15. Here, too, I have chosen to provide my own translation in order to highlight some specific features for the purpose of my analysis. It is also instructive to consider the original Japanese:

> Nemurō to *ishiki* sureba suru hodo, gyaku ni me ga samete kuru. . . . Watashi wa nemuri no fuchi no yō na mono o yubi no saki ni wazuka ni kanjiru. Soshite watashi no *ishiki* wa kakusei shite iru. Watashi wa honoka ni madoromu. De mo usui kabe ni hedaterareta tonari no heya de, sono *ishiki* wa ariari to kakusei shi, jitto watashi o mimamotteiru. Watashi no nikutai wa furafura to hakumei no naka o tadayoinagara, watashi jishin no *ishiki* no shisen to ikizukai o sugu soko ni kanjitsuzukete iru. Watashi wa nemurō to suru nikutai de ari, sore to dōji ni kakusei shiyō to suru *ishiki* de aru. . . . *Ishiki* ga sutto watashi no karada kara hanarete iku. . . . Kakusei ga itsu mo watashi no soba ni iru. Watashi wa sono hiyayaka na kage o kanjitsuzukeru. Sore wa watashi jishin no kage da. Kimyō da, to watashi wa madoromi no naka de omou. Watashi wa watashi jishin no kage no naka ni iru no da.
>
> ("Nemuri," 146–47; emphasis mine)

16. Interestingly, the word *kanashibari* does not have an equivalent in any Western language. After his sojourn at Tufts University in the 1990s, Murakami commented that he was surprised by the fact that his American students had never heard of this phenomenon, which in Japan is considered fairly common.

17. Strecher, "Magical Realism," 295.

18. Napier, *The Fantastic in Modern Japanese Literature*, 223.

19. Ibid., 112.

20. Tetsuo Najita also discusses the vision of technology among Meiji intellectuals, arguing that "Technology as a system of knowledge and production belongs to the Western Other, and has been directly imported into the native historical stream, rendering much of that history artificial." Najita, "On Culture and Technology in Postmodern Japan," 11. Interestingly, in American science fiction from the 1970s and later by authors such as William Gibson, Japan became in turn the symbol of technology and its dangers.

21. Napier, *The Fantastic in Modern Japanese Literature*, 126.

22. "Il y a un phénomène étrange qu'on peut expliquer de deux manières, par des types de causes naturelles et surnaturelles. La possibilité d'hésiter entre les deux crée l'effet fantastique." Todorov, 30.

23. Jackson, *Fantasy*, 307.

24. Ibid., 52.

25. Yoda, "A Roadmap to Millennial Japan," 635.

26. "Superfrog Saves Tokyo," in Murakami Haruki, *after the quake,* 87; "Kaeru-kun," in Murakami Haruki, *Kami no kodomotachi wa mina odoru,* 135. All subsequent citations will appear in the text.

27. The exchange in Japanese:

> "Nee, Kaeru-san," to Katagiri wa itta.
> "Kaeru-kun," to Kaeru-kun wa mata yubi o ippon tatete teisei shita.
> "Nee, Kaeru-kun . . ."

This pattern appears several times in "Superfrog," 84, 89, 92, 93, 94; "Kaeru-kun" 132, 139, 143, 144, 146. The suffix "-san" is more formal than "-kun"; Kaeru-kun, called this way also by the narrator (as well as in the title), introduces himself to Katagiri by saying "Call me Kaeru-kun," although he calls Katagiri "Katagiri-san" and uses honorific language (*sonkeigo*) when addressing him.

28. Murakami Haruki, *Dance Dance Dance,* 83–84; *Dansu dansu dansu,* 148–50.

29. Shibata, "Murakami Haruki rongu intabyū," 36–37; translation mine.

30. Ibid., 37.

31. These quotations include the following:

> "As Nietzsche said, the highest wisdom is to have no fear."
> ("Superfrog," 90; "Kaeru-kun," 154)
>
> "As Joseph Conrad once wrote, true terror is the kind that men feel toward their imagination." ("Superfrog," 92; "Kaeru-kun," 143)
>
> "My chances of beating him by myself are perhaps just slightly better than Anna Karenina's chances of beating that speeding locomotive. Have you read Anna Karenina, Mr. Katagiri?" When he heard that Katagiri had not read the novel, Frog gave him a look as if to say "What a shame." Apparently, Frog was very fond of Anna Karenina.
> ("Superfrog," 94; "Kaeru-kun," 146–47)
>
> "But as Ernest Hemingway saw so clearly, the ultimate value of our lives is decided not by how we win but by how we lose."
> ("Superfrog," 98; "Kaeru-kun," 153)

Conclusion

1. Murakami has also become increasingly active in promoting his own translations. Interestingly, his policy seems to be to give priority to the American market. A good example is the anthology of short stories *The Elephant Vanishes,* a selection of stories published in America that has been the basis for similar anthologies in Europe: even though the stories were translated from the original, the European

publishers were asked to use the same selection of stories, based on the idea that those would be the ones that most appealed to an "international audience." The authority of the selection was further reinforced by the issue of a Japanese version, *Zō no shōmetsu*, on the occasion of the twenty-fifth anniversary of its publication in the United States for the Japanese edition. Murakami even retranslated one of the stories, "Lederhosen," arguing that Birnbaum's version in the collection was so interesting that he considered it to be an original work and therefore wanted to (re)translate it into Japanese. In this sense, once again, Murakami's work seems to be representative of the shift of the "civilizing mission" from Europe to America and of the fact that, for Japan, America has become the center of the Western world, while at the same time reappropriating and exploiting such mechanisms.

2. Hirata, "Amerika de yomareru Murakami Haruki," 103.

3. This in turn has affected his position in Japan. As it often happens with novelists whose works are translated into English and sell well on the international market, his role as an international writer, widely read abroad, has positively influenced his reception at home, further increasing both his popularity and his image as a modern cosmopolitan intellectual. Consequently, his role in introducing Western culture to Japan has acquired further significance.

4. Karatani, "Murakami Haruki no fūkei," 98.

5. See Miura, *Murakami Haruki to Shibata Motoyuki.*

6. Rubin, "New Akutagawa Translation," 15.

7. Murakami Haruki, Introduction to Akutagawa, *Rashōmon*, xxvi.

8. Ibid., xxvii.

9. Ibid., xxvi.

10. Ibid., xxvii.

11. Ibid., xxviii.

12. My thanks to Murakami Haruki for giving me permission to look at the Japanese original of his essay, and to Jay Rubin for providing me with the actual text.

13. Murakami Haruki, Introduction to *Rashōmon*, xxix.

14. Powers, keynote speech at the symposium *Murakami Haruki o meguru bōken: sekai wa Murakami bungaku o dō yomu ka.* My deepest thanks to Anna Elliott for kindly providing me with a copy of the paper.

15. Kelts, "Heart of Darkness," 3.

Works Cited

Akutagawa Ryūnosuke. *Rashōmon and Seventeen Other Stories, with an Introduction by Haruki Murakami.* Trans. Jay Rubin. London and New York: Penguin, 2006.

Allison, Anne. "A Challenge to Hollywood? Japanese Character Goods Hit the U.S." *Japanese Studies* 20, no. 1 (May 2000): 67–88.

Amitrano, Giorgio. *The New Japanese Novel: Popular Culture and Literary Tradition in the Works of Murakami Haruki and Yoshimoto Banana.* Kyoto, Italian School of East Asian Studies (ISEAS) Occasional Papers 7 (1996).

Arensberg, Ann. "Just the Myths, Ma'am." *New York Times Book Review*, 3 December 1989, 82.

Atkins, E. Taylor. "Can Japanese Sing the Blues? 'Japanese Jazz' and the Problem of Authenticity." In *Japan Pop! Inside the World of Japanese Popular Culture*, ed. Timothy J. Craig, 27–59. Armonk, NY: M.E. Sharpe, 2000.

Auster, Paul. *I Thought My Father Was God: And Other True Tales from National Public Radio's National Story Project.* New York: Picador, 2002.

Barkan, Elazar. *The Retreat of Scientific Racism: Changing Concepts of Race in Britain and the United States between the World Wars.* Cambridge, UK: Cambridge University Press, 1992.

Befu, Harumi. "Globalization as Human Dispersal: From the Perspective of Japan." In *Globalization and Social Change in Contemporary Japan*, ed. Jerry S. Eades, Tom Gill, and Harumi Befu, 17–40. Melbourne: Trans Pacific Press, 2000.

———. "Globalization Theory from the Bottom Up: Japan's Contribution." *Japanese Studies* 23, no. 1 (May 2003): 3–22.

Befu, Harumi and Sylvie Guichard-Anguiss, eds. *Globalizing Japan: Ethnography of the Japanese Presence in Asia, Europe and America.* London: Routledge, 2001.

Benedict, Ruth. *The Crysanthemum and the Sword.* Boston, MA: Houghton Mifflin, 1946. Republished with a foreword by Ezra F. Vogel, 1989.

Birnbaum, Alfred, ed. *Monkey Brain Sushi: New Tastes in Japanese Fiction.* Tokyo: Kodansha International, 1991.

Bloom, Harold. *The Anxiety of Influence: A Theory of Poetry.* Oxford, London, and New York: Oxford University Press, 1973.

Bradbury, Malcolm and James McFarlane, eds. *Modernism, 1890–1930.* London: Penguin Books, 1976.

Brooks, Peter. *Body Work: Objects of Desire in Modern Narrative.* Cambridge, MA: Harvard University Press, 1993.

Caryl, Christian. "Gods of the Mall, a Review of Murakami Haruki's *Blind Willow, Sleeping Woman.*" *New York Review of Books,* 1 March 2007, 30–33.

Castelli, Jean-Christophe. "Tokyo Prose." *Harper's Bazaar,* March 1993, 278–79.

Chave, Graham Bruce. "An Overview of the Hard-boiled Fiction of Murakami Haruki." http://www.gbctrans.com/essay/essay.html. Accessed 5 February 2008.

Chopin, Kate. *The Awakening and Selected Stories, with an Introduction by Sandra M. Gilbert.* London: Penguin 1983.

Devereaux, Elizabeth. "PW Interviews Murakami Haruki." *Publisher's Weekly,* 21 September 1991, 1–12.

Edwards, Gareth. *The Use of Certain Fantastic Concepts in the Fiction of Murakami Haruki.* B.A. diss., 1998. http://dottocomu.com/b/documents/dissertation.pdf. Accessed 5 February 2008.

Ellery Queen. *Cat of Many Tails.* New York: Little, Brown and Company, 1949.

Ellis, Toshiko. "Questioning Modernism and Postmodernism in Japanese Literature." In *Japanese Encounters with Postmodernity,* ed. Yoshio Sugimoto and Jóhann P. Árnason, 133–53. London: Kegan Paul International, 1995.

Eliot, T. S. "Tradition and the Individual Talent." In *Selected Essays,* 13–22. London: Faber & Faber, 1951.

———. "*Ulysses,* Order and Myth." *Dial* 75, no. 5 (1923): 480–83.

Fallows, James. *More Like Us: Making America Great Again*. Boston, MA: Houghton Mifflin, 1989.

Fisch, Michael. "In Search of the Real: Technology, Shock and Language in Murakami Haruki's *Sputnik Sweetheart*." *Japan Forum* 16, vol. 3 (November 2004): 361–83.

Flanagan, Kathleen. "The Orient as Pretext for Aesthetic and Cultural Revolution in Modern American Poetry." In *Cohesion and Dissent in America*, ed. Carol Colatrella and Joseph Alkana, 114–30. Albany, NY: State University of New York Press, 1994.

Friedman, Susan Stanford. "Definitional Excursions: The Meanings of Modern/Modernity/Modernism." *Modernism/Modernity* 8, no. 3 (2001): 493–513.

Glazer, Nathan "From Ruth Benedict to Herman Kahn: The Postwar Japanese Image in the American Mind." In *Mutual Images: Essays in American-Japanese Relations*, ed. Akira Iriye, 138–67. Cambridge, MA: Harvard University Press, 1975.

Goody, Jack and Ian Watt. "The Consequences of Literacy." In *Literacy in Traditional Societies*, ed. Jack Goody and Ian Watt, 27–68. Cambridge, UK: Cambridge University Press, 1968.

Gray, John. *False Dawn: The Delusions of Global Capitalism*. New York: The New Press, 1998.

Haarmann, Harald. *Symbolic Values of Foreign Language Use: From the Japanese Case to a General Sociolinguistic Perspective*. Berlin and New York: Mouton de Gruyter, 1989.

Halloran, Richard. *Japan: Images and Realities – The Inner Dynamics of Power in a Nation of Outward Change*. New York: Knopf, 1969. Republished Tokyo: Tuttle, 1970.

Hammond, Phil, ed. *Cultural Difference, Media Memories: Anglo-American Images of Japan*. London and Washington: Cassell, 1997.

Harootunian, Harry D. *Overcome by Modernity: History, Culture, and Community in Interwar Japan*. Princeton, NJ: Princeton University Press, 2000.

——. "Visible Discourses/Invisible Ideologies." In *Postmodernism and Japan*, ed. Masao Miyoshi and H. D. Harootunian, 63–92. Durham, NC and London: Duke University Press, 1989.

Harris, Neil. "All the World a Melting Pot? Japan at American Fairs, 1876–1904." In *Mutual Images: Essays in American-Japanese Relations*, ed. Akira Iriye, 24–54. Cambridge, MA: Harvard University Press, 1975.

Hatanaka Yoshiaki. "Murakami Haruki no namae o meguru bōken" (Adventure in Search of the Name(s) of Murakami Haruki). *Yuriika*, June 1989 (Special Issue), 138–43.

Hidaka Rokurō, ed. *Kindaishugi* (Modernism). Tokyo: Chūō kōronsha, 1964.

Hirata, Hosea. "Amerika de yomareru Murakami Haruki" (Murakami Haruki as read in America). *Kokubungaku* 40, no. 4 (1995): 100–104.

——. *Discourses of Seduction: History, Evil, Desire, and Modern Japanese Literature*. Cambridge, MA: Harvard University Press, 2005.

Holquist, Michael. "Whodunit and Other Questions: Metaphysical Detective Stories in Post-War Fiction." *New Literary History: A Journal of Theory and Interpretation* 3, no. 1 (1971): 35–56. Republished in *Two Centuries of Detective Fiction: A New Comparative Approach*, ed. Maurizio Ascari, 157–80. Bologna: Cotepra, 2000.

Huntington, Samuel. "The Clash of Civilisations." *Foreign Affairs* 72, no. 1 (1993): 22–50.

Hutcheon, Linda. *A Poetics of Postmodernism*. London and New York: Routledge, 1988.

Ivy, Marilyn. *Discourses of the Vanishing: Modernity, Phantasm, Japan*. Chicago: The University of Chicago Press, 1995.

Iwabuchi, Koichi. "Complicit Exoticism: Japan and Its Other." *Continuum* 8, no. 2 (1994): 49–82.

——. "Marketing 'Japan': Japanese Cultural Presence under a Global Gaze." *Japanese Studies* 18, no. 2 (September 1998): 165–80.

——. "Multinationalizing the Multicultural: the Commodification of 'Ordinary Foreign Residents' in a Japanese TV Talk Show." *Japanese Studies* 25, no. 2 (September 2005): 103–18.

——. *Recentering Globalization: Popular Culture and Japanese Transnationalism*. Durham and London: Duke University Press, 2002.

Iwamoto, Yoshio. "A Voice from Postmodern Japan: Haruki Murakami." *World Literature Today* 67, no. 2 (1993): 295–301.

Iyer, Pico. "Tales of the Living Dead." *Time*, 3 November 1997, 114.

Jackson, Rosemary. *Fantasy: The Literature of Subversion*. London: Methuen, 1981.

James, Jamie. "East Meets West." *New York Times Book Review*, 2 November 1997, 8.

Jameson, Frederic. "Postmodernism, or the Cultural Logic of Late Capitalism." *New Left Review* 146 (1984): 53–92.

Johnson, Chalmers. "Japan's Woes Are Political, and the U.S. Is Not Helping." *International Herald Tribune*, 27 March 2001.

——. *MITI and the Japanese Miracle: The Growth of Industrial Policy, 1925–1975*. Stanford, CA: Stanford University Press, 1982. Republished Tokyo: Tuttle, 1986.

Johnson, Sheila K. *The Japanese Through American Eyes*. London, Tokyo, and New York: Kodansha International, 1988.

Karatani Kōjin. "Murakami Haruki no fūkei" (Murakami Haruki's Landscape). In *Shūen o megutte* by Murakami Haruki, 89–135. Tokyo: Kōdansha, 1995.

——. "Nihongo no kanōsei ni tsuite" (On the potential of the Japanese language). *Kōkoku hihyō* 161 (1993): 40–46.

——. *Origins of Modern Japanese Literature*. Trans. Brett de Bary. Durham, NC and London: Duke University Press, 1993.

——. *Shinpojiumu*. Tokyo: Shinchōsha, 1989.

——. *Tankyū I*. Tokyo: Kōdansha, 1986.

——. *Tankyū II*. Tokyo: Kōdansha, 1988.

Katō Koichi. "Shishatachi no okurimono." *Gunzō* (August 1983): 202–15.

Kawakami Tetsutarō and Takeuchi Yoshimi, eds. *Kindai no chōkoku* (Overcoming Modernity). Tokyo: Fuzanbō, 1979.

Kawamoto Saburō. *Toshi kanjusei*. Tokyo: Chikuma bunko, 1988.

Kelts, Roland. "Heart of Darkness: interview with Murakami Haruki." *Kansai Time Out*, November 1999.

Kern, Robert. *Orientalism, Modernism, and the American Poem*. Cambridge, UK: Cambridge University Press, 1996.

Kodama Sanehide. *America no japonisme* (The Japonisme of America). Tokyo: Chūō kōronsha, 1995.

Komori Yōichi. *Murakami Haruki ron: Umibe no Kafuka o seidoku suru* (On Murakami Haruki: A Close Reading of *Kafka on the Shore*). Tokyo: Heibonsha, 2006.

Konishi Keita. *Murakami Haruki no ongaku zukan* (Illustrated Guide to the Music of Murakami Haruki). Tokyo: Japan Mix KK, 1998.

Kuroko Kazuo. *Murakami Haruki: za rosuto warudo* (Murakami Haruki: The Lost World). Tokyo: Rokkō shuppan, 1989.

Leavitt, David. "As Japanese as Burt Bacharach." *New York Times Book Review*, 28 March 1993, 8.

Lewis, Bernard. "The Roots of Muslim Rage." *Atlantic Monthly* 266, no. 3 (September 1990): 47–60.

Lind, William. "Defending Western Culture." *Foreign Policy* 84 (1991): 2–11.

Lippit, Seiji M. *Topographies of Japanese Modernism*. New York: Columbia University Press, 2002.

Lyotard, Jean-François. *La condition postmoderne*. Paris: Minuit, 1979.

Marukawa Tetsushi. "Jidai no bunsekii." *Yuriika*, March 2000 (Special Issue), 122–25.

Maruyama Masao. *Senchū to sengo no aida 1936–1957*. Tokyo: Chūō kōronsha, 1976.

Matsumoto Ken'ichi, ed. *Kindai no chōkoku*. Tokyo: Chikuma shobō, 1979.

Matsuoka, Naomi. "Murakami Haruki and Raymond Carver: The American Scene." *Comparative Literature Studies* 30, vol. 4 (1993): 423–38.

McHale, Brian. *Postmodernist Fiction*. London: Methuen, 1987. Republished London and New York: Routledge, 1989.

McInerney, Jay. "Roll over Bashō: Who Japan Is Reading, and Why—A Conversation between Jay McInerney and Murakami Haruki." *New York Times Book Review*, 27 September 1992, 1.

Miller, Laura. "The Salon Interview—Haruki Murakami: An Interview with Laura Miller." *Salon*, 16 December 1997, 1–12.

Minear, Richard. "Orientalism and the Study of Japan." *Journal of Asian Studies* 39, no. 3 (1980): 507–17.

Mitgang, Herbert. "Looking for America, or Is It Japan?" *New York Times Book Review*, 3 January 1994.

Miura Masashi. *Murakami Haruki to Shibata Motoyuki no mō hitotsu no Amerika* (Murakami Haruki and Shibata Motoyuki's Other America). Tokyo: Shinshokan, 2003.

Miyawaki Hiroyuki. "Kyū nan'yō guntō ni okeru Nihonka kyōiku no kōzō to jittai oyobi zanzon keitai" (The Structure, Conditions, and Surviving Forms of Japanization Education in the Former South Sea Islands). *Miyagi Gakuin Joshi Daigaku jinbun shakai kagaku ronsō* 4 (1995): 53–105.

———. "Maraya, Shingapōru no kōminka to Nihongo kyōiku (1942–1945)" (Imperialization and Japanese-Language Education in Malaya and Singapore, 1942–1945). In *Bunka no naka no shokuminchi* (Colonies within Culture). Vol. 7 of *Iwanami kōza: kindai Nihon to shokuminchi* (Iwanami Lectures: Modern Japan and Its Colonies), ed. Ōe Shinobu, Asada Kyōji, et al., 193–208. Tokyo: Iwanami shoten, 1993.

———. "Nihon no 'Manshūkoku' tairiku senryōchi ni okeru kyōiku kan'yo" (Japan's Influence on Education in 'Manchukuo' and

Occupied Areas on the Continent). *Seijō Gakuen kyōiku kenkyūjo kenkyū nenpō* 20 (1998): 118–61.

Miyoshi, Masao. *Off Center: Power and Culture Relations between Japan and the United States*. Cambridge, MA: Harvard University Press, 1991.

Moeran, Brian. "The Orient Strikes Back: Advertising and Imagining Japan." *Theory, Culture & Society* 13, no. 3 (1996): 77–112.

Morimoto Takako. "*Pan'ya saishūgeki*—fuzai no na ni mukete" (*The Second Bakery Attack*—Toward the Name of Absence). *Kokubungaku* 40, no. 4 (1995): 90–95.

Murakami Fuminobu. *Postmodernist, Feminist and Postcolonial Currents in Contemporary Japanese Culture: A Reading of Murakami Haruki, Yoshimoto Banana, Yoshimoto Takaaki, and Karatani Kōjin*. London and New York: Routledge, 2005.

Murakami Haruki. *1973-nen no pinbōru*. Tokyo: Kōdansha, 1980. Trans. Alfred Birnbaum under the title *Pinball, 1973* (Tokyo: Kodansha English Library, 1985).

——. *Afutādāku*. Tokyo: Shinchōsha, 2004.

——. *Andāguraundo*. Tokyo: Kōdansha, 1997.

——. *Chūgokuyuki no surō bōto*. Tokyo: Chūō kōronsha, 1983.

——. *Dansu dansu dansu*. Tokyo: Kōdansha, 1988. Trans. Alfred Birnbaum under the title *Dance Dance Dance* (Tokyo and New York: Kodansha International, 1994).

——. *The Elephant Vanishes*. Trans. Alfred Birnbaum and Jay Rubin, ed. Gary Fiskjeton. New York: Knopf, 1993.

——. *Hon'yaku yawa*, with Shibata Motoyuki. Tokyo: Bungei shunjū, 2000.

——. *Hon'yaku yawa 2: Sarinjā senki*, with Shibata Motoyuki. Tokyo: Bungei shunjū, 2003.

——. *Hotaru, Naya o yaku, sono ta no tanpen*. Tokyo: Shinchōsha, 1984.

——. *Kaiten mokuba no deddo hīto*. Tokyo: Kōdansha, 1985.

——. *Kami no kodomotachi wa mina odoru*. Tokyo: Shinchōsha, 2000. Trans. Jay Rubin under the title *after the quake* (New York: Knopf, 2002).

——. *Kangarū biyori*. Tokyo: Heibonsha, 1983, Kōdansha, 1986.

——. *Kaze no uta o kike*. Tokyo: Kōdansha, 1979. Trans. under the title *Hear the Wind Sing* (Tokyo: Kodansha English Library, 1987).

——. "Kigō to shite no Amerika." *Gunzō* 38, no. 4 (April 1983): 246–50.

——. "Mēkingu obu Nejimakidori kuronikuru." *Shinchō*, November 1995, 288.

———. *Murakami Haruki zensakuhin 1979–89*. 8 vols. Tokyo: Kōdansha, 1991.

———. *Murakami Haruki zensakuhin 1990–2000*. 7 vols. Tokyo, Kōdansha, 2002.

———. *Nejimakidori kuronikuru*. 3 vols. Tokyo: Shinchōsha, 1994–95. *The Wind-Up Bird Chronicle* (New York, Knopf, 1997).

———. *Pan'ya saishūgeki*. Tokyo: Bungei shunjū, 1986.

———. *Rekishinton no yūrei*. Tokyo: Bungei shunjū, 1996.

———. *Sekai no owari to hādoboirudo wandārando*. Tokyo: Shinchōsha, 1985. Trans. Alfred Birnbaum under the title *Hard-Boiled Wonderland and the End of the World* (Tokyo and New York: Kodansha International, 1991).

———. *Tōkyō kitanshū*. Tokyo: Shinchōsha, 2005.

———. *TV pīpuru*. Tokyo: Bungei shunjū, 1990.

———. *Umibe no Kafuka*. Tokyo: Shinchōsha, 2002. Trans. Philip Gabriel under the title *Kafka on the Shore* (New York: Knopf, 2005).

———. *Wakai dokusha no tame no tanpen shōsetsu annai*. Tokyo: Bungei shunjū, 1997.

———. *Yagate kanashiki gaikokugo*. Tokyo: Kōdansha, 1997.

———. *Yakusoku sareta basho de – Underground 2*. Tokyo: Bungei shunjū, 1998. Trans. Alfred Birnbaum and Philip Gabriel under the title *Underground* (New York: Random House, Vintage International, 2000).

———. *Yoru no kumozaru*. Tokyo: Heibonsha, 1995.

Nagahara Takamichi. "Hotaru, Naya o yaku, sono ta no tanpen: moshi kare no kotoba ga misuterī sākuru de attara" ("Firefly," "Barn Burning," and Other Stories: If His Words were Mystery Circles). *Yuriika*, March 2000 (Special Issue), 110–13.

Najita, Tetsuo. "On Culture and Technology in Postmodern Japan." In *Postmodernism and Japan*, ed. Masao Miyoshi and H. D. Harootunian, 3–20. Durham, NC and London: Duke University Press, 1989.

Najita, Tetsuo and H. D. Harootunian. "Japanese Revolt against the West: Political and Cultural Criticism in the Twentieth Century." In *The Cambridge History of Japan, Volume 6: The Twentieth Century*, ed. Peter Duus, 711–74. Cambridge, UK: Cambridge University Press, 1988.

Nakamura Fumiaki. *Yoshimoto Takaaki*. Tokyo: Izara shobō, 1973.

Napier, Susan J. *The Fantastic in Modern Japanese Literature: The Subversion of Modernity*. London and New York: Routledge, 1996.

Norizuki Rintarō. "Andāguraundo: many tales—takusan no monogatari." *Yuriika*, March 2000 (Special Issue), 185–93.

North, Sam. "Haruki Murakami—Outside Looking In." *Hackwriters.com.* http://www.hackwriters.com/murakami.htm. Accessed 5 February 2008.

Nozumi Yukiko. *Nihon shakai ni afureru katakanago* (The Abundance of *Katakana* Words in Japanese Society). Tokyo: Shinpūsha, 1998.

Numano Mitsuyoshi. "Dōnattsu, bīru, supagetti—Murakami Haruki to Nihon o meguru sanshō" (Doughnuts, Beer, Spaghetti—Three Chapters on Murakami Haruki and Japan). *Yuriika*, June 1989 (Special Issue), 144–57.

Ōe Kenzaburō. *Japan, the Ambiguous and Myself: The Nobel Prize Speech and Other Lectures.* Tokyo, London, and New York: Kodansha International, 1995.

Ōga Kazumasa. "E-mēru intabyū: kotoba to iu hageshii buki" (E-mail Interview: Words as Fierce Weapons). *Yuriika*, March 2000 (Special Issue), 8–27.

Olson, Lawrence. "Intellectuals and 'The People'; On Yoshimoto Takaaki." *Journal of Japanese Studies* 4, no. 2 (Summer 1978): 327–57.

Ouchi, William. *Theory Z: How American Business Can Meet the Japanese Challenge.* Reading, MA: Addison-Wesley, 1981.

Parry, Richard Lloyd. "Haruki Murakami: An Interview by Richard Lloyd Parry." In *Tokyo Voices, Tokyo Journal's Conversations.* Tokyo: Yohan Publications, 1995.

Powers, Richard. Keynote speech at the symposium *Murakami Haruki o meguru bōken: sekai wa Murakami bungaku o dō yomu ka.* Tokyo, March 26, 2006. Unpublished.

Prestowitz, Clyde. *Trading Places: How We Allowed Japan to Take the Lead.* New York: Basic Books, 1988. Republished as *Trading Places: How America is Surrendering its Future to Japan and How to Win It Back.* Tokyo: Charles E. Tuttle, 1991.

Qian, Zhaoming. *Orientalism and Modernism: The Legacy of China in Pound and Williams.* Durham, NC: Duke University Press, 1995.

Rebuck, Mark. "The Function of English Loanwords in Japanese." *NUCB Journal of Language, Culture, and Communication* 4, no. 1 (2002): 53–64.

Reischauer, Edwin O. *Japan Past and Present.* New York: Alfred A. Knopf, 1946.

Revell, Lynn. "*Nihonjinron*: Made in the U.S.A." In *Cultural Differences, Media Memories: Anglo-American Images of Japan*, ed. Phil Hammond, 52–74. London: Cassell, 1997.

Rubin, Jay. *Haruki Murakami and the Music of Words*. London: Harvill, 2002.

——. "New Akutagawa Translation Reveals Short Story Master's Modern Roots." *Asahi Shinbun* (English Edition), 26 April 2006, 15.

——. "The Other World of Murakami Haruki." *Japan Quarterly* 39, no. 4 (1992): 490–500.

Rycroft, David. "Tsubouchi Shōyō's Translation of *Hamlet*." In *Shakespeare in Japan*, ed. Tetsuo Anzai, Soji Iwasaki, Holger Klein, and Peter Millward, 187–227. Lewiston, NY: Edwin Mellen Press, 1999.

Said, Edward. *Culture and Imperialism*. London: Chatto and Windus, 1993.

——. *Orientalism*. New York: Pantheon Books, 1978 (reprinted New York: Vintage Books, 1979).

Sakai, Naoki. *Translation and Subjectivity: On "Japan" and Cultural Nationalism*. Minnaeapolis, MN and London: University of Minnesota Press, 1997.

——. "'You Asians': On the Historical Role of the West and Asia Binary." *South Atlantic Quarterly* 99, no. 4 (2000): 789–818.

Seeley, Christopher. *A History of Writing in Japan*. Leiden and New York: Brill, 1991.

Sengoku Hideyo. *Airon o kakeru seinen: Murakami Haruki to Amerika* (Young Men Who Iron: Murakami Haruki and America). Tokyo: Sairyūsha, 1991.

Sherif, Ann. "Japanese Without Apology: Yoshimoto Banana and Healing." In *Ōe and Beyond: Fiction in Contemporary Japan*, ed. Stephen Snyder and J. Philip Gabriel, 278–300. Honolulu, HI: University of Hawai'i Press, 1999.

Shibata Motoyuki. "Murakami Haruki rongu intabyū: yagi-san yūbin mitai ni meiroka shita sekai no naka de—shōsetsu no kanōsei—" (Long Interview with Murakami Haruki: Inside the Labyrinthine World of Mr. Goat's Letter—The Possibilities of the Novel—). *Yuriika*, June 1989 (Special Issue), 10–37.

Shiraishi, Saya S. "Japan's Soft Power: Doraemon Goes Overseas." In *Network Power: Japan and Asia*, ed. Peter Katzenstein and Takashi Shiraishi, 234–70. Ithaca, NY: Cornell University Press, 1997.

Shirakawa Masayoshi. *Yoshimoto Takaaki ron* (On Yoshimoto Takaaki). Tokyo: Nagai shuppan kikaku, 1971.

Smith, Henry D. *Learning from Shōgun: Japanese History and Western Fantasy*. Santa Barbara, CA: University of California Program in Asian Studies, 1980.

Snyder, Stephen and Philip Gabriel, eds. *Ōe and Beyond: Fiction in Contemporary Japan*. Honolulu, HI: University of Hawai'i Press, 1999.

Strecher, Matthew. *Dances With Sheep: The Quest for Identity in the Fiction of Murakami Haruki*. Ann Arbor, MI: University of Michigan, Center for Japanese Studies, 2002.

——. "Magical Realism and the Search for Identity in the Fiction of Murakami Haruki." *Journal of Japanese Studies* 25, no. 2 (1999): 263–98.

Suzuki Tomi. *Narrating the Self: Fictions of Japanese Modernity*. Stanford, CA: Stanford University Press, 1996.

Takeuchi Yoshimi. "Kindai no chōkoku" (Overcoming Modernity). *Takeuchi Yoshimi zenshū*. Tokyo: Chikuma shobō, 1980.

Tanaka, Keiko. *Advertising Language: A Pragmatic Approach to Advertisements in Britain and Japan*. London and New York: Routledge, 1994.

Tani, Stefano. *The Doomed Detective: The Contribution of the Detective Novel to Postmodern American and Italian Fiction*. Carbondale, IL: Southern Illinois University Press, 1984.

Todorov, Tzvetan. *Introduction à la littérature fantastique*. Paris: Seuil, 1982.

Tsurumi, Patricia. *Japanese Colonial Education in Taiwan*. Cambridge, MA: Harvard University Press, 1977.

Twine, Nanette. *Language and the Modern State: The Reform of Written Japanese*. London and New York: Routledge, 1991.

Van Wolferen, Karel. *The Enigma of Japanese Power: People and Politics in a Stateless Nation*. London: MacMillan, 1989.

Vogel, Ezra. *Japan as Number One: Lessons for America*. Cambridge, MA: Harvard University Press, 1979.

Wallerstein, Immanuel. "Culture as the Ideological Battleground of the Modern World System." *Theory, Culture and Society* 7 (1990): 31–55.

Walley, Glynne. "Two Murakamis and Their American Influence." *Japan Quarterly* 44 (1999): 41–51.

Waugh, Patricia. *Metafiction: The Theory and Practice of Self-Conscious Fiction*. London: Methuen, 1984.

Williams, David. "Modernity, Harootunian, and the Demands of Scholarship." *Japan Forum* 15, no. 1 (2003): 147–62.

Wright, Sarah. "Dancing as Fast as He Can." Review of *Dance, Dance, Dance*, by Murakami Haruki. *Boston Magazine*, January 1994, 34–35.

Yamamoto Masahide. *Genbun itchi no rekishi ronkō* (Treatise on the History of *Genbun Itchi*). Tokyo: Seiryūsha, 1971.

Yoda, Tomiko. "A Roadmap to Millennial Japan." *South Atlantic Quarterly* 99, no. 4 (2000): 629–68.

Yoshida Haruo. *Murakami Haruki tenkai suru* (Murakami Haruki Changes). Tokyo: Sairyūsha, 1997.

——. *Murakami Haruki to Amerika* (Murakami Haruki and America). Tokyo: Sairyūsha, 2001.

Yoshioka Hiroshi. "Samurai and Self-colonization in Japan." In *The Decolonization of Imagination: Culture, Knowledge, and Power*, ed. Jan Nederveen Pieterse and Bhikhu Parekh, 99–112. London: Zed Books, 1995.

Index

Harvard East Asian Monographs

(*out-of-print)

*1. Liang Fang-chung, *The Single-Whip Method of Taxation in China*
*2. Harold C. Hinton, *The Grain Tribute System of China, 1845–1911*
3. Ellsworth C. Carlson, *The Kaiping Mines, 1877–1912*
*4. Chao Kuo-chün, *Agrarian Policies of Mainland China: A Documentary Study, 1949–1956*
*5. Edgar Snow, *Random Notes on Red China, 1936–1945*
*6. Edwin George Beal, Jr., *The Origin of Likin, 1835–1864*
7. Chao Kuo-chün, *Economic Planning and Organization in Mainland China: A Documentary Study, 1949–1957*
*8. John K. Fairbank, *Ching Documents: An Introductory Syllabus*
*9. Helen Yin and Yi-chang Yin, *Economic Statistics of Mainland China, 1949–1957*
10. Wolfgang Franke, *The Reform and Abolition of the Traditional Chinese Examination System*
11. Albert Feuerwerker and S. Cheng, *Chinese Communist Studies of Modern Chinese History*
12. C. John Stanley, *Late Ching Finance: Hu Kuang-yung as an Innovator*
13. S. M. Meng, *The Tsungli Yamen: Its Organization and Functions*
*14. Ssu-yü Teng, *Historiography of the Taiping Rebellion*
15. Chun-Jo Liu, *Controversies in Modern Chinese Intellectual History: An Analytic Bibliography of Periodical Articles, Mainly of the May Fourth and Post-May Fourth Era*
*16. Edward J. M. Rhoads, *The Chinese Red Army, 1927–1963: An Annotated Bibliography*
*17. Andrew J. Nathan, *A History of the China International Famine Relief Commission*
*18. Frank H. H. King (ed.) and Prescott Clarke, *A Research Guide to China-Coast Newspapers, 1822–1911*
*19. Ellis Joffe, *Party and Army: Professionalism and Political Control in the Chinese Officer Corps, 1949–1964*

*20. Toshio G. Tsukahira, *Feudal Control in Tokugawa Japan: The Sankin Kōtai System*

*21. Kwang-Ching Liu, ed., *American Missionaries in China: Papers from Harvard Seminars*

*22. George Moseley, *A Sino-Soviet Cultural Frontier: The Ili Kazakh Autonomous Chou*

23. Carl F. Nathan, *Plague Prevention and Politics in Manchuria, 1910–1931*

*24. Adrian Arthur Bennett, *John Fryer: The Introduction of Western Science and Technology into Nineteenth-Century China*

*25. Donald J. Friedman, *The Road from Isolation: The Campaign of the American Committee for Non-Participation in Japanese Aggression, 1938–1941*

*26. Edward LeFevour, *Western Enterprise in Late Ching China: A Selective Survey of Jardine, Matheson and Company's Operations, 1842–1895*

27. Charles Neuhauser, *Third World Politics: China and the Afro-Asian People's Solidarity Organization, 1957–1967*

*28. Kungtu C. Sun, assisted by Ralph W. Huenemann, *The Economic Development of Manchuria in the First Half of the Twentieth Century*

*29. Shahid Javed Burki, *A Study of Chinese Communes, 1965*

30. John Carter Vincent, *The Extraterritorial System in China: Final Phase*

31. Madeleine Chi, *China Diplomacy, 1914–1918*

*32. Clifton Jackson Phillips, *Protestant America and the Pagan World: The First Half Century of the American Board of Commissioners for Foreign Missions, 1810–1860*

*33. James Pusey, *Wu Han: Attacking the Present Through the Past*

*34. Ying-wan Cheng, *Postal Communication in China and Its Modernization, 1860–1896*

35. Tuvia Blumenthal, *Saving in Postwar Japan*

36. Peter Frost, *The Bakumatsu Currency Crisis*

37. Stephen C. Lockwood, *Augustine Heard and Company, 1858–1862*

38. Robert R. Campbell, *James Duncan Campbell: A Memoir by His Son*

39. Jerome Alan Cohen, ed., *The Dynamics of China's Foreign Relations*

40. V. V. Vishnyakova-Akimova, *Two Years in Revolutionary China, 1925–1927*, trans. Steven L. Levine

41. Meron Medzini, *French Policy in Japan During the Closing Years of the Tokugawa Regime*

42. Ezra Vogel, Margie Sargent, Vivienne B. Shue, Thomas Jay Mathews, and Deborah S. Davis, *The Cultural Revolution in the Provinces*

43. Sidney A. Forsythe, *An American Missionary Community in China, 1895–1905*

*44. Benjamin I. Schwartz, ed., *Reflections on the May Fourth Movement.: A Symposium*

*45. Ching Young Choe, *The Rule of the Taewŏngun, 1864–1873: Restoration in Yi Korea*

46. W. P. J. Hall, *A Bibliographical Guide to Japanese Research on the Chinese Economy, 1958–1970*

47. Jack J. Gerson, *Horatio Nelson Lay and Sino-British Relations, 1854–1864*

48. Paul Richard Bohr, *Famine and the Missionary: Timothy Richard as Relief Administrator and Advocate of National Reform*
49. Endymion Wilkinson, *The History of Imperial China: A Research Guide*
50. Britten Dean, *China and Great Britain: The Diplomacy of Commercial Relations, 1860–1864*
51. Ellsworth C. Carlson, *The Foochow Missionaries, 1847–1880*
52. Yeh-chien Wang, *An Estimate of the Land-Tax Collection in China, 1753 and 1908*
53. Richard M. Pfeffer, *Understanding Business Contracts in China, 1949–1963*

*54. Han-sheng Chuan and Richard Kraus, *Mid-Ching Rice Markets and Trade: An Essay in Price History*

55. Ranbir Vohra, *Lao She and the Chinese Revolution*
56. Liang-lin Hsiao, *China's Foreign Trade Statistics, 1864–1949*

*57. Lee-hsia Hsu Ting, *Government Control of the Press in Modern China, 1900–1949*

*58. Edward W. Wagner, *The Literati Purges: Political Conflict in Early Yi Korea*

*59. Joungwon A. Kim, *Divided Korea: The Politics of Development, 1945–1972*

60. Noriko Kamachi, John K. Fairbank, and Chūzō Ichiko, *Japanese Studies of Modern China Since 1953: A Bibliographical Guide to Historical and Social-Science Research on the Nineteenth and Twentieth Centuries, Supplementary Volume for 1953–1969*
61. Donald A. Gibbs and Yun-chen Li, *A Bibliography of Studies and Translations of Modern Chinese Literature, 1918–1942*
62. Robert H. Silin, *Leadership and Values: The Organization of Large-Scale Taiwanese Enterprises*
63. David Pong, *A Critical Guide to the Kwangtung Provincial Archives Deposited at the Public Record Office of London*

*64. Fred W. Drake, *China Charts the World: Hsu Chi-yü and His Geography of 1848*

*65. William A. Brown and Urgrunge Onon, translators and annotators, *History of the Mongolian People's Republic*

66. Edward L. Farmer, *Early Ming Government: The Evolution of Dual Capitals*

*67. Ralph C. Croizier, *Koxinga and Chinese Nationalism: History, Myth, and the Hero*

*68. William J. Tyler, tr., *The Psychological World of Natsume Sōseki*, by Doi Takeo

69. Eric Widmer, *The Russian Ecclesiastical Mission in Peking During the Eighteenth Century*

*70. Charlton M. Lewis, *Prologue to the Chinese Revolution: The Transformation of Ideas and Institutions in Hunan Province, 1891–1907*

71. Preston Torbert, *The Ching Imperial Household Department: A Study of Its Organization and Principal Functions, 1662–1796*
72. Paul A. Cohen and John E. Schrecker, eds., *Reform in Nineteenth-Century China*
73. Jon Sigurdson, *Rural Industrialism in China*
74. Kang Chao, *The Development of Cotton Textile Production in China*

75. Valentin Rabe, *The Home Base of American China Missions, 1880–1920*
*76. Sarasin Viraphol, *Tribute and Profit: Sino-Siamese Trade, 1652–1853*
77. Ch'i-ch'ing Hsiao, *The Military Establishment of the Yuan Dynasty*
78. Meishi Tsai, *Contemporary Chinese Novels and Short Stories, 1949–1974: An Annotated Bibliography*
*79. Wellington K. K. Chan, *Merchants, Mandarins and Modern Enterprise in Late Ch'ing China*
80. Endymion Wilkinson, *Landlord and Labor in Late Imperial China: Case Studies from Shandong by Jing Su and Luo Lun*
*81. Barry Keenan, *The Dewey Experiment in China: Educational Reform and Political Power in the Early Republic*
*82. George A. Hayden, *Crime and Punishment in Medieval Chinese Drama: Three Judge Pao Plays*
*83. Sang-Chul Suh, *Growth and Structural Changes in the Korean Economy, 1910–1940*
84. J. W. Dower, *Empire and Aftermath: Yoshida Shigeru and the Japanese Experience, 1878–1954*
85. Martin Collcutt, *Five Mountains: The Rinzai Zen Monastic Institution in Medieval Japan*
86. Kwang Suk Kim and Michael Roemer, *Growth and Structural Transformation*
87. Anne O. Krueger, *The Developmental Role of the Foreign Sector and Aid*
*88. Edwin S. Mills and Byung-Nak Song, *Urbanization and Urban Problems*
89. Sung Hwan Ban, Pal Yong Moon, and Dwight H. Perkins, *Rural Development*
*90. Noel F. McGinn, Donald R. Snodgrass, Yung Bong Kim, Shin-Bok Kim, and Quee-Young Kim, *Education and Development in Korea*
*91. Leroy P. Jones and Il SaKong, *Government, Business, and Entrepreneurship in Economic Development: The Korean Case*
92. Edward S. Mason, Dwight H. Perkins, Kwang Suk Kim, David C. Cole, Mahn Je Kim et al., *The Economic and Social Modernization of the Republic of Korea*
93. Robert Repetto, Tai Hwan Kwon, Son-Ung Kim, Dae Young Kim, John E. Sloboda, and Peter J. Donaldson, *Economic Development, Population Policy, and Demographic Transition in the Republic of Korea*
94. Parks M. Coble, Jr., *The Shanghai Capitalists and the Nationalist Government, 1927–1937*
95. Noriko Kamachi, *Reform in China: Huang Tsun-hsien and the Japanese Model*
96. Richard Wich, *Sino-Soviet Crisis Politics: A Study of Political Change and Communication*
97. Lillian M. Li, *China's Silk Trade: Traditional Industry in the Modern World, 1842–1937*
98. R. David Arkush, *Fei Xiaotong and Sociology in Revolutionary China*
*99. Kenneth Alan Grossberg, *Japan's Renaissance: The Politics of the Muromachi Bakufu*
100. James Reeve Pusey, *China and Charles Darwin*

101. Hoyt Cleveland Tillman, *Utilitarian Confucianism: Chen Liang's Challenge to Chu Hsi*
102. Thomas A. Stanley, *Ōsugi Sakae, Anarchist in Taishō Japan: The Creativity of the Ego*
103. Jonathan K. Ocko, *Bureaucratic Reform in Provincial China: Ting Jih-ch'ang in Restoration Kiangsu, 1867–1870*
104. James Reed, *The Missionary Mind and American East Asia Policy, 1911–1915*
105. Neil L. Waters, *Japan's Local Pragmatists: The Transition from Bakumatsu to Meiji in the Kawasaki Region*
106. David C. Cole and Yung Chul Park, *Financial Development in Korea, 1945–1978*
107. Roy Bahl, Chuk Kyo Kim, and Chong Kee Park, *Public Finances During the Korean Modernization Process*
108. William D. Wray, *Mitsubishi and the N.Y.K, 1870–1914: Business Strategy in the Japanese Shipping Industry*
109. Ralph William Huenemann, *The Dragon and the Iron Horse: The Economics of Railroads in China, 1876–1937*

*110. Benjamin A. Elman, *From Philosophy to Philology: Intellectual and Social Aspects of Change in Late Imperial China*

111. Jane Kate Leonard, *Wei Yüan and China's Rediscovery of the Maritime World*
112. Luke S. K. Kwong, *A Mosaic of the Hundred Days:. Personalities, Politics, and Ideas of 1898*

*113. John E. Wills, Jr., *Embassies and Illusions: Dutch and Portuguese Envoys to K'ang-hsi, 1666–1687*

114. Joshua A. Fogel, *Politics and Sinology: The Case of Naitō Konan (1866–1934)*

*115. Jeffrey C. Kinkley, ed., *After Mao: Chinese Literature and Society, 1978–1981*

116. C. Andrew Gerstle, *Circles of Fantasy: Convention in the Plays of Chikamatsu*
117. Andrew Gordon, *The Evolution of Labor Relations in Japan: Heavy Industry, 1853–1955*

*118. Daniel K. Gardner, *Chu Hsi and the "Ta Hsueh": Neo-Confucian Reflection on the Confucian Canon*

119. Christine Guth Kanda, *Shinzō: Hachiman Imagery and Its Development*

*120. Robert Borgen, *Sugawara no Michizane and the Early Heian Court*

121. Chang-tai Hung, *Going to the People: Chinese Intellectual and Folk Literature, 1918–1937*

*122. Michael A. Cusumano, *The Japanese Automobile Industry: Technology and Management at Nissan and Toyota*

123. Richard von Glahn, *The Country of Streams and Grottoes: Expansion, Settlement, and the Civilizing of the Sichuan Frontier in Song Times*
124. Steven D. Carter, *The Road to Komatsubara: A Classical Reading of the Renga Hyakuin*
125. Katherine F. Bruner, John K. Fairbank, and Richard T. Smith, *Entering China's Service: Robert Hart's Journals, 1854–1863*

126. Bob Tadashi Wakabayashi, *Anti-Foreignism and Western Learning in Early-Modern Japan: The "New Theses" of 1825*
127. Atsuko Hirai, *Individualism and Socialism: The Life and Thought of Kawai Eijirō (1891–1944)*
128. Ellen Widmer, *The Margins of Utopia: "Shui-hu hou-chuan" and the Literature of Ming Loyalism*
129. R. Kent Guy, *The Emperor's Four Treasuries: Scholars and the State in the Late Chien-lung Era*
130. Peter C. Perdue, *Exhausting the Earth: State and Peasant in Hunan, 1500–1850*
131. Susan Chan Egan, *A Latterday Confucian: Reminiscences of William Hung (1893–1980)*
132. James T. C. Liu, *China Turning Inward: Intellectual-Political Changes in the Early Twelfth Century*
*133. Paul A. Cohen, *Between Tradition and Modernity: Wang T'ao and Reform in Late Ching China*
134. Kate Wildman Nakai, *Shogunal Politics: Arai Hakuseki and the Premises of Tokugawa Rule*
*135. Parks M. Coble, *Facing Japan: Chinese Politics and Japanese Imperialism, 1931–1937*
136. Jon L. Saari, *Legacies of Childhood: Growing Up Chinese in a Time of Crisis, 1890–1920*
137. Susan Downing Videen, *Tales of Heichū*
138. Heinz Morioka and Miyoko Sasaki, *Rakugo: The Popular Narrative Art of Japan*
139. Joshua A. Fogel, *Nakae Ushikichi in China: The Mourning of Spirit*
140. Alexander Barton Woodside, *Vietnam and the Chinese Model: A Comparative Study of Vietnamese and Chinese Government in the First Half of the Nineteenth Century*
*141. George Elison, *Deus Destroyed: The Image of Christianity in Early Modern Japan*
142. William D. Wray, ed., *Managing Industrial Enterprise: Cases from Japan's Prewar Experience*
*143. T'ung-tsu Ch'ü, *Local Government in China Under the Ching*
144. Marie Anchordoguy, *Computers, Inc.: Japan's Challenge to IBM*
145. Barbara Molony, *Technology and Investment: The Prewar Japanese Chemical Industry*
146. Mary Elizabeth Berry, *Hideyoshi*
147. Laura E. Hein, *Fueling Growth: The Energy Revolution and Economic Policy in Postwar Japan*
148. Wen-hsin Yeh, *The Alienated Academy: Culture and Politics in Republican China, 1919–1937*
149. Dru C. Gladney, *Muslim Chinese: Ethnic Nationalism in the People's Republic*
150. Merle Goldman and Paul A. Cohen, eds., *Ideas Across Cultures: Essays on Chinese Thought in Honor of Benjamin L Schwartz*
151. James M. Polachek, *The Inner Opium War*
152. Gail Lee Bernstein, *Japanese Marxist: A Portrait of Kawakami Hajime, 1879–1946*

- *153. Lloyd E. Eastman, *The Abortive Revolution: China Under Nationalist Rule, 1927–1937*
- 154. Mark Mason, *American Multinationals and Japan: The Political Economy of Japanese Capital Controls, 1899–1980*
- 155. Richard J. Smith, John K. Fairbank, and Katherine F. Bruner, *Robert Hart and China's Early Modernization: His Journals, 1863–1866*
- 156. George J. Tanabe, Jr., *Myōe the Dreamkeeper: Fantasy and Knowledge in Kamakura Buddhism*
- 157. William Wayne Farris, *Heavenly Warriors: The Evolution of Japan's Military, 500–1300*
- 158. Yu-ming Shaw, *An American Missionary in China: John Leighton Stuart and Chinese-American Relations*
- 159. James B. Palais, *Politics and Policy in Traditional Korea*
- *160. Douglas Reynolds, *China, 1898–1912: The Xinzheng Revolution and Japan*
- 161. Roger R. Thompson, *China's Local Councils in the Age of Constitutional Reform, 1898–1911*
- 162. William Johnston, *The Modern Epidemic: History of Tuberculosis in Japan*
- 163. Constantine Nomikos Vaporis, *Breaking Barriers: Travel and the State in Early Modern Japan*
- 164. Irmela Hijiya-Kirschnereit, *Rituals of Self-Revelation: Shishōsetsu as Literary Genre and Socio-Cultural Phenomenon*
- 165. James C. Baxter, *The Meiji Unification Through the Lens of Ishikawa Prefecture*
- 166. Thomas R. H. Havens, *Architects of Affluence: The Tsutsumi Family and the Seibu-Saison Enterprises in Twentieth-Century Japan*
- 167. Anthony Hood Chambers, *The Secret Window: Ideal Worlds in Tanizaki's Fiction*
- 168. Steven J. Ericson, *The Sound of the Whistle: Railroads and the State in Meiji Japan*
- 169. Andrew Edmund Goble, *Kenmu: Go-Daigo's Revolution*
- 170. Denise Potrzeba Lett, *In Pursuit of Status: The Making of South Korea's "New" Urban Middle Class*
- 171. Mimi Hall Yiengpruksawan, *Hiraizumi: Buddhist Art and Regional Politics in Twelfth-Century Japan*
- 172. Charles Shirō Inouye, *The Similitude of Blossoms: A Critical Biography of Izumi Kyōka (1873–1939), Japanese Novelist and Playwright*
- 173. Aviad E. Raz, *Riding the Black Ship: Japan and Tokyo Disneyland*
- 174. Deborah J. Milly, *Poverty, Equality, and Growth: The Politics of Economic Need in Postwar Japan*
- 175. See Heng Teow, *Japan's Cultural Policy Toward China, 1918–1931: A Comparative Perspective*
- 176. Michael A. Fuller, *An Introduction to Literary Chinese*
- 177. Frederick R. Dickinson, *War and National Reinvention: Japan in the Great War, 1914–1919*

178. John Solt, *Shredding the Tapestry of Meaning: The Poetry and Poetics of Kitasono Katue (1902–1978)*
179. Edward Pratt, *Japan's Protoindustrial Elite: The Economic Foundations of the Gōnō*
180. Atsuko Sakaki, *Recontextualizing Texts: Narrative Performance in Modern Japanese Fiction*
181. Soon-Won Park, *Colonial Industrialization and Labor in Korea: The Onoda Cement Factory*
182. JaHyun Kim Haboush and Martina Deuchler, *Culture and the State in Late Chosŏn Korea*
183. John W. Chaffee, *Branches of Heaven: A History of the Imperial Clan of Sung China*
184. Gi-Wook Shin and Michael Robinson, eds., *Colonial Modernity in Korea*
185. Nam-lin Hur, *Prayer and Play in Late Tokugawa Japan: Asakusa Sensōji and Edo Society*
186. Kristin Stapleton, *Civilizing Chengdu: Chinese Urban Reform, 1895–1937*
187. Hyung Il Pai, *Constructing "Korean" Origins: A Critical Review of Archaeology, Historiography, and Racial Myth in Korean State-Formation Theories*
188. Brian D. Ruppert, *Jewel in the Ashes: Buddha Relics and Power in Early Medieval Japan*
189. Susan Daruvala, *Zhou Zuoren and an Alternative Chinese Response to Modernity*
*190. James Z. Lee, *The Political Economy of a Frontier: Southwest China, 1250–1850*
191. Kerry Smith, *A Time of Crisis: Japan, the Great Depression, and Rural Revitalization*
192. Michael Lewis, *Becoming Apart: National Power and Local Politics in Toyama, 1868–1945*
193. William C. Kirby, Man-houng Lin, James Chin Shih, and David A. Pietz, eds., *State and Economy in Republican China: A Handbook for Scholars*
194. Timothy S. George, *Minamata: Pollution and the Struggle for Democracy in Postwar Japan*
195. Billy K. L. So, *Prosperity, Region, and Institutions in Maritime China: The South Fukien Pattern, 946–1368*
196. Yoshihisa Tak Matsusaka, *The Making of Japanese Manchuria, 1904–1932*
197. Maram Epstein, *Competing Discourses: Orthodoxy, Authenticity, and Engendered Meanings in Late Imperial Chinese Fiction*
198. Curtis J. Milhaupt, J. Mark Ramseyer, and Michael K. Young, eds. and comps., *Japanese Law in Context: Readings in Society, the Economy, and Politics*
199. Haruo Iguchi, *Unfinished Business: Ayukawa Yoshisuke and U.S.-Japan Relations, 1937–1952*
200. Scott Pearce, Audrey Spiro, and Patricia Ebrey, *Culture and Power in the Reconstitution of the Chinese Realm, 200–600*
201. Terry Kawashima, *Writing Margins: The Textual Construction of Gender in Heian and Kamakura Japan*
202. Martin W. Huang, *Desire and Fictional Narrative in Late Imperial China*

203. Robert S. Ross and Jiang Changbin, eds., *Re-examining the Cold War: U.S.-China Diplomacy, 1954–1973*
204. Guanhua Wang, *In Search of Justice: The 1905–1906 Chinese Anti-American Boycott*
205. David Schaberg, *A Patterned Past: Form and Thought in Early Chinese Historiography*
206. Christine Yano, *Tears of Longing: Nostalgia and the Nation in Japanese Popular Song*
207. Milena Doleželová-Velingerová and Oldřich Král, with Graham Sanders, eds., *The Appropriation of Cultural Capital: China's May Fourth Project*
208. Robert N. Huey, *The Making of 'Shinkokinshū'*
209. Lee Butler, *Emperor and Aristocracy in Japan, 1467–1680: Resilience and Renewal*
210. Suzanne Ogden, *Inklings of Democracy in China*
211. Kenneth J. Ruoff, *The People's Emperor: Democracy and the Japanese Monarchy, 1945–1995*
212. Haun Saussy, *Great Walls of Discourse and Other Adventures in Cultural China*
213. Aviad E. Raz, *Emotions at Work: Normative Control, Organizations, and Culture in Japan and America*
214. Rebecca E. Karl and Peter Zarrow, eds., *Rethinking the 1898 Reform Period: Political and Cultural Change in Late Qing China*
215. Kevin O'Rourke, *The Book of Korean Shijo*
216. Ezra F. Vogel, ed., *The Golden Age of the U.S.-China-Japan Triangle, 1972–1989*
217. Thomas A. Wilson, ed., *On Sacred Grounds: Culture, Society, Politics, and the Formation of the Cult of Confucius*
218. Donald S. Sutton, *Steps of Perfection: Exorcistic Performers and Chinese Religion in Twentieth-Century Taiwan*
219. Daqing Yang, *Technology of Empire: Telecommunications and Japanese Expansionism, 1895–1945*
220. Qianshen Bai, *Fu Shan's World: The Transformation of Chinese Calligraphy in the Seventeenth Century*
221. Paul Jakov Smith and Richard von Glahn, eds., *The Song-Yuan-Ming Transition in Chinese History*
222. Rania Huntington, *Alien Kind: Foxes and Late Imperial Chinese Narrative*
223. Jordan Sand, *House and Home in Modern Japan: Architecture, Domestic Space, and Bourgeois Culture, 1880–1930*
224. Karl Gerth, *China Made: Consumer Culture and the Creation of the Nation*
225. Xiaoshan Yang, *Metamorphosis of the Private Sphere: Gardens and Objects in Tang-Song Poetry*
226. Barbara Mittler, *A Newspaper for China? Power, Identity, and Change in Shanghai's News Media, 1872–1912*
227. Joyce A. Madancy, *The Troublesome Legacy of Commissioner Lin: The Opium Trade and Opium Suppression in Fujian Province, 1820s to 1920s*

228. John Makeham, *Transmitters and Creators: Chinese Commentators and Commentaries on the Analects*
229. Elisabeth Köll, *From Cotton Mill to Business Empire: The Emergence of Regional Enterprises in Modern China*
230. Emma Teng, *Taiwan's Imagined Geography: Chinese Colonial Travel Writing and Pictures, 1683–1895*
231. Wilt Idema and Beata Grant, *The Red Brush: Writing Women of Imperial China*
232. Eric C. Rath, *The Ethos of Noh: Actors and Their Art*
233. Elizabeth Remick, *Building Local States: China During the Republican and Post-Mao Eras*
234. Lynn Struve, ed., *The Qing Formation in World-Historical Time*
235. D. Max Moerman, *Localizing Paradise: Kumano Pilgrimage and the Religious Landscape of Premodern Japan*
236. Antonia Finnane, *Speaking of Yangzhou: A Chinese City, 1550–1850*
237. Brian Platt, *Burning and Building: Schooling and State Formation in Japan, 1750–1890*
238. Gail Bernstein, Andrew Gordon, and Kate Wildman Nakai, eds., *Public Spheres, Private Lives in Modern Japan, 1600–1950: Essays in Honor of Albert Craig*
239. Wu Hung and Katherine R. Tsiang, *Body and Face in Chinese Visual Culture*
240. Stephen Dodd, *Writing Home: Representations of the Native Place in Modern Japanese Literature*
241. David Anthony Bello, *Opium and the Limits of Empire: Drug Prohibition in the Chinese Interior, 1729–1850*
242. Hosea Hirata, *Discourses of Seduction: History, Evil, Desire, and Modern Japanese Literature*
243. Kyung Moon Hwang, *Beyond Birth: Social Status in the Emergence of Modern Korea*
244. Brian R. Dott, *Identity Reflections: Pilgrimages to Mount Tai in Late Imperial China*
245. Mark McNally, *Proving the Way: Conflict and Practice in the History of Japanese Nativism*
246. Yongping Wu, *A Political Explanation of Economic Growth: State Survival, Bureaucratic Politics, and Private Enterprises in the Making of Taiwan's Economy, 1950–1985*
247. Kyu Hyun Kim, *The Age of Visions and Arguments: Parliamentarianism and the National Public Sphere in Early Meiji Japan*
248. Zvi Ben-Dor Benite, *The Dao of Muhammad: A Cultural History of Muslims in Late Imperial China*
249. David Der-wei Wang and Shang Wei, eds., *Dynastic Crisis and Cultural Innovation: From the Late Ming to the Late Qing and Beyond*
250. Wilt L. Idema, Wai-yee Li, and Ellen Widmer, eds., *Trauma and Transcendence in Early Qing Literature*
251. Barbara Molony and Kathleen Uno, eds., *Gendering Modern Japanese History*

252. Hiroshi Aoyagi, *Islands of Eight Million Smiles: Idol Performance and Symbolic Production in Contemporary Japan*
253. Wai-yee Li, *The Readability of the Past in Early Chinese Historiography*
254. William C. Kirby, Robert S. Ross, and Gong Li, eds., *Normalization of U.S.-China Relations: An International History*
255. Ellen Gardner Nakamura, *Practical Pursuits: Takano Chōei, Takahashi Keisaku, and Western Medicine in Nineteenth-Century Japan*
256. Jonathan W. Best, *A History of the Early Korean Kingdom of Paekche, together with an annotated translation of* The Paekche Annals *of the* Samguk sagi
257. Liang Pan, *The United Nations in Japan's Foreign and Security Policymaking, 1945–1992: National Security, Party Politics, and International Status*
258. Richard Belsky, *Localities at the Center: Native Place, Space, and Power in Late Imperial Beijing*
259. Zwia Lipkin, *"Useless to the State": "Social Problems" and Social Engineering in Nationalist Nanjing, 1927–1937*
260. William O. Gardner, *Advertising Tower: Japanese Modernism and Modernity in the 1920s*
261. Stephen Owen, *The Making of Early Chinese Classical Poetry*
262. Martin J. Powers, *Pattern and Person: Ornament, Society, and Self in Classical China*
263. Anna M. Shields, *Crafting a Collection: The Cultural Contexts and Poetic Practice of the* Huajian ji 花間集 *(Collection from Among the Flowers)*
264. Stephen Owen, *The Late Tang: Chinese Poetry of the Mid-Ninth Century (827–860)*
265. Sara L. Friedman, *Intimate Politics: Marriage, the Market, and State Power in Southeastern China*
266. Patricia Buckley Ebrey and Maggie Bickford, *Emperor Huizong and Late Northern Song China: The Politics of Culture and the Culture of Politics*
267. Sophie Volpp, *Worldly Stage: Theatricality in Seventeenth-Century China*
268. Ellen Widmer, *The Beauty and the Book: Women and Fiction in Nineteenth-Century China*
269. Steven B. Miles, *The Sea of Learning: Mobility and Identity in Nineteenth-Century Guangzhou*
270. Lin Man-houng, *China Upside Down: Currency, Society, and Ideologies, 1808–1856*
271. Ronald Egan, *The Problem of Beauty: Aesthetic Thought and Pursuits in Northern Song Dynasty China*
272. Mark Halperin, *Out of the Cloister: Literati Perspectives on Buddhism in Sung China, 960–1279*
273. Helen Dunstan, *State or Merchant? Political Economy and Political Process in 1740s China*
274. Sabina Knight, *The Heart of Time: Moral Agency in Twentieth-Century Chinese Fiction*

275. Timothy J. Van Compernolle, *The Uses of Memory: The Critique of Modernity in the Fiction of Higuchi Ichiyō*
276. Paul Rouzer, *A New Practical Primer of Literary Chinese*
277. Jonathan Zwicker, *Practices of the Sentimental Imagination: Melodrama, the Novel, and the Social Imaginary in Nineteenth-Century Japan*
278. Franziska Seraphim, *War Memory and Social Politics in Japan, 1945–2005*
279. Adam L. Kern, *Manga from the Floating World: Comicbook Culture and the* Kibyōshi *of Edo Japan*
280. Cynthia J. Brokaw, *Commerce in Culture: The Sibao Book Trade in the Qing and Republican Periods*
281. Eugene Y. Park, *Between Dreams and Reality: The Military Examination in Late Chosŏn Korea, 1600–1894*
282. Nam-lin Hur, *Death and Social Order in Tokugawa Japan: Buddhism, Anti-Christianity, and the* Danka *System*
283. Patricia M. Thornton, *Disciplining the State: Virtue, Violence, and State-Making in Modern China*
284. Vincent Goossaert, *The Taoists of Peking, 1800–1949: A Social History of Urban Clerics*
285. Peter Nickerson, *Taoism, Bureaucracy, and Popular Religion in Early Medieval China*
286. Charo B. D'Etcheverry, *Love After* The Tale of Genji*: Rewriting the World of the Shining Prince*
287. Michael G. Chang, *A Court on Horseback: Imperial Touring & the Construction of Qing Rule, 1680–1785*
288. Carol Richmond Tsang, *War and Faith:* Ikkō Ikki *in Late Muromachi Japan*
289. Hilde De Weerdt, *Competition over Content: Negotiating Standards for the Civil Service Examinations in Imperial China (1127–1279)*
290. Eve Zimmerman, *Out of the Alleyway: Nakagami Kenji and the Poetics of Outcaste Fiction*
291. Robert Culp, *Articulating Citizenship: Civic Education and Student Politics in Southeastern China, 1912–1940*
292. Richard J. Smethurst, *From Foot Soldier to Finance Minister: Takahashi Korekiyo, Japan's Keynes*
293. John E. Herman, *Amid the Clouds and Mist: China's Colonization of Guizhou, 1200–1700*
294. Tomoko Shiroyama, *China During the Great Depression: Market, State, and the World Economy, 1929–1937*
295. Kirk W. Larsen, *Tradition, Treaties and Trade: Qing Imperialism and Chosŏn Korea, 1850–1910*
296. Gregory Golley, *When Our Eyes No Longer See: Realism, Science, and Ecology in Japanese Literary Modernism*

Harvard East Asian Monographs

297. Barbara Ambros, *Emplacing a Pilgrimage: The Ōyama Cult and Regional Religion in Early Modern Japan*
298. Rebecca Suter, *The Japanization of Modernity: Murakami Haruki between Japan and the United States*